# OUR LAST BEST CHANCE

## THE PURSUIT OF PEACE IN A TIME OF PERIL

## KING ABDULLAH II

**THORNDIKE PRESS**

*A part of Gale, Cengage Learning*

GALE
CENGAGE Learning

Detroit • New York • San Francisco • New Haven, Conn • Waterville, Maine • London

**GALE**
CENGAGE Learning™

Thorndike Press® Large Print Nonfiction.

The text of this Large Print edition is unabridged.

Other aspects of the book may vary from the original edition.

Set in 16 pt. Plantin.

**LIBRARY OF CONGRESS CATALOGING-IN-PUBLICATION DATA**

Abdullah II, King of Jordan, 1962–
    Our last best chance : the pursuit of peace in a time of peril /
by King Abdullah II.
        p. cm. — (Thorndike Press large print nonfiction)
    Originally published: New York : Viking, 2010.
    Includes index.
    ISBN-13: 978-1-4104-3603-0 (hardcover)
    ISBN-10: 1-4104-3603-9 (hardcover)
    1. Abdullah II, King of Jordan, 1962– 2. Jordan — Kings and
rulers — Biography. 3. Jordan — Politics and government.
4. Peace-building — Middle East. 5. Arab-Israeli conflict —
1993 — Peace. I. Title.
DS154.6.A23A3 2011
956.9504′4092—dc22
[B]
                                                          2011002815

Published in 2011 by arrangement with Viking, a member of Penguin
Group (USA) Inc.

Printed in the United States of America
1 2 3 4 5 6 7 15 14 13 12 11

# PREFACE

Two years ago, when I started writing this book, I hoped it would reveal the inner workings of how, against great odds, the United States, Israel, and the Arab and Muslim world had brokered peace in the Middle East. As I write these words, however, I can only say that this is a story about how peace has continued to elude our grasp. And yet, in my region, where optimism is even more precious than water, we cannot afford to give up hope.

Why would a head of state want to write a book? There are countless reasons why doing so may be ill-advised. Running a country, after all, even a small one, is a full-time job. Added to that is the requirement of getting along with neighbors — many of whom could easily be offended by an honest presentation of the facts as viewed from another nation's perspective. And then there are those who will want their actions either to go unmentioned or to be praised beyond their worth.

I have decided to put aside these arguments and write this book because the Middle East, the very tough neighborhood in which I live, is facing a moment of real crisis. I believe we still have one last chance to achieve peace. But the window is rapidly closing. If we do not seize the opportunity presented by the now almost unanimous international consensus on the solution, I am certain we will see another war in our region — most likely worse than those that have gone before and with more disastrous consequences.

People around here have long memories. They readily remember previous failed attempts to bring together the parties to the conflict. Many of the same players are still on the stage, and likely will remain so for years to come. This could be seen as a compelling reason not to speak publicly about sensitive issues, but I believe the world must know the risks of doing nothing.

My father's generation reeled from the blast of war about once a decade. Following the war triggered by the creation of Israel in 1948, there was Suez in 1956, the disastrous 1967 war, when Israel seized the West Bank, the Sinai, and the Golan Heights, and the war of 1973, when Egypt and Syria tried and failed to win back the territory they had lost in 1967. These were followed by the Iran-Iraq War and the Israeli invasion of Lebanon in the 1980s, and the Gulf War in 1991. The periods in between could be called "peace" only in the loosest of senses. In the eleven years since I became King of Jordan, I have seen five conflicts: the Al Aqsa intifada in 2000, the U.S. invasion of Afghanistan in 2001, the U.S. invasion of Iraq in 2003, the Israeli invasion of Lebanon in 2006, and the Israeli attack on Gaza in 2008–9. Every two or three years, it seems, another conflict besets our troubled region. As I look forward, my greatest fear is that we will soon see another war between Israel and its neighbors, triggered by a yet unknown flashpoint, that will escalate in terrifying ways.

The conflict between the Israelis and the Palestinians goes back to the early years of the twentieth century, but the impact of their struggle is felt very much in the present. Since the breakdown of the peace process in 2000, about a thousand Israelis and over sixty-five hundred Palestinians have been killed, and many thousands more injured. Today the whole Middle East faces the critical challenge of resolving a conflict that has almost defined the modern history of the region. If we succeed, I believe we will strike at one of the main roots of violence and instability in the Middle East.

Many in the West, when they look at our region, view it as a series of separate challenges: Iranian expansionism, radical terrorism, sectarian tensions in Iraq and Lebanon, and a long-festering conflict between Israel and the Palestinians. But the truth is that all of these are interconnected. The thread that links them is the Israeli-Palestinian conflict.

For Muslims, the Arab-Israeli conflict is qualitatively different from any other in which they are involved. Contrary to what some like to say, it is not a religious struggle. It is a political conflict over rights and land. In 1900 there were around 60,000 Jews and 510,000 Arabs in the land of historic Palestine. Following a century of mass immigration, there are now over 6 million Jews and only 5 million Arabs. Many Jewish immigrants came during the persecution by the Nazi regime that culminated in one of the greatest tragedies in history — the Holocaust. Many more came later, when Israel opened its doors to Jews from all over the world. The 1948 war resulted in the displacement of hundreds of thousands of Palestinians, most of whom have never been allowed to return to their homes. The 1967 war put many more — especially those living in the West Bank, which had been part of Jordan — under Israeli occupation. Millions of Palestinians live today under Israeli occupation, and Israeli actions are threatening the identity of Jerusalem, one of three holy cities in Islam. The importance of Jerusalem in part explains the centrality of the Palestinian issue to Arabs and Muslims the world over.

A point not well understood in the West is that this is a global issue. When I go to Indonesia or China and meet with Muslims, they want to talk about Jerusalem. When I went to New Delhi in 2006 and met with the Muslim community of India, I was asked: When are the Arabs going to solve the Israeli-Palestinian problem? When Pakistanis list their grievances, right after India comes Israel. The Palestinian issue is a cause that resonates among all the world's 1.5 billion Muslims.

This explains (but does not justify) why radical groups like Al Qaeda, claiming to want to "liberate" Jerusalem, can manipulate the cause and draw others to commit acts of terrorism in the name of defending Islam and the Palestinians. It also explains why groups like Hezbollah and Hamas, although very different from Al Qaeda in mandate and ideology, arm themselves against Israel, and why calls for resistance are embraced by a growing number of Arabs and Muslims. This call for armed struggle against the occupation gains more credibility as efforts by Arab countries like Jordan, Egypt, and the Kingdom of Saudi Arabia to achieve a negotiated peace fail to deliver.

But if Israel could make peace with the Palestinians, then what moral justification would any government or resistance group have for continuing the struggle? If Jerusalem were a shared city, with East Jerusalem as the capital of a viable, sovereign, and independent Palestinian state, what possible rationale could the government of Iran, for example, have for its anti-Israeli rhetoric and actions?

One of the best weapons against violent extremists is to undercut their rallying cries. Solving the Muslim world's most emotional problem by establishing a Palestinian state based on the pre-1967 boundaries, with East Jerusalem as its capital, would help remove one of the biggest reasons for conflict in the Muslim world. Achieving a just and lasting peace is one of our most powerful tools against extremism. It won't stop every fanatic, but it will radically transform the playing field. As such, it should be an American priority as well as an Arab one.

Another often misunderstood aspect of the conflict is its impact on the Christian community and holy sites in Jerusalem. Before the 1967 war, Jordan administered the West Bank, including East Jerusalem, and it remains the legal and political guardian of all the holy sites in the Old City, Christian and Muslim alike. So when Israelis attempt to consolidate their illegal occupation of East Jerusalem by building more settlements, Jordan is a staunch defender of the rights of the Christian and Muslim communities. Today there are only about eight thousand Christians left in Jerusalem, compared to some thirty thousand in 1945. Israeli policies and social and economic pressures have forced the majority of Christians to leave. Most native Christians in Jerusalem are Arabs, and while Israel welcomes foreign Christians who come to visit Jerusalem, it makes life very difficult for Christian Jerusalemites. This is ironic, since the Arab Christian community is the oldest Christian community in the world, and its presence in Jerusalem dates back to the time of Jesus Christ. Palestinian Christians and Palestinian Muslims have suffered equally under the occupation, and they share the same aspirations for freedom and the Kingdom of statehood.

■■■■

The prevailing approach in past peace efforts has been for all sides to take incremental steps, to work on small issues and leave the tough ones, like the final status of Jerusalem, to a later date. The problem is that we will never get to the end if we keep kicking the big problems down the road. We need to resolve immediately the final status issues: Jerusalem, refugees, borders, and security. At this point, it is our only hope of rescuing the two-state solution. There is no other option.

I have been highly critical at times of Israel's behavior and intransigence, but it goes without saying that there is plenty of blame to go around on both sides for the failure of the peace process. Arabs and Israelis need to recognize each other's respective needs. A two-state solution is predicated on the recognition by Israelis of the rights of the Palestinians to freedom and statehood and the recognition by Palestinians and the rest of the Muslim world of Israel's right to security. We have no choice but to live together. Both sides have a moral responsibility to strive for peace. They also have a very compelling pragmatic imperative to do so: the alternative is more conflict and violence.

Geography, history, and international law all dictate that Jordan should be involved in the process of finding a solution to the conflict. We are home to over 1.9 million Palestinian refugees, the most of any country, and have friendly relations with Israel's Arab neighbors and the United States. We are also one of only two Arab countries to have a peace treaty with Israel.

Resolution of the Palestinian conflict is the key to normalizing relations between Israel and the entire Muslim world. My father, in the last years of his reign, developed a proposal offering Israel a comprehensive peace with all twenty-two Arab countries in return for full Israeli withdrawal from occupied Arab land and the establishment of a Palestinian state. Unfortunately, his proposal did not gain momentum, and it stalled with his death. On becoming king, I revived my father's plan and had our government discuss it with Egypt and Saudi Arabia. Eventually the Saudis developed the idea and took it one step further, when Crown Prince Abdullah bin Abdulaziz Al Saud presented it to the Arab League Summit in Beirut in 2002. The summit collectively adopted the Saudi proposal, which came to be known as the Arab Peace Initiative.

The initiative called for full Israeli withdrawal from all Arab territories occupied since 1967, a negotiated settlement of the issue of Palestinian refugees, and the establishment of a sovereign, independent Palestinian state with East Jerusalem as its capital. In return, all twenty-two Arab countries said they would "consider the Arab-Israeli conflict ended, enter into a peace agreement with Israel, and provide security for all the states of the region." In addition, they stated, they would "establish normal relations with Israel in the context of this comprehensive peace." I was surprised that the Israelis, and even some members of the American administration, shot down the initiative out of hand. My later discussions with many of them showed that they had not even read it. On the issues of refugees, for example, the initiative proposed "the achievement of a just solution to the Palestinian refugee problem to be agreed upon in accordance with UN General Assembly resolution 194." The operative words here are "agreed upon"; when I would mention that to the Israelis, they would say "oh," and some would admit they had never bothered to look at the text. The Arab Peace Initiative was subsequently approved by all fifty-seven member states of the Organization of the Islamic Conference (OIC). Unfortunately, Israel never took it seriously and never acknowledged it for the unprecedented opportunity it represented. We are still stuck in the old ways, negotiating lower-priority issues and putting off the difficult decisions. Israel seems to feel it has all the time in the world. But its delays, reversals, and stalling tactics have come at a price.

The events of the last eleven years have destroyed confidence on both sides. Today the credibility of the peace process is in tatters. And once trust has vanished completely between the two sides, it may prove impossible to rebuild. All friends of Israel should encourage it to engage fully and expeditiously to make peace. And the United States, as an old, true friend of Israel, should not hesitate to push, aggressively if needed, to get both sides to the negotiating table and to reach a final settlement.

The American president, Barack Obama, with his willingness to listen and to offer an outstretched hand to the Muslim and Arab world, opened up a brief window of hope. But Arabs and Palestinians are frustrated that so little concrete progress has been made. President Obama has been criticized for pressing Israel's prime minister, Benjamin Netanyahu, to freeze settlements, and American prestige in the region was hurt by Israel's intransigence. But it would be a terrible mistake for Obama to pull back. If America does not exert its moral and political strength now to broker a two-state solution, we may never see another such chance. The window is closing, and if we do not act soon, future generations will condemn our failure to seize this last chance for peace.

Peace for its own sake would be prize enough. But in my mind, I see benefits that far outweigh that precious commodity. There can be little doubt that terrorist organizations exploit the injustice resulting from the continuation of occupation. Resolving this conflict would deprive these organizations of their appeal. Many will argue that the hatred sown and nurtured by extremist factions on both sides in the Holy Land cannot be overcome. But history has shown that peace can prevail even among the fiercest of enemies. Not long ago observers might have thought that tensions across the Berlin Wall or between the factions in Northern Ireland would never be eased — and yet those struggles are now mostly memories. Why not aim to do the same in the Middle East?

Bringing peace is not the only struggle we face. Among our greatest challenges are political reform and the improvement of our economies. We need to learn to make things the rest of the world wants to buy, and to raise the living standards for all our people. Providing proper education and good jobs for young people is one of the most effective defenses against the siren call of the extremists. We cannot afford to have so many unemployed young men. And we must let women play a greater role in our economies. The impulse to hold women back for so-called religious or cultural reasons, to keep them out of the workforce, comes from a deep insecurity. It is unacceptable for half of society to be denied their rights and for half the workforce to stay at home.

Think of a world where the managerial expertise of the Israelis, the professionalism of the Jordanians, Lebanese entrepreneurship, and the education of the Palestinians could be combined effectively. I see the association of these potential partners as producing a regional economic powerhouse — a Middle Eastern Benelux. All this can be achieved. But the situation on the ground is rapidly getting away from us, rendering this outcome more and more unlikely. If current trends are not reversed soon, there will be no land left to swap for peace — no reason for Palestinians to cast their lot with moderate leaders rather than with the extremists. Our future will be doomed to war and conflict.

There is a tendency in life and in politics to default to the status quo. But in this case the seeming stability is misleading. I hear the mounting frustration and anger, and I fear it will soon eclipse all dreams of peace and reconciliation. I do not think most Americans and Europeans recognize the urgency of the situation. It is because of this sense of urgency that I have decided to write this book. In the eleven years since I succeeded my father, I have seen and learned a great deal. I am determined to share my story openly and honestly, in the hope that it can help make a difference.

In my region, we live history, for better and for worse. What may seem abstract and intangible at a distance is part of the fabric of our everyday lives. I have decided that the best and most persuasive way to tell this story is through the story of my own life — by sharing what I have seen, what I have done — to show how the personal and the political are often intertwined.

I never intended to hold the position I am now entrusted with, and expected instead that I would spend my life in the army. Part of my story is about that military experience and what it taught me about Jordan and about leadership more generally. I have tried to tell my story simply, using the straight-forward language and imagery of a military man rather than the long-winded phrases and vocabulary beloved by politicians.

I hope in this book to challenge some of the false ideas about the region in which I live. Too often, when people in the West hear the words "Arab," "Muslim," or "Middle East" they think of terrorism, suicide bombers, and wild-eyed fanatics hiding in caves. But I want them to associate our region with multimillion-dollar IT start-ups in Jordan, Nobel literature prize winners in Egypt, and the historic architecture of Damascus.

One of the most dangerous ideas to have emerged in recent years is the suggestion that the West and the Muslim world are two separate blocs, heading inevitably on a collision course with each other. This concept is ill-informed, inflammatory, and wrong. For over a thousand years Muslims, Jews, and Christians have lived together peacefully, enriching one another's cultures. For sure, there have been conflicts, such as the Crusades or the European colonization of many Middle Eastern countries after World War I. But these are political, rooted in the motivations of a certain time and context, rather than manifestations of an eternal cultural hostility.

After my military education at Sandhurst, I served for a year in Britain's 13th/18th Hussars, a proud regiment that traces its history back to almost six decades before the battle of Waterloo. The regiment also fought bravely in the Crimean War in the nineteenth century. In that conflict, made famous by Alfred Tennyson's poem "The Charge of the Light Brigade," Britain and France fought alongside the Ottoman Empire to protect it from invasion by the Russians. More than half of the Ottoman Empire's thirty million subjects were Christian, with many serving in the Ottoman army. And Muslim soldiers fought bravely on both sides of the conflict, including in the French and Russian armies.

This pernicious idea of a clash of cultures bleeds into the modern political arena, giving strength to extremists on all sides and empowering those who wish to set men and armies against each other. If an Algerian, an Afghan, or a Jordanian carries out a terrorist attack, he is inevitably described in the West as a "Muslim terrorist." But if a similar attack is carried out by an Irishman or a Sri Lankan, they are rarely called a "Christian terrorist" or a "Hindu terrorist." Rather, they are described according to the political motivations of their group, as an Irish Republican Army activist or a Tamil separatist.

People with a narrow view of history assume that the way things are now is the way they have always been. But the economic and technological ascendancy of the West is relatively recent, born out of an amazing flourishing of innovation in Europe and America in the nineteenth and twentieth centuries. To those who take a longer view, things can look quite different. In the Middle Ages, when Washington, D.C., was just a swamp, the great cities of Jerusalem, Baghdad, and Damascus were the world's leading centers of learning and knowledge. Over the centuries, the pendulum of history swung toward the West, and by the twentieth century the Arab world had fallen far behind.

My family, the Hashemites, are descended from the Prophet Mohammad, and for generations have been leaders and rulers in our region. In the sixth century, my ancestor Qusai was the first ruler of Mecca. My heritage is one of tolerance and acceptance of different cultures and faiths. The Holy Quran says:

God Almighty said: "Mankind! We created you from a pair of a male and female, and made you into nations and tribes that ye may know each other." (Al Hujurat: 13)

I have never felt that interacting with Western culture comes at the expense of my identity as an Arab or a Muslim. As somebody born in the East but educated in the West, I feel a deep affinity for both cultures. My hope is that this book can, in a small way, act as a bridge between them. All too often extremists on both sides frame the discussion and dominate the debate. All too often the voices of moderate Arabs are drowned out by those who shout the loudest. I will not shout, but I do want my message to be heard. I want to tell the world that while there are great problems in our region, there is also cause for hope.

■■■■

# PART I

■■■■

# CHAPTER 1
# THE CONFLICT BEGINS

One constant in my life ever since I was a small child has been the conflict between the Israelis and the Palestinians. Some people in the West and Israel like to portray this as the continuation of a centuries-old struggle. They are wrong. It is a relatively recent conflict, rooted in Jewish immigration into Palestine in the early twentieth century. In the Middle East, perhaps more than any other place, history matters, though far too many people use historical grievances as an excuse for not dealing with current problems. If you want to understand where you are going, it helps to know where you have come from. So before I try to explain the situation we find ourselves in today, and offer some suggestions on how to get out of the current stalemate, I would like to say a few words about the distance we have come.

As the Ottoman Empire, which extended over much of the Middle East from the early sixteenth century, was taking its last breath toward the end of World War I, the Arabs began to follow new nationalist leaders. One of these was my great-great-grandfather, Sharif Hussein bin Ali, the sharif of Mecca. A member of the Hashemite family, which had ruled Mecca since the tenth century, Sharif Hussein was an outspoken supporter of Arab nationalism. He was believed by other Arab nationalists to have the religious status and political experience to lead the Arab nationalist movement and the planned revolt against Ottoman rule, and to represent his people in negotiations with the British to secure an independent Arab state. His role was formalized by the Charter of Damascus in 1915. Negotiations between Sharif Hussein and the British High Commissioner in Egypt, Sir Henry McMahon, resulted in the secret Hussein-McMahon correspondence of 1915–16 in which Sharif Hussein was promised support for a united and independent Arab kingdom under his rule. The agreement with McMahon was later subject to differing interpretations by the British and Arabs.

In June 1916, Sharif Hussein launched the Great Arab Revolt, initiating the revolutionary push for a single independent unified Arab state, and was declared King of the Arabs. His vision was to establish a new Arab country that would stretch from Palestine to Yemen. He believed that the Arab peoples could be united based on their shared culture and Islamic ideals, and he embraced a tradition of tolerance and respect for minorities. He hoped to bring about an Arab Renaissance. His four sons, Princes Ali, Faisal, Abdullah, and Zeid, led the Arab armies against the Ottoman forces. They were eventually victorious and succeeded in driving the Turks from Arabia in 1918. Faisal became king of Syria and then Iraq, and Abdullah became emir of Transjordan. Following Sharif Hussein's abdication in 1924, Ali became king of the Hijaz (later part of modern Saudi Arabia). Zeid worked with Faisal in Iraq, and served as Iraq's ambassador to Turkey, Germany, and the United Kingdom.

The Arab Revolt brought to prominence a young British officer who went by the name of T. E. Lawrence. He was later immortalized as "Lawrence of Arabia," played onscreen by Peter O'Toole in the 1962 film, parts of which were shot in Jordan. My great-great-uncle Prince Faisal was played in the film by Alec Guinness.

My mother briefly worked on the production of the film, but she left to marry my

31

father in the summer of 1961. A few months later, she took him back to visit the set. The director was filming the scene in which Prince Faisal's camp is bombed by Turkish airplanes while his forces are en route to Damascus. My mother and father watched from a hill overlooking the set. When the word spread that my father was there, the bedouin extras left the camp and rushed up to him, shouting out their loyalty and admiration. Once things had settled down, the crew prepared to film the scene again. As the airplanes flew overhead, one of my father's retainers, a very tall old Nigerian man, turned to my father and said, "Sir, that's not the way it happened." My father asked him how he knew this. "Well," he replied, "I was a child in that camp at the time, and the planes came from the other direction." After their visit, the production crew politely asked my father not to visit the set again.

The film was tremendously popular in the West, less so in Jordan, where it is viewed by many people as a partial and inaccurate retelling of history. And although Lawrence is seen today by many in the West as a romantic hero who played a key role in leading the Arab people to freedom, the view in my family of the historical record is considerably more measured. My great-grandfather King Abdullah I regarded Lawrence as a "strange character," eager to mold people to suit his interests. In his memoir he wrote:

> His intrigues went as far as an attempt to influence me against my own father on the pretext that my father was obstinate. I sent his messenger back with this reply: "Tell your friend that my father is my lord and king. I shall be content with this relationship to the end of my days." In fact Lawrence rendered the Arabs the greatest service by reiterating that my father was determined in his aims. Lawrence appeared only to require people who had no views of their own, that he might impress his personal ideas upon them.

At the end of World War I, the fate of the Arabs was complicated by Great Power rivalries, since Britain had made secret promises not only to the sharif of Mecca but also to the French. Under the terms of the Sykes-Picot Agreement of 1916, modern-day Syria and Lebanon would fall under a French sphere of influence and modern-day Jordan, Iraq, Palestine, and what is now western Saudi Arabia into a British sphere. The San Remo Conference of 1920 formalized the new regional map as the French and British claimed responsibility for League of Nations mandates over these territories. On November 2, 1917, contravening promises made to the Arabs, British Foreign Secretary Arthur Balfour had publicly stated his government's support for "the establishment in Palestine of a national home for the Jewish people."

Sharif Hussein felt that he could not in good conscience consent either to the British Mandate over Palestine or to the Balfour Declaration, as both represented a betrayal of the Arab Revolt. These pledges and arrangements would fuel the cause of Arab nationalism for several decades.

The new regional order was in part determined by Britain's colonial secretary, Winston Churchill. My great-grandfather Abdullah had a much higher opinion of Churchill than of Lawrence, describing him as "unique among the men Great Britain has produced in recent times." In 1921, Abdullah became the emir of Transjordan, which encompassed the lands to the east of the Jordan River. All the lands to the west of the Jordan, comprising modern-day Israel, the West Bank, Jerusalem, and the Gaza Strip, remained under British control as the British Mandate of Palestine.

Many thousands of Jewish immigrants

began to arrive in Palestine, their movement encouraged and facilitated by the Balfour Declaration. At that time the Arabs accounted for some 90 percent of the population of Palestine. In 1897, the Zionist movement, at its first Congress in Basle, had defined its purpose as establishing "a home for the Jewish people in Palestine." By 1947, the number of Jews in Palestine had grown to about 600,000, the increase encouraged by the Zionist movement and reinforced by persecution in Europe. The large influx created tensions with the 1.2 million Muslim and Christian Palestinians. For the first time, America stepped into the arena, insisting that Palestine open its doors to 100,000 Jewish immigrants.

In a prophetic article written in the now defunct *American* magazine in 1947, six months before the first Arab-Israeli war, my great-grandfather warned of the dangers of unchecked immigration:

No people on earth have been less "anti-Semitic" than the Arabs. The persecution of the Jews has been confined almost entirely to the Christian nations of the West. Jews, themselves, will admit that never since the Great Dispersion did Jews develop so freely and reach such importance

as in Spain when it was an Arab posses-
sion. With very minor exceptions, Jews
have lived for many centuries in the Middle
East, in complete peace and friendliness
with their Arab neighbors. . . .

I have the impression that many Americans believe the trouble in Palestine is very
remote from them, that America had little
to do with it, and that your only interest
now is that of a humane bystander.

I believe that you do not realize how directly you are, as a nation, responsible in
general for the whole Zionist move and
specifically for the present terrorism. I call
this to your attention because I am certain
that if you realize your responsibility you
will act fairly to admit it and assume it.

The present catastrophe may be laid
almost entirely at your door. Your government, almost alone in the world, is insisting
on the immediate admission of 100,000
more Jews into Palestine — to be followed
by countless additional ones. This will have
the most frightful consequences in bloody
chaos beyond anything ever hinted at in
Palestine before.

I have the most complete confidence
in the fair-mindedness and generosity of
the American public. We Arabs ask no
favors. We ask only that you know the

full truth, not half of it. We ask only that when you judge the Palestine question, you put yourselves in our place. What would your answer be if some outside agency told you that you must accept in America many millions of utter strangers in your midst — enough to dominate your country — merely because they insisted on going to America, and because their forefathers had once lived there some 2,000 years ago?

Our answer is the same.

And what would be your action if, in spite of your refusal, this outside agency began forcing them on you?

Ours will be the same.

From the beginning, the conflict in Palestine has been a struggle between Jewish immigrants and the existing Arab Palestinian people, not, as it is often portrayed, the continuation of ancient hatreds between Jews and Arabs.

Throughout the 1930s and early 1940s the British tried to limit the number of Jewish immigrants pouring into Palestine. Zionist organizations such as Haganah, the Irgun, and Lohamei Herut Israel (also known as the Stern Gang) conducted assassinations, planted bombs, and engaged in other acts of terrorism and sabotage to scare Palestinians from their land, force the British to leave Palestine, and impose a Jewish state.

In November 1944, the Stern Gang assassinated the British minister of state for the Middle East, Lord Moyne, in Cairo. Two years later, members of the Irgun planted a bomb in Jerusalem's King David Hotel, which housed the British Mandate secretariat and British military intelligence headquarters. Ninety-one people were killed. And in August 1947, in retaliation for the execution of three Jewish terrorists, the Irgun kidnapped two British sergeants and hanged them from eucalyptus trees in a forest south of the coastal town of Netanya. They booby-trapped the bodies, so that when British troops tried to cut them down a bomb exploded and injured another officer. This barbaric incident was widely condemned. The leader of the Irgun, Menachem Begin, would later go on to found the right-wing Herut Movement and become prime minister of Israel.

The British announced on September 23, 1947, that they would terminate their Mandate in Palestine by May 15, 1948. They had decided to hand over the problem of who should rule Palestine to the new United Nations, set up in 1945. Interestingly, the UN came up with a two-state solution. On November 29, 1947, the UN General Assembly voted to partition Palestine into two states, one Arab and one Jewish, with Jerusalem designated as an international city under UN control. Under Resolution 181 half the territory, including the valuable coastline, was given to the Jews, who at the time controlled only 6 percent of the land. Conflict was inevitable.

Even before the formal outbreak of hostilities in May 1948, there were bloody clashes between Jewish and Arab communities. On April 9, 1948, Jewish terrorists from the Stern Gang and the Irgun attacked the village of Deir Yassin, several miles to the west of Jerusalem, and massacred 250 people, mostly women and children. To protect the Palestinians from such atrocities, my great-grandfather, King Abdullah I, began in late April to move Arab Legion forces across the River Jordan. At the same time, the Jewish leaders began to marshal their forces, including their nascent army, the Haganah, the Irgun, and the Stern Gang.

On May 14, 1948, the day the British Mandate ended, the Jewish People's Council declared the establishment of the state of Israel. Eleven minutes later, this new entity was recognized by U.S. president Harry Truman, followed by the Soviet Union. The tensions between Jews and Arabs did not take long to escalate into armed conflict. On the night Israel declared its independence, Egypt, Jordan, Syria, and Iraq sent troops into Palestine to try to protect the rights of Arab Palestinians. The new Israeli army outnumbered Arab troops and slowly gained the upper hand, profiting from a lack of coordination among the Arab forces.

Jerusalem, with its religious significance for Muslims, Jews, and Christians and its strategic importance for the center of Palestine, was the main focus of the fighting. One of the fiercest battles was around the village of Latrun, allotted to the Arabs under the partition plan, where Jordanian and Israeli forces fought for control of a key road leading into Jerusalem. The Jordanian forces, commanded by Habis Majali, repelled several attacks by the Israeli forces. In one engagement, a young Israeli platoon commander was shot and severely wounded by the Jordanian forces. His name was Ariel Sharon, and he would go on to become a prominent military and political figure — defense minister, and then prime minister.

The Arab Legion, commanded by my

great-grandfather, was among the best-equipped and -trained but also one of the smallest of the Arab armies. It managed to hold the West Bank, including East Jerusalem, and even made gains. In the spring of 1949, after more than eight months of fierce fighting punctuated by intermittent pauses, representatives of Israel and the Arab states met on the Greek island of Rhodes. The Hashemite Kingdom of Jordan and Israel signed a general armistice agreement on April 3. The West Bank had been allocated to the Arabs by the UN, and in recognition of my great-grandfather's role in protecting the Palestinians and holding the West Bank, a group of Palestinian leaders now called for unity with the East Bank under my great-grandfather, who on May 25, 1946, was proclaimed King of Jordan by Parliament, which also changed the name of the country from the Emirate of Transjordan to the Hashemite Kingdom of Jordan. So in April 1950, in an Act of Union of the two banks of the Jordan, the West Bank formally became part of the Hashemite Kingdom of Jordan, and gained representation in the Jordanian parliament and government.

Before, during, and after the 1948 war some 750,000 Palestinian Arab refugees fled the fighting or were evicted from their homes. They settled in the West Bank, Jordan, Syria, Lebanon, the Gulf states, and elsewhere in the region and beyond. In many countries they remained stateless refugees, unable to travel or work, and living in United Nations refugee camps, but my great-grandfather welcomed the Palestinian refugees to Jordan, granting them Jordanian citizenship. More than sixty years later, the right of these refugees and their descendants to return to their homes in what is now Israel remains one of the most contentious issues between Israel and the Palestinians.

Famous for his compassion and kindness, my great-grandfather took a special interest in my father. He understood English but did not speak it, so he would sometimes call my father to his office in the palace to act as his translator. In the evening, my great-grandfather would discuss the events of the day over dinner, explaining to my father the intricacies and subtleties of the diplomatic negotiations he had been translating.

My father was sent away to boarding school in Egypt. He went to Victoria College in Alexandria, which at the time was probably the best school in the region. In the summer of 1951 he was back in Jordan when tragedy struck. On July 20, on a visit to Jerusalem for Friday prayers, my great-grandfather was assassinated by a Palestinian gunman at the entrance to the Al Aqsa Mosque. The assassin, a member of the radical group Jihad Muqaddas, shot my great-grandfather in the head and killed him. My father was at his side. He was then fifteen. He chased the murderer, who opened fire on him. A second bullet from the assassin's gun miraculously bounced off a medal that was pinned to his chest — it missed killing him by the narrowest of margins — and a third clipped his ear. The assassin was then killed by my great-grandfather's guards. Six other men were later arrested and sentenced to death for their parts in the plot. Four were executed, but two somehow managed to find refuge in Egypt, which refused to hand them over.

My great-grandfather's tragic murder was mourned across the region and the world. My grandfather, Talal bin Abdullah, who had attended the Royal Military Academy Sandhurst in the United Kingdom and served in the Arab Legion as a cavalry officer, became king, and in accordance with the Constitution, which states that succession passes to the king's eldest son, my father became crown prince.

At the time, Egypt was publicly antagonistic toward the Jordanian government, and it was felt that it was too risky for my father to continue his schooling in Alexandria. So he was sent to Harrow in England. Although my father knew that he would someday assume official duties, his personal hope was that he would be able to finish his education and begin a career, living an ordinary life for a time. But my grandfather, who suffered from schizophrenia, was unable to rule for long due to poor health, and he abdicated a year after he assumed office. On August 12, 1952, my father was on summer holiday from Harrow in Switzerland with his mother, Queen Zein Al Sharaf. He was staying at the Beau Rivage Hotel on Lake Geneva when he received a telegram addressed to "His Majesty King Hussein."

Back in Amman, my father discussed with his uncle Sharif Nasser bin Jamil how best to fill his time, as it would be six months before he would reach the legal age to accede to the throne. Their conversation turned to Sandhurst, which was famous for educating leaders in all walks of life. His uncle said, "Your father went to Sandhurst. I remember him telling me that Sandhurst was the greatest military academy in the world and the finest place for a man to learn to be a king."

My father's mind flashed back to when he was a child playing toy soldiers, and he remembered my grandfather saying, "No man can rule a country without discipline. No man can be a good soldier without discipline. And nowhere in the world do they teach men discipline like they do at Sandhurst."

So on September 9, 1952, Officer Cadet King Hussein arrived at Sandhurst and joined Inkerman Company. The regular yearlong course was compressed into six months. Although my father had a demanding schedule, with extra drills and marching, that time was one of the happiest and most formative periods of his life. For a brief moment longer, he would be a cadet among other cadets.

On May 2, 1953, when he reached the age of eighteen, my father assumed his responsibilities as king. He would rule Jordan for forty-six years and would see four major wars between Israel and the Arab states. He would eventually reach a peace treaty with Israel, and would see his Israeli partner assassinated for seeking peace, but he would not live to see the end of the conflict he had so yearned to help settle.

My father's first test, three years after he assumed the throne, was the Suez crisis. Following the Egyptian revolution of 1952, which toppled King Farouk and led to the rise of Gamal Abdel Nasser, nationalist sentiment was running high in Egypt. In 1956 Nasser nationalized the Suez Canal, which until then had been controlled by Britain and France. In reaction, the two countries cooked up a secret plan with Israel. Israel would attack Egypt, and in response Britain and France would send "peacekeeping troops" that would retake control of the canal.

The Israelis kept their side of the bargain, advancing into the Sinai Peninsula in October 1956. An Anglo-French task force deployed shortly afterward and seized the canal. While militarily successful, the operation became a political fiasco as news of the plot leaked. Under pressure from the United States, Britain and France were forced to remove their troops, and British prime minister Anthony Eden resigned. The Suez crisis strengthened Nasser's Arab nationalist credentials and heightened tensions between Israel and the Arab world. It also suggested the usefulness of a crisis as a pretext for intervention by Western powers. Thankfully, Jordan avoided being drawn into the Suez affair. But we were not so fortunate the next time Egypt and Israel fought each other, in the spring of 1967.

# CHAPTER 2
# THE 1967 WAR

From my room, I heard a muffled bang, followed by several others. Grabbing my telescope, I ran down the corridor to the window. I could see a black column of smoke in the distance and heard another explosion, this time louder. Israeli jets were attacking Palestinian guerrillas outside Salt, a town fifteen miles northwest of Amman. My father rushed up and took the telescope from me. After twisting it and realizing that it was a toy, he impatiently threw it to the floor and ran off to change into his military uniform.

I was five years old and this was my first experience of war. About forty minutes later I heard the staccato cough of anti-aircraft guns as the Jordanian army fired at the Israeli planes.

When my father returned that evening, he looked distraught and went straight into his bedroom. Although I was young, I could sense something was terribly wrong. I followed him and found him sitting on the bed with his face in his hands. He looked up as I entered, and I could see that his eyes were damp. That was one of the very few times I ever saw my father cry. I asked him what was wrong and why there was so much noise and so many airplanes flying overhead.

He patiently explained that the Israelis were trying to hit Palestinian guerrilla fighters who were living in Jordan. I had no understanding at that time as to what guerrillas were or why the Israelis were trying to kill them. All I knew was that things were bad. Rather than selecting specific military targets, the Israelis were bombing communities full of families, devastating the roads and houses.

Many of their munitions did not explode immediately. My father told me about a little girl who, thinking the danger was over, had approached one of the bombs; it then exploded. He rushed to free her from the rubble, but when he dug her out he found that she was badly injured. She had lost one of her legs. Gently cradling her, he ran to a nearby ambulance, but it was too late. She died in his arms.

We lived in a small, tree-lined compound in a district called Hummar, twenty minutes up into the hills outside of Amman. The relative seclusion provided some protection from those who wanted to hurt us, but not from Israeli planes: for that we had to rely on four .50 caliber quad guns mounted on turrets in the garden. The soldiers manning the guns kindly allowed my four-year-old brother, Feisal, and me to think we were part of the defensive effort. Our job was to carry oil cans and lubricate the guns if they started firing. We enjoyed our role as the most junior members of the military unit — an association that came to an abrupt halt when someone showed my mother a photo of us posing by the guns with cigarettes dangling from our mouths. My mother still lives in that house, but the area where the anti-aircraft guns were is now a vegetable garden; one gun was mounted on what is now a compost heap.

Although as a child I could perceive the emotional impact of the war, at that time I had little idea of its meaning and implications.

In the spring of 1967 it was already clear to many in the region that Israel and its Arab neighbors were racing headlong toward a collision. In November 1966 Israeli forces launched a devastating attack on Samu, a village near Hebron, as a reprisal for the killing by landmine of three soldiers, raising concerns in Amman about Israeli intentions. In early May, President Nasser deployed troops in the Sinai Peninsula and requested that the UN remove its peacekeeping troops (the United Nations Emergency Force, UNEF) from the Sinai, where they had been positioned since the Suez crisis more than a decade earlier. Not long after that, he closed the Straits of Tiran, Israel's only access to the Red Sea, to Israeli shipping.

The Arab forces were not a cohesive army but a collection of separate national armies that had recently joined together. Following a series of failed attempts at closer political union among the Arab states during the 1960s, the Egyptians, the Syrians, and the Iraqis had joined their militaries together to form the United Arab Command in 1964. Egypt and Syria then signed a defense treaty in November 1966.

In late May 1967, sensing the looming possibility of a conflict, and given the highly charged Arab nationalist sentiment at the time, my father felt he had no choice but to announce his support for Arab leaders in the face of Israeli aggression. He went to Cairo and, in a fateful decision, committed Jordan to a mutual defense treaty with Egypt. From then on, the Jordanian Armed Forces would be under the command of an Egyptian officer, General Abdul Monim Riad. The Israelis decided on a preemptive strike, claiming that Nasser was planning to attack. They had already prepared the way.

At that time, the Middle East was a focus of intense competition between the rival superpowers locked in a cold war. The region was divided into two broad areas of influence: a pro-Soviet camp, led by Nasser and the Egyptians, and a pro-Western camp, to which my father belonged. According to declassified U.S. documents, on June 1, 1967, General Meir Amit, the head of the Mossad, the Israeli foreign intelligence service, visited Washington, D.C., and met with Richard Helms, the director of the Central Intelligence Agency.

Drawing upon American fears of Soviet expansionism, Amit portrayed Egypt and Nasser as a threat not just to Israel but to the whole region. According to Helms, Amit's view was that the Egyptian president would, if left unimpeded, draw the entire Middle East into the Soviet sphere of influence. Jordan's forced accommodation with Egypt was by this logic a sign of things to come. Saudi Arabia and Lebanon would be next, after which it would be the turn of Turkey and Iran. Even Tunisia and Morocco would eventually topple to Nasser. Summarizing their conversation in a memo to U.S. president Lyndon Johnson, Helms said, "Amit thinks the Israelis' decision will be to strike."

General Amit's visit was a warning from Israel to America. Unless President Johnson told them not to do so, Israel would attack Egypt.

On June 3, President Johnson wrote to Prime Minister Levi Eshkol of Israel, saying, "I must emphasize the necessity for Israel not to make itself responsible for the initiation of hostilities." Then Johnson added, "We have completely and fully exchanged views with General Amit." The next day Amit returned to Israel, and Johnson's letter was delivered to the Israeli government.

One of Israel's greatest talents has been exaggerating the threat posed by countries it considers strategic enemies, perpetuating the story of it being a tiny nation surrounded by hostile powers. This myth has allowed the Israelis to portray their own calculated acts of aggression as self-defense and, in some cases, to persuade other nations to attack its enemies in its stead.

In 1967, in military terms, Israel was certainly a match for its Arab adversaries. The Israeli army was some 300,000 strong, with 800 tanks and 197 fighter aircraft. The combined Arab armies had some 240,000 men, 900 tanks, and 385 aircraft of all types. But simply comparing combat strength is misleading. For one thing, the largest Arab army, the Egyptian army, at over 100,000 strong, had around one-fifth of its men in Yemen at the time, supporting the Republican forces in the ongoing civil war. By telling the Americans that Egypt posed a threat to the entire region, Israel had at best misled and at worst purposefully lied to a nation that was and still is one of its closest allies.

Learning of the impending conflict from NATO intelligence, Turkey's ambassador to Jordan warned my father of an imminent Israeli attack. My father immediately told Nasser, who refused to heed the warning.

In implementation of the defense pact Jordan had entered with Egypt, General Riad assumed command of our armed forces. He was at a severe disadvantage, as he did not know the terrain in Jordan or Palestine well, nor did he have a good sense of the capabilities of the men under his command. In addition, he took his orders from Cairo, not Amman. If Israel were to attack Egypt, Riad would order Jordanian troops into battle, and we would be at war with Israel.

On June 5, 1967, Israeli jets flew into Egypt and struck at the Egyptian air force. Egyptian planes were not their only targets. That same day two Israeli Mystère jets attacked the royal palace in Amman, targeting my father's private office with rockets and machine-gun fire. Thankfully, he was at army headquarters at the time. If he had been at the palace, he would have been killed.

Our whole extended family, including my uncle Prince Muhammad and his two sons, Talal and Ghazi, lived in our house during the war, camping out in sleeping bags in the basement. My uncle Muhammad, who was in charge of my father's security, slept on the floor with a machine gun outside my father's bedroom. To a five-year-old it all seemed like a great adventure; I was too young to understand the tragic events that were unfolding.

One afternoon my brother Feisal and I were hiding in the basement with assorted aunts, cousins, and other relatives. It was another Israeli air raid, and we could hear the explosions outside. My brother dared me to run across the lawn, touch the fence, and return. With Feisal goading me on, I dashed onto the lawn and ran as fast as my legs would carry me. There was a huge explosion. I burst into tears and ran back into the house.

Throughout the day of June 5, 1967, the Israeli air force attacked our bases in Amman and Mafraq, destroying our landing fields and our fleet of Hawker Hunter aircraft. For the next two days Jordanian forces fought bravely to defend the West Bank and East Jerusalem, but, outmanned and outgunned, and with no air cover, they were overwhelmed by the Israelis. The Royal Jordanian Air Force also did an amazing job considering its limited resources and the superiority of Israeli airpower, shooting down eight Israeli planes and launching two attacks on central Israeli cities. It was the only Arab air force that downed Israeli planes during this war.

Pressing on, the Israeli armed forces, commanded by Yitzhak Rabin, attempted to seize control of the whole of the West Bank. Determined to be on the front line, my father headed down to the Jordan Valley to be with his men. When he got there, a terrible sight awaited him, which he later described: "Roads clogged with trucks, jeeps, and all kinds of vehicles twisted, disemboweled, dented, still smoking, giving off that particular smell of metal and paint burned by exploding bombs — a stink that only powder can make."

Throughout the evening of June 5 and into

the next day our soldiers and tank drivers, including the 40th Armoured Brigade in which I would later serve as a young soldier, showed great courage, but they were helpless under the bombardment of Israeli fighters. Most of their tanks were destroyed by Israeli bombs. My father later described the battle, saying, "That night was hell. It was clear as day. The sky and the earth glowed with the light of the rockets and the constant explosions of the bombs pouring from Israeli planes."

The war was disastrous for Jordan and for other Arab states. When the fighting stopped on June 10, Israel had taken the West Bank and East Jerusalem from Jordan, the Sinai Peninsula and Gaza Strip from Egypt, and the Golan Heights from Syria. Much of the territory it seized in 1967 is still illegally occupied by Israel today. Some two hundred thousand to three hundred thousand Palestinians crossed to the East Bank of the River Jordan, increasing the total number of Palestinian refugees in Jordan to around three-quarters of a million. The Jordanian Armed Forces were devastated. Seven hundred were killed and some six thousand wounded, and we lost all of our air force and most of our tanks. Following the end of the war, Jordan's weakened armed forces underwent a vigorous program of restructuring and retraining, assisted by a Pakistani advisory mission headed by Brigadier Zia-ul-Haq, who later became president of Pakistan.

Seizing the West Bank was in no way necessary if Israel simply intended to respond to a perceived threat from Egypt. But Israeli leaders wanted defense in depth, as they put it, so when the chance arose to acquire more territory, they took it. And once they had it, they were determined to hang on to it.

The consequences of Israel's occupation of the West Bank and East Jerusalem continue to resonate across the region and the world to this day. The loss of Jerusalem was particularly painful to my father. My family belongs to the Prophet Mohammad's branch of the Quraish tribe and directly descends from the Prophet through the male line of his elder grandson, Al Hasan. ("Hashem" was actually the great-grandfather of the Prophet; hence the family name, "Hashemites.") From AD 965 until 1925 the Hashemites ruled the Hijaz in western Arabia and served as the guardians of the holy cities of Mecca and Medina, making us the second-oldest ruling dynasty in the world after the Japanese imperial family. As the head of the Hashemite family, responsible for safeguarding Jerusalem, my father was devastated by his inability to protect Jerusalem and the Al Aqsa Mosque, one of the three holiest sites in Islam, from the encroaching Israeli army.

As soon as the war ended, the negotiations for peace began. The Arab Summit in Khartoum in late August, though famous for its "three nos" — no to peace, no to recognition of Israel, and no to negotiation with Israel — had in fact provided a framework for the pursuit of diplomacy. Talks in November continued at the Waldorf-Astoria in New York, home of the U.S. ambassador to the UN, Arthur Goldberg, who hosted private meetings between the Israeli, Egyptian, and Jordanian delegations. A former justice of the Supreme Court, the ambassador was a prominent supporter of Israel and as such was viewed with suspicion by my father and the Egyptians. Their suspicion turned out to be justified.

According to notes from one of my father's close advisers who was involved in the discussions, Goldberg sent an oral message to my father that if the Arabs would accept a UN Security Council resolution, the United States would push for Israeli withdrawal from the occupied territories, and that any changes to the prewar borders would be "minor, reciprocal border rectifications."

Goldberg indicated that the Israelis were onboard. My father flew to Cairo and discussed the proposal with Nasser, who asked him to support the resolution.

In early November my father returned to New York to meet with the UN secretary-general, U Thant, and to confer with the other Arab delegations in the run-up to the next Security Council meeting. He met with President Johnson at the White House on November 8; then, after spending ten days in the United States, he left for Europe. The final result of the negotiations, UN Resolution 242, was adopted by the UN Security Council in a unanimous vote on November 22, 1967. The resolution called for Israel's withdrawal from territories (the Arabic text called for withdrawal from "the" territories, while the English text spoke only of territories) it had occupied in exchange for peace, thereby launching the land-for-peace formula that would underpin Jordan's future foreign policy. The resolution's preamble stressed the inadmissibility of the acquisition of territory by force and said:

[T]he fulfillment of Charter principles requires the establishment of a just and lasting peace in the Middle East which should

60

include the application of both the following principles:

(i) Withdrawal of Israeli Armed Forces from territories occupied in the recent conflict;

(ii) Termination of all claims or states of belligerency and respect for and acknowledgment of the sovereignty, territorial integrity and political independence of every State in the area and recognized boundaries free from threats or acts of force.

The resolution also made clear the necessity of achieving a just settlement of the refugee problem. Over forty years later, UN Security Resolution 242, which Jordan played an important role in formulating, is still the primary reference point for building a lasting peace between the Israelis and Palestinians.

For most of the Arab world the conflict was over, but for those of us living in Jordan the troubles were just beginning. Another storm was brewing, only this time, rather than involving an external enemy, it would set brother against brother.

# CHAPTER 3
# DARK CLOUDS OVER AMMAN

In the aftermath of the 1967 war some three hundred thousand refugees from the West Bank poured into Jordan. Yasser Arafat, a Palestinian who had lived in Egypt before moving to Kuwait in 1957, where he cofounded the Fatah movement before relocating to Syria in the early 1960s, also moved to Jordan in the aftermath of the war. Fatah, along with a number of armed Palestinian factions loosely gathered under the umbrella of the Palestine Liberation Organization (PLO), began to call for armed resistance against Israel. Fatah and other Palestinian guerrillas, known as the fedayeen, recruited disaffected young men from the refugee camps and began launching attacks across the Jordan River against Israeli forces.

The following year, the Israeli army decided to hit back. In the early hours of the morning of March 21, 1968, expecting an easy victory, Israel sent two armored brigades across the River Jordan. Their plan was to strike at the refugee camp at Karameh, twenty miles west of Amman, where some of these Palestinian fedayeen were based, and then to continue on toward the capital. The Jordanian army, which was still recovering from the 1967 war, engaged the Israeli forces in fierce fighting and inflicted heavy enough losses on them that in a few hours they started screaming for a cease-fire. My father insisted that there would be no cease-fire until the last Israeli soldier withdrew from Karameh. Fifteen hours after the attack, the Israeli invading troops completed their withdrawal in tattered regiments. In the battle of Karameh, the Israelis suffered their first defeat by an Arab army. Although the fedayeen took part in the fighting, the victory was achieved by the army. But Arafat and his guerrillas were quick to claim the credit. They soon came to believe in their own rhetoric and to flex their muscles, so much so that the fedayeen, as an armed movement, began to represent a challenge to the country. They threatened security, broke laws, and sought to establish a state within the state.

During the 1950s and early 1960s Jordan was tremendously vulnerable to regional political upheavals. This was the age of Arab nationalism. Revolutionary Nasserites in Egypt and the secular Baathists who took over Syria and Iraq were then very popular. They had grand visions of Arab unity, and their aspirations for geopolitical dominance extended to Jordan. Between the time my father was eighteen, when he became king, and thirty, when I was three years old, there were eighteen documented assassination attempts against him, including two by traitors inside the Royal Court. The assassins were working for Gamal Abdel Nasser and his United Arab Republic, a three-year union between Egypt and Syria (1958–61). The UAR was allied with the Soviet Union. My father was an ally of the West, and by killing him Nasser and the Soviet Union hoped to create instability in Jordan and to push the country into their orbit.

The first inside job involved acid. My father, who was in his mid-twenties at the time, suffered from sinus problems, so he would regularly use saline solution in nose drops. Somebody with access to his personal bathroom switched the saline solution for hydrochloric acid. By accident, one of the containers fell into the sink. When the enamel began to steam and crack under the powerful acid, my father realized that he had narrowly escaped a very painful death.

The second assassination attempt involved poison. My father noticed that dead cats began to litter the palace grounds. When his staff investigated this curious development, they found that an assistant chef in the palace kitchen had been hired to kill him. The chef, a good cook but a poor poisoner, had been practicing his art on the unfortunate cats, trying to judge the correct dose.

Partly because of the high probability that one of these assassins might eventually succeed, and in order to protect the monarchy, my father decided in 1965 to remove the title of crown prince from me when I was just three years old. He designated his brother Prince Hassan, who was then eighteen, as his successor instead. Although I was oblivious to the change at the time, it was one of the best things he ever did for me, as it allowed me to lead a relatively normal life. One of the few traces of my brief time as heir apparent is a set of stamps with my image as a three-year-old. But I did not need formal titles to enjoy my childhood.

My father had a silver Mercedes-Benz 300SL gull-wing roadster, which he had raced in hill climbs in Lebanon in the 1950s. I loved the way the doors lifted upward like something out of a movie. He was really into fast cars and was always racing around on a motorcycle, in a car — or by helicopter. In those days we did not have the wide array of TV channels that we have today — in fact, there were only two hours of TV a day in Jordan, so we had to make much of our own entertainment. In calmer moments my father, mother, and I would sometimes drive out north. Since my father's 300SL was only a two-seater, I would sit on his lap. Speeding along on desert roads, he would beep the horn to keep the beat as we sang "Popeye the Sailor Man," the theme song to one of my favorite shows. At dusk we often stopped for a picnic next to a wheat field. The soldiers guarding us would go into the field, pick heads of wheat, and roast the kernels on leaves over a wood fire. Ever since then, I have loved the smell of roasting wheat.

Every boy at some level thinks his father is a king. I knew my father was special, and I understood he was a leader, although I did not really comprehend what he did all day. But I cherished those moments we spent together. My parents tried their best to let my brother Feisal and me experience normal lives as children. They would bring us to a small farm down in the Jordan Valley on Fridays, along with friends and their children. Another family activity we enjoyed was target practice. We had a shooting range at the bottom of the garden, and my father, my mother, Feisal, and I would take turns firing at targets.

My mother grew up in an army family. Her father, a British officer, had fought in World War II and after that in Malaya, and had taught her to shoot as a young girl. She was an excellent shot. When she was a teenager her father was posted to Jordan, and she met my father at a diplomatic reception. She was just nineteen at the time, and he was twenty-five. He was entranced by her beauty and charm and would invite her to the palace from time to time to watch a movie with his mother and family. My mother reciprocated by inviting him to her parents' house, where he was served cakes and strong English tea. They discovered a shared interest in motor sports, and got to know each other better on trips to the Amman Go-Kart Club, where my father taught her to drive. Soon she was competing in the ladies' races. About a year after they first met, my father proposed and, too overcome to speak, she simply nodded her assent. Born Antoinette Gardiner, my mother converted to Islam before the wedding, became a Jordanian citizen, and took the name Muna Al Hussein.

Two days before the wedding they were discussing my mother's future role in the royal family when she said, "Does it sound ridiculous if I say that I don't really want the title of queen?" Delighted that she was marrying for love rather than a title, my father gladly assented, and they were wed on May 25, 1961, in a simple ceremony at Zahran Palace in Amman. After the wedding my mother became Princess Muna, and the next year, I arrived.

Amman in 1968 was not the safest of cities. Yasser Arafat and his guerrilla fighters were launching attacks from Jordanian territory into Israel, and the Israeli army retaliated periodically, striking targets inside Jordan. Apart from Israeli bombs, there were various Egyptians and Syrians with nefarious designs: Soviet-sponsored communist agitators and hired assassins determined to destabilize moderate governments like ours. Amman became a gathering place for all types of radicals, from the German Baader-Meinhof Gang and the Japanese Red Army to the Venezuelan terrorist Carlos the Jackal, many of them attracted by Jordan's proximity to the Israeli-occupied West Bank and the possibility of striking at Israel. With the Jordanian army patrolling the borders, the guerrillas and radicals took over parts of the city. They established roadblocks and brought whole neighborhoods under their control. I remember when we drove down from our house into Amman at night in my mother's old white Mercedes, we had to cover the headlights lest roving guerrillas open fire. My mother never left the house without a Kalashnikov in the passenger seat and a small Colt revolver in the glove box.

The situation in Jordan was especially dispiriting because the country had welcomed Yasser Arafat and his men with open arms after the 1967 war and had allowed the PLO to enjoy freedom of movement. But Arafat failed to repay this generosity. His forces started to undermine the state. They levied taxes and ignored the laws. Many guerrilla groups under the PLO acted with impunity. If they were hungry, guerrilla fighters would break into a house while the owner was at work and force his wife to cook lunch for them at gunpoint. They would kidnap people for ransom, kill people at random, confiscate cars, occupy homes, and attack hotels, hoping to take foreign nationals hostage.

I was six years old at the time and my parents decided to send me out of the country to escape the mounting violence and chaos inside Jordan. Since my father had gone to Harrow, England was a natural choice. I still remember arriving in the evening at St. Edmund's School, a large country house in Surrey set in extensive grounds. Driving from Heathrow Airport through the green fields and tightly packed hedgerows, I felt a long way from the dusty desert roads of Jordan.

Although the teachers were friendly and welcoming, I was not happy at St. Edmund's. Part of my dislike was due to leaving my parents at such a young age and part of it was due to the language. Arabic is my first language, and since we had a Swiss nanny I spoke a fair amount of French at home. English was the weakest of the three languages I grew up speaking. And yet before too long I had mastered English and picked up a British accent that has stayed with me. A year and a half later my brother Feisal joined me, but we were not going to stay in England for long.

Tensions had been growing between my father and the guerrilla forces. As Arafat stepped up his efforts to seize control of Jordan, his men began to turn their attention to its king.

In September 1970, as my father headed into Amman accompanied by Zaid Rifai, the stately Harvard-educated chief of the

Royal Court, and Sharif Nasser bin Jamil, a heavy, barrel-chested man who at that time was chief of staff of the Jordanian army, he was stopped at a crossroads by a roadblock. When one of his men got out to move the roadblock, guerrillas who had been hiding in the hills opened fire with a variety of weapons, including a Russian-made Dushka heavy machine gun. The soldier trying to remove the barricade was killed, and my father saw the bullets coming closer, hitting the ground like hail. Everybody piled out and began to return fire. My father shouted, "Shame on them!" — which may seem like an odd thing to say when you are being attacked, but he had a strong sense of personal honor and believed that his assailants were nothing more than cowardly bandits. Zaid Rifai and Sharif Nasser pleaded with him to take shelter in a nearby ditch. When the attackers saw my father take cover, they swung the heavy machine gun around to target him. Zaid Rifai and the commander of the Royal Guard dove to protect him, colliding in midair, and both fell on top of him. My father felt his back buckle under the weight.

Once they had beaten back the attackers, my father and his men jumped back into their cars. My father was in the front seat when he realized his beret had fallen off and was lying in the dirt. He was so furious about being ambushed that he got out and, with bullets flying, strode over to pick it up. He placed it on his head, then calmly got back into his car and drove off. As they headed back to our house in Hummar he turned to Zaid Rifai and said, "Next time, I'll take my chances with the fedayeen. You two did more damage than they did!" From that point on, he often complained of a bad back.

By this time, following two failed cease-fires, it was clear that Jordan could not coexist with Arafat's guerrillas. At the time, the PLO and its affiliates numbered around 100,000 men: 25,000 full-time fighters and some 75,000 armed militia. And they kept getting bolder. On September 6, 1970, the radical Popular Front for the Liberation of Palestine (PFLP) hijacked three international airliners that had taken off from Frankfurt, Zurich, and Amsterdam en route to New York and diverted two of them to Dawson's Field, a remote airfield in the desert in the Azraq area in northeast Jordan — the third was diverted to Cairo and blown up. Three days later, a third civilian airliner was hijacked to the same strip. The guerrillas demanded the release of Palestinian militants held in

European jails. When their demands were not met, on September 12, under the gaze of the world media, the guerrillas blew up the three planes after releasing all the passengers. Two days later the PLO called for the establishment of a "national authority" in Jordan.

For my father, this was the final straw. Eight days later, on September 17, he ordered the army to move aggressively against the fedayeen in Amman and other cities. It would be a mistake to characterize this confrontation as a civil war between Jordanians and Palestinians. Many Jordanians of Palestinian origin fought bravely in the army. And some Jordanians from the East Bank had joined the guerrilla forces fighting against the army. As chief of staff of the army, Sharif Nasser led the struggle. A powerful man and a fierce warrior, he looked like he could punch a horse and knock it out cold. One of his favorite tricks was to grab an onion in one hand and crush it into a pulp, squeezing it over his dinner plate to add a little spice to a bland meal.

The fighting between the Jordanian forces and the fedayeen was fierce. Before long, we were not only contending with internal enemies. In the fall of 1970, Syria attacked northern Jordan with three armored brigades, a brigade of commandos, and a brigade of Palestinian guerrillas, seeking to help Arafat's men. Although heavily outnumbered, the Jordanian soldiers of the 40th Armoured Brigade, who were responsible for defending the border, fought back fiercely and held their ground. Syria's invasion threatened to create an international crisis out of a domestic conflict. On September 23, the Syrians were driven back. But while we had defended our northern border, inside Jordan the conflict with the fedayeen continued to rage.

In the end, the Jordanian Armed Forces, with their superior professionalism, training, and equipment, prevailed. The fighting with the guerrillas continued off and on until the summer of 1971, but Jordan won. The army regained control of the country and legitimacy prevailed. My father and Sharif Nasser learned that Arafat was hiding in the Egyptian embassy in Amman, which was hosting a visiting delegation from the Arab League. As the delegation members were leaving, they appeared to have gained an extra member: a stocky woman covered from head to toe in a black *abayah* and head scarf. My father's intelligence service reported that the mystery woman was likely Arafat trying to escape.

Sharif Nasser wanted to capture and kill Arafat and argued that he did not deserve to live. But my father told his men to let Arafat leave Jordan. He always believed that it was important to leave open the possibility of reconciliation.

Twenty years later my father would save Arafat's life for a second time. In April 1992, Arafat's plane crashed in the Libyan desert during a sandstorm, killing three of the passengers. By then, much had changed in their relationship. My father would have been a doctor had life not led him into politics, and when he saw Arafat two months later he noticed that he seemed unwell. He sent him to the King Hussein Medical Center. It turned out that Arafat had a blood clot in his brain, which the doctors safely removed in an emergency operation.

When the Palestinian guerrillas were chased out of Jordan, many of them made their way to Lebanon, which would become the next arena of an even more bloody war. Meanwhile, back home, a handful of radical guerrillas formed a sophisticated new internationally funded terrorist organization. Calling themselves Black September, after the month in which the conflict between Jordan and the PLO began, they vowed to take revenge for their defeat. One of their first acts was to assassinate the Jordanian prime minister, Wasfi Tal, on a visit to Cairo in November 1971.

The following month Zaid Rifai, who had recently become Jordan's ambassador to the UK, received an urgent telegram from my father saying that a Black September assassination squad had been dispatched to London to attack a Jordanian target. Rifai arranged for extra security at the embassy and drew up a list of potential targets, including me and my brother Feisal, who had recently joined me at school in England. Although I was almost ten, I quickly got the sense something was wrong when policemen with guard dogs came to my school and stayed with me around the clock.

The next day, Rifai left his home in Regent's Park later than usual. The car drove past Christmas shoppers on Kensington High Street, and as it slowed to make a sharp turn, a gunman sprang into the road, pulled out a Sten gun, and started spraying bullets. Realizing that he was the target, Rifai threw himself on the floor of the car while the gunman kept firing at the backseat. After the shooting stopped, Zaid Rifai yelled at the driver to take him to a hospital. The car sped away; then, after a few minutes, it stopped. "What's the matter?" Zaid asked. "Your Excellency," said the driver, who was an Englishman, "we have a red light."

Rifai survived, but his wounds were quite extensive, and he required eleven operations on his hand and arm. There was little doubt as to who was responsible: Black September. My parents came to the conclusion that England was no longer safe. They decided to send Feisal and me even farther away: to America.

# CHAPTER 4
## ARRIVING IN AMERICA

Nineteen seventy-two was a difficult year for my family, and not just because of threats from terrorists. That was when my parents decided, after ten years of marriage and four children (my twin sisters Aisha and Zein were born in 1968), to divorce. The fact that my brother and I were away at boarding school did not shield us from the uncertainty that all children from divorced families must face. But we were fortunate that our parents always remained very close and were united in their concern and support for us.

In September 1972, Black September carried out another attack, taking hostages and subsequently killing eleven Israeli athletes at the summer Olympic Games in Munich. The attack took place in the spotlight of the assembled media from across the globe, and now the whole world had witnessed their brutality.

In October my brother Feisal and I went

to America. On our first trip to the United States a few years earlier we had been to Florida with our parents and little sisters and had visited Cypress Gardens and the recently opened Disney World. So I was excited at the thought of returning to the States — in my mind, it was one big theme park. But New England in the fall was not quite Disney World.

My new school, Eaglebrook, a prep school in western Massachusetts, was perched on a hill in the Pocumtuck range overlooking the town of Deerfield. The school had the feeling of a Swiss mountain resort, complete with chalets and its own ski run. Feisal and I shared a dorm room, and he went to school at Bement, just down the hill. Another change that took a bit of getting used to was the food. One of my favorite snacks in Jordan was bread and *zeit ou zatar,* olive oil mixed with dried thyme. But here I was introduced to the delights of peanut butter and jelly sandwiches.

I did not like St. Edmund's in the UK, but I never got into a fight there. Eaglebrook was different. I was the first Arab the school had ever seen, and there were several Jewish students. Pretty soon, some of them let me know I was not welcome. I did not understand their animosity and was too young to have encountered the concept of irrational prejudice. In later years I would become all too familiar with people who judge individuals on the basis of their identity, but to a child it made no sense. I knew that Jordanians and Israelis were enemies, but we were now in the United States, and these were Americans. In my mind there was no connection between an Israeli and a Jew. But even in western Massachusetts, it seemed, I could not escape the conflicts of the Middle East.

I got into a number of scrapes. Although I had security guards who accompanied me everywhere, their instructions were to protect me from terrorists and assassins, not from aggressive ten-year-olds. Sometimes I did not help my case. In one confrontation, my antagonist said, "Yeah, you and whose army?" I replied, "Me and my dad's army!"

One afternoon one of the proctors — older students who were responsible for keeping discipline — kicked my brother out of our dorm room, brought in an older boy from down the hallway, and said, "You and he will fight." I was enthusiastic, but I did not know how to fight and neither did he, so we locked arms and pounded each other on the back. The proctors let us go at it until we were out of breath, separated us, and then made us go at it again. I jumped onto a bed and leaped at my antagonist, knocking him over. He fell and hit his head hard on the floor. We were all scared something had happened to him, and the proctors hauled him away. It was completely by chance, but because I had taken down a much bigger boy, the others began to show me a little more respect.

I had just arrived at Eaglebrook when my father married Alia Toukan, the daughter of a Jordanian diplomat from a prominent family of Palestinian origin. Tragically, Queen Alia was killed in a helicopter crash in 1977, when she was just twenty-eight years old. The following year my father married Lisa Halaby, the daughter of an Arab-American businessman and senior U.S. Defense Department official, and she took the name Queen Noor.

I have quite a large family. In addition to my older sister Alia, from my father's first marriage in the 1950s to Sharifa Dina Abdel Hamid, there were my brother Feisal and my twin sisters Aisha and Zein. My father's marriage to Queen Alia produced another sister, Haya, and another brother, Ali, and they adopted an orphan girl, Abir. Later on, after my father married Queen Noor, we were joined by two more brothers, Hamzah and Hashim, and two more sisters, Iman and Raiyah. In all we were twelve children, five boys and seven girls, but very much one family. My four brothers and I like to say we are like five fingers on a hand. If you are well-meaning, we extend the hand of friendship, but when outsiders try to harm the family, we band together and become a fist.

Nineteen seventy-two was as turbulent a year for the region as it was at home. The United States under President Nixon, preoccupied with its overtures to China, ceased most diplomatic activity aimed at mediating a resolution to the Arab-Israeli conflict. In Egypt and Syria, impatience over the stalemate was growing. Anwar Sadat, who had succeeded Nasser as president of Egypt in 1970, declared in a speech in late March, "War is inevitable." In September 1973, Sadat and Syrian president Hafez al-Assad agreed to coordinate a simultaneous attack on Israel so both could regain territory they had lost in the 1967 war.

On October 6, 1973, Egyptian troops attacked the Sinai while Syrian forces targeted the Golan Heights. After recovering from the surprise attack, three weeks into the war the Israeli forces gained the upper hand. Though neither Sadat nor Assad had informed my father of their war plan, Jordan was drawn into the fray as the whole Arab world supported the war. My father's priority was Jordan's safety. He put Jordanian forces on high alert, and sent the 40th Armoured Brigade to support the Syrian army in the Golan Heights rather than risk opening a third front by crossing the border into the West Bank. Three days later Jordanian forces briefly engaged Israeli forces and one company suffered heavy losses. A ceasefire was declared on October 22. The war did not change the status quo; if anything, it cemented it. That would be the last war between Israel and its neighbors for nearly a decade. Four years later, in November 1977, President Sadat would become the first Arab leader to visit Israel. In September 1978, Egypt and Israel signed the historic Camp David Accords, which were partly brokered by President Jimmy Carter. A year later, the two countries signed a peace treaty. Israel returned the Sinai Peninsula to Egypt. In exchange, Egypt became the first Arab country to recognize Israel.

Although the conflict was five thousand miles away, its reverberations managed to reach as far as the hills of western Massachusetts. One of Eaglebrook's cherished traditions was for the younger students to help out at mealtimes. Shortly after the war began, I was in the dining hall when the headwaiter, one of the older students, stared at me and told me to come over. As I walked up, he hit me. The dining hall was bustling with students, and I stared at him in disbelief. He said, "You're an Arab, and I hate you!" and then turned and walked away. When I returned to Amman for the holidays, my mother asked me about my time at school, and although I would sometimes say I was not enjoying it that much, I never got into the specifics. I had been brought up to believe that you never told tales, and that you should fight your own battles.

While back in Jordan on holiday, I hurt my wrist in a boating accident. After the local doctor patched me up, putting my arm in a sling, I walked into the house feeling sorry for myself. I saw my father and was about to tell him all about the accident, when he gave me a look that said, "What are you whining about?" He was from that generation that believed in being personally tough. Not wishing to appear weak, I took the sling off, which caused my arm to swell up badly. Three days later I got it X-rayed and discovered that it was fractured and required a cast.

That accident finally established me at

Eaglebrook. With my broken wrist I could not take part in ski classes. When the cast came off there were about three weeks left to the term, and I was thrown in with the wrestling team. My father, a physical fitness buff, had given me some exercises to do called Commando 7, based on a Canadian army training program. I took to wrestling and discovered that I could be good at it. The next year, as I began to get stronger and fitter, I joined the wrestling team. While they may not have respected titles, my fellow students greatly respected sporting ability. In addition to wrestling, I took up track and field. In those days I was a pretty good sprinter, and I would eventually become captain of both my high school track and wrestling teams. Sport provided me with a way to escape the narrow prejudices of some of my classmates and gave me an early opportunity for leadership.

Though I may have had bumpy times with my fellow students at Eaglebrook, the same was not true with my teachers, who were excellent. I thrived under their care and still have fond memories of many of them, especially the dorm masters, my French teacher, and my wrestling coaches. They taught me a lot and helped me acclimatize to the United States.

When it came time to go to high school, I went down the hill, to Deerfield Academy, while Feisal, who was a year and a half younger than me, stayed behind at Eaglebrook. Although only about a mile away, it was a different world. With two hundred years of tradition behind it, Deerfield was dedicated to high academic standards but also to personal development. There was an atmosphere of genuine respect and tolerance and a strong sense of community among the students. I can truly say that the years I spent at Deerfield were some of the happiest of my life.

I had good sports credentials for a new boy and made it onto the school wrestling team in my sophomore year. But not without a struggle. In those days, wrestling was very regimented by weight. The coach told me that if I could get down to 118 pounds, I would make the team. The problem was, I weighed 130 pounds and was in good shape. I realized that the only way I could lose all that weight was to stop eating, so for three weeks I ate nothing but wafer crackers and diet Jell-O. I made the team, won all my matches, and in the third match pulled off a victory by pinning my opponent in a record eleven seconds. But my success was short-lived. Because I had been undereating, I could not concentrate in class and my grades took a sudden turn for the worse. Also, I started passing out and went on sick leave for a time. As a result, they took me off the team and put me on the backup squad.

Although it was hard being so far away from home and from my family, the egalitarian spirit of America was refreshing. Back in Jordan I would always be the eldest son of the King, and this would bear on all my interactions, whether with teachers or fellow classmates. But at Deerfield it did not matter whether you were the son of a chief executive officer, a scholarship kid from Chicago's South Side, or one of the Rockefellers — everyone had the same tasks to perform and the same opportunity to shine. Each day at mealtimes some students acted as waiters, serving their classmates. At one point, when it was my turn to serve, I was not doing a very good job. Jim Smith, who ran the dining hall and was also the football coach, good naturedly yelled, "Abdullah, I don't care if your father is the King of Jordan, I am the king in this dining hall!" I got the message and my performance improved. Smith was quite popular with the students. He had a large family himself, several boys and a girl, and looked on the school as an extension of his family. He would frequently break out into song in the dining hall — and although he had a fine voice, the students enjoyed pretending that it reminded them of the sound of fingernails on a blackboard.

At Deerfield I made my first close American friends: George "Gig" Faux, from outside Boston; Chip Smith, a preppy New Englander; and Perry Vella, who had come on a scholarship from Queens, New York. My classmates knew my background, but they did not stand on ceremony. To them, I was just Abdullah or, as they more often called me, "Ab." Deerfield allowed me to have a normal childhood and gave me the tools to turn into the man I needed to become. To this day, some of my closest friends are my old Deerfield classmates.

Since Jordan was too far to go for anything but the longer holidays, I spent many vacations with Gig and his family. Halfway around the world from home, I valued the chance to spend time in a family atmosphere. Back then you had to schedule an international phone call days in advance, so I managed to speak to my father only once or twice a semester.

My security guards lived close by, in a house on the edge of campus. They gave me an early taste for "covert action": I used to delight in finding new and innovative ways to escape from the dorm at night without being observed. Although we did not often succeed, it provided great training for Gig and me when in our senior year we became dorm proctors. By that point we knew most of the tricks, sometimes the hard way. Gig's father was an air force fighter pilot, and Gig had somehow managed to get his hands on a military distress flare. Curious to see how it worked, one night we snuck out of our dorms along with two other friends and set the thing off. The flare soared through the New England night, illuminating the campus with a bright red glow, and headed toward the white-pillared entrance to the Old Gym, a magnificent, sturdy building that housed the squash courts and wrestling facilities. Panicked that it would burn down the gym and maybe hit the neighboring dining hall, we sprinted toward the building as fast as we could. I can still remember my relief when we figured out that the flare had shot over the roof of the gym and landed in the playing field.

Although my guards had not been terribly useful in protecting me from the other students at Eaglebrook, they did have one overwhelming virtue: their own car. Gig and I would ask them to take us to his parents' house whenever we had a long weekend. The first time we visited, Gig's parents were a little nervous to see us pull up in a car accompanied by armed bodyguards. Thankfully, Gig's younger brother Chris broke the tension as I got out of the car — by shooting me with a BB gun. After that, we all laughed and relaxed into the chaotic family atmosphere of the Faux home. Gig's mother, Mary, an Italian American, had cooked a delicious lasagna that I would come to know well. After each visit, she would give us a large tray to take back with us to Deerfield, and to this day I cannot eat anyone else's lasagna.

One of my favorite teachers was Dan Hodermarsky, the exuberant, white-bearded head of the art department. He was a warm, gregarious character and beloved by many of the students. Like so many of the Deerfield teachers, "Hodo" looked after us as if we were his own, often delighting in our antics but reeling us in with gentle admonitions.

When it came time for him to go to high school, Feisal, not wanting to forever be known as "Abdullah's younger brother," decided not to follow me to Deerfield. When we were children he was determined to do everything the opposite of me. If I wore a T-shirt and jeans, he would wear a suit.

Very academic and gifted at math, he went to high school at St. Albans in Washington, D.C., before studying electrical engineering at Brown University in Providence, Rhode Island. After Brown, he forever differentiated himself from me by attending the Royal Air Force College in Cranwell, England, graduating top of his class and winning five of seven possible awards for cadets. He later joined the Jordanian Air Force as a pilot.

My time at Deerfield passed quickly, and before I knew it I was coming to the end of my senior year. I was planning to attend Dartmouth with Gig, but my life was about to take a quite different turn. Shortly before graduation I sat down with my father, and he asked me how school was going and what I planned to do next. I told him about my plans for university, and how I wanted to study law and international relations. After listening quietly for some time, he said, "Have you ever considered the military?" Coming from my father, this was more of a command than a suggestion. So I began to look at options. I went to visit the Citadel, the military college in South Carolina, but was put off by the thought of four years of its strict, Prussian-style curriculum. When I walked through the dining hall, the cadets seemed very stiff and formal. It was a long way from what I had experienced at Deer-field.

Back in Amman one evening I was watching a movie with my father and Feisal. Sensing that I was not excited by the thought of an American military education, my father said, "What about Sandhurst? It's where your grandfather and I went. Why don't you go there?"

# PART II

PART II

# CHAPTER 5
## SANDHURST

The gravel crunched beneath the car's tires as I pulled up to the gate. I got out of the car, picked up my bag, and walked through with the academy adjunct, who was responsible for welcoming new students. Back in the United States in the fall of 1980 my Deerfield friends were discovering the delights of pop, dancing to Fleetwood Mac and the Blues Brothers. Some of my peers in the UK were engaging in body piercing and dyeing their hair purple. But I was about to undergo quite a different experience. Walking through the gates of the Royal Military Academy Sandhurst, I was in for the shock of my life.

The first five weeks were hell. We marched for hours on the parade ground, woke up before dawn to go running in the pouring rain, and shined our boots endlessly, with color sergeants shouting at us constantly. I thought, "What the hell have I got myself into?" All my classmates from Deerfield were freshmen at places like Dartmouth, Brown, and Columbia, where the toughest thing they had to contend with was another freezing winter. And here I was running around the Barossa training ground, mud on my face, carrying a rifle. It was surreal. Alongside the training ground was an old Roman road nicknamed Devil's Highway. After a couple of hours out there in the cold I had a pretty good idea how it had gotten its name.

In those days most incoming cadets were high school graduates, all about eighteen. I do not think most of us had any idea of what was in store. Half of the cadets dropped out of my platoon within the first five months. The training course was designed to be tough, and the military brass fully expected people to quit. They were weeding us out and wanted to keep only the ones who would not cave in. I remember training one afternoon under the watchful eye of Color Sergeant Lawley. He ran us down to the main gate, from where we could see the Staff College at Camberley, which provided postgraduate military education for senior officers. It looked like a little palace. He made us all do push-ups, and as we lay facedown in the mud, he said, "That is Staff College over there. And looking at the bunch of you, this is about as close as you are ever going to get!"

Sergeant Lawley was a philosopher in a soldier's sort of way. We were in the middle of a live-fire exercise in the countryside and things were going from bad to worse. My section of cadets was about to assault a hill, and we were waiting for the order. He and I were sitting slightly apart from the others, off to one side behind a few trees. He said, "Mr. Abdullah, there's something I've been meaning to tell you." He paused for effect. "You're always going to be in the shit. It's just the depth that's going to vary." I adopted that as my motto, and to this day still think of his words whenever I am facing a tough situation.

Those of us who made it through basic training became commissioned officers. Then, for those planning on a career in the military, another five or six months of officer training followed, covering leadership, British military doctrine, and international relations. After receiving my commission as an officer in the British army from Queen Elizabeth, I would have to choose a regiment. I was encouraged to join the Coldstream Guards, a historic infantry regiment, one of the oldest in the British army and part of the queen's personal guard. It was thought a fitting regiment for a prince — and, more important, my color sergeant was a Coldstreamer. So I began making preparations to sign up.

The problem was, the day-to-day life of an infantryman was proving less than glamorous. On a rare weekend break from Sandhurst, I met up with the crown prince of Bahrain at the Dorchester Hotel in London. Hamad Bin Isa Al Khalifa was a close friend of my father, and I looked on him as an uncle. A fellow Sandhurst graduate, he smiled in recognition when I told him about the punishing training we were being put through. As I said my good-byes, he provided me with a welcome surprise: a hamper of sandwiches from the Dorchester kitchens. I was the most popular cadet in my platoon that evening, although I am not sure the other cadets believed me when I told them the sandwiches were a gift from the crown prince of Bahrain.

Years later, on a trip to London, I too bought a hamper of sandwiches from the Dorchester. I knew that the grandson of Sheikh Hamad, who had by then become the king of Bahrain, would welcome the gift. He was attending Sandhurst and I had all too vivid recollections of what he was going through.

In the spring of 1981, a week before I had to make my final choice of regiment, I was on an exercise with my platoon at a training area near the Welsh border. We had been dug in for four days and the weather was foul — snow, sleet, and freezing fog. I had trench foot, and we were all miserable. The nights were so cold and awful that some of the cadets actually wept.

At dawn, after we had put in a counterattack against one of our positions taken by the Gurkhas, a Scorpion light tank pulled up next to our trench, part of a reconnaissance party for another regiment's exercise. Rumors circulated among the infantry that inside tanks were anything from TV sets to washing machines, even kettles so that tank commanders could serve up their own hot drinks. A cavalry officer popped his head out of the turret of the Scorpion, holding a steaming cup of tea. He took one look at us, disappeared back into the turret, and reappeared a few seconds later holding a small glass of port. He raised his glass to us in a silent toast, then slammed the top shut and drove off.

"That's it, to hell with the infantry," I thought. "I'm joining the cavalry!" The next day I transferred to reconnaissance and signed up for the 13th/18th Royal Hussars, which later merged with another regiment, the 15th/19th, the King's Royal Hussars, to form the Light Dragoons. (A few years ago Her Majesty Queen Elizabeth honored me by making me the Light Dragoons' colonel-in-chief.)

I joined as a second lieutenant, and after two months went for a young officer's basic course before returning to my regiment. I completed my armor training at Bovington Camp in Dorset, and served a year as an officer in the British army, in the UK and West Germany. At that time, in the early 1980s, the cold war was still at its height, and as an armored regiment one of our missions would have been to repel a Russian advance through the Fulda Gap into the heart of West Germany.

One afternoon I was traveling with my regiment on the M4 highway, the main motorway from London to the west, in Fox armored cars, which, although they have turrets equipped with 30mm cannons, move on wheels, not tracks. To a civilian, however, they look like tanks. These armored cars had a reputation for being fast, so I thought I would test them out. We were barreling along well over the speed limit when I looked out of the turret and saw a police car driving alongside us, siren blaring and lights flashing. I gave the order to pull over, and the convoy stopped at the side of the motorway. The policeman got out and walked over, shaking his head. "I have no idea how I'm going to write this up," he said. "Nobody would believe me if I told them I'd pulled over five tanks for speeding on the M4!" We were let off with a warning and told to mind our speed and get on our way.

During the Falklands war, which began in April 1982, when Britain and Argentina fought over control of the Falkland Islands, we were given "dog tags" for the first time — metal tags that soldiers wear around their neck with personal information so they can be identified if they are killed in battle. I called my father and told him they were issuing us with dog tags and it looked like we might be deployed. Without a pause, he said, "If they go, you go with them." As it turned out, another unit was sent, and we spent the conflict on a training exercise in Fort Polk, Louisiana.

In June 1982, as the Falklands war was ending, halfway around the globe another war was beginning. On June 6, the Israeli army invaded southern Lebanon — just four years after it had last crossed the border and occupied southern Lebanon with the purpose of destroying PLO bases and expanding the buffer zone it had established where a surrogate force, under the leadership of a renegade Lebanese army officer, was providing support. By June 1978, Israeli forces had been replaced by the United Nations Interim Force in Lebanon (UNIFIL), established under UN Security Council Resolution 425. Their mandate was to confirm Israel's withdrawal and to assist the government of Lebanon with restoring peace and security.

This time, in contravention of a cease-fire brokered by U.S. envoy Philip Habib in July 1981, the Israeli army, under the command of Defense Minister Ariel Sharon, conducted an aggressive campaign — Israel called it "Operation Peace for Galilee" — in pursuit of Yasser Arafat and his PLO guerrilla fighters. Sharon pushed all the way to Beirut. This was one of the first Middle Eastern wars to be televised, and millions watched in disbelief as for the first time Israeli tanks rolled into the streets of an Arab capital. For me and for all Arabs, this was a tragic, traumatic event. It was a defining moment, and to this day people can tell you exactly what they were doing when the invasion took place. I watched on television in the officers' mess at Carver Barracks in Saffron Walden, just south of Cambridge, as Israeli forces shelled Beirut. They were using eight-inch artillery, which are not known for their accuracy, and I knew that there would be many civilian casualties. But what none of us could know was that civilians would be deliberately and brutally targeted.

By the end of August 1982, PLO forces had been evacuated from Beirut. Then, on September 14, the Christian Lebanese president-elect Bachir Gemayel was assassinated. Two days later, Israeli forces entered West Beirut, and Sharon authorized a group of Christian militia fighters to go into the Sabra and Shatila Palestinian refugee camps to settle some old scores. In the resulting tragedy some eight hundred refugees were massacred. As stories and pictures began to make their way to a horrified world, gruesome scenes unfolded to match the worst of human history. We saw pictures of bodies piled upon each other in the streets, women and children hacked to death with knives and axes, and old men lined up against a wall and shot. Throughout it all, the Israeli army surrounded the camps, firing flares at night to illuminate the way for the murderers going about their sickening work. I was furious, and for days after that I had trouble sleeping. Every time I closed my eyes I was haunted by visions of mutilated bodies.

Across the globe people were horrified by what had taken place. How could Israel claim to be a democratic, law-abiding nation and let its soldiers stand idly by while such crimes were committed? Ariel Sharon, who supervised the operation as defense minister, was viewed by many as a murderer and war criminal. A subsequent Israeli commission of inquiry into the incident (the Kahan Commission), which was established in September 1982, concluded at the end of its work in February 1983 that Sharon bore "personal responsibility" for failing to prevent the massacre and recommended that he be removed as defense minister. Sharon resigned as minister of defense but stayed in the government as a minister without portfolio.

I had thought that perhaps after Sandhurst I would go to university in the United States, but somehow life took a different course. After completing a year in the British army, I went to study international relations at Pembroke College, Oxford. I spent a year among the grassy quads and honey-colored stone buildings of that venerable institution, studying Middle Eastern politics. My time was spent mostly working one-on-one with excellent tutors. I learned a great deal about the challenges of the region and the intricacies of its politics, but this was not the kind of college experience I had hoped for. At the completion of the course I returned to Jordan and my army career. By the age of twenty-one I was pretty much a full-time army officer.

One of my few regrets in life is that I never had a chance to enjoy four years as an undergraduate like my friends from Deerfield. My initiation into the responsibilities of adulthood was accelerated. A military education forces you to mature quickly, challenges you to rise to the demands of leadership, and requires you to look after others. Little did I know then how useful those skills would prove to be.

At Sandhurst and during my year in the British army I was treated very much like the other cadets and second lieutenants. That was important, because it meant that when I went back to Jordan I could easily spot when people tried to give me special treatment. I was determined to make the military a full-time career. I did not want to roll up in a Mercedes from time to time and inspect the troops as an honorary colonel of a regiment. I wanted, as much as I could, to be just another army officer, to lead and fight with my men.

# CHAPTER 6
## QATRANEH NIGHTS

When I returned home in 1983, I joined the 40th Armoured Brigade, a unit with a proud history. The second oldest armored unit in the Jordanian army, it has fought to the last three times, in 1967, 1970, and 1973. I was based near Qatraneh, a small town in the desert sixty miles south of Amman. In the early years of the twentieth century the town had been a stop on the Hijaz railway, the Ottoman-constructed line that connected Damascus in Syria with Medina in Saudi Arabia. It had not seen much action since then. The first night, I was down at brigade headquarters when I heard a bustle of activity coming from the officers' mess. I went to find out what was going on. All the chairs were lined up outside the mess, the officers had been given a cup of tea, and everyone was preparing to watch the sunset. Frustrated that the only excitement the place had to offer after a long day was a cup of tea at sunset, I went back to my room, put my tracksuit on, and went for a run.

The reason I was so far out in the desert had little to do with my military ability. Some senior officers felt threatened by my joining the military, figuring that in time I might encroach on their established ways, and even on their positions. Throughout my military career I had major problems with some very high-ranking officers whose decisions, in my view, had not served the armed forces well. I believed that we needed to modernize and take advantage of the latest developments in military technology and tactics. Staunch defenders of the status quo, these officers saw no need for change and seemed determined to make my life miserable. I think they figured that by piling on pressure with unreasonable requests and surprise inspections, and by isolating me in the desert, they could convince me to quit the regular army in a few months and assume a more ceremonial role.

I was determined to prove them wrong. I felt I could not mention any of this to my father for fear he would secretly intervene to make things easier for me. As it turned out, one of the biggest favors anyone ever did for me was to put me out where the real army was. That is where I stayed, usually for months at a time. Many younger officers do not want to spend much time out in the desert and would rather be back at headquarters in the relative comfort of Amman. Those who serve at headquarters make valuable contributions too, but if you want to learn about your service, the best place to do so is out in the field. Part of learning about the army is being assigned to the back of beyond, having to go through the daily routine and dealing with all the difficult and unpleasant problems that arise. It ruins your social life but teaches you a lot about leadership.

As a twenty-one-year-old second lieutenant I felt a high degree of responsibility for my men, especially as we were all lumped together in a remote location. I was responsible for their training, for making sure that they were fed and clothed, and, to a degree, for ensuring that their dependents were well taken care of. At that time, our army was a mix of professional soldiers and conscripts doing their national service. As with all conscript armies, we had our challenges. Conscripted men sometimes shot themselves in the foot to get out of their obligations. One soldier even injected kerosene into his leg (I had to cut it open with a knife to drain it). An army is a reflection of a country. In

Jordan the army has been a traditional path for advancement, and my men came from all over the country and from all strata of society. They were mainly very poor, and some faced tremendous problems.

One of my fellow lieutenants, who had come up through the ranks, was dealing with a family crisis soon after I arrived. His brother had died. This fellow had a wife and eight children, and his brother also had a wife and eight children, so this one man suddenly had eighteen dependents to take care of on a meager officer's wages. I gave him half of my salary for the whole time I was there — about a year. At the time the army maintained a high state of readiness — at any time a third of our units had to be ready to go on fifteen minutes' notice for a possible war, which meant a lot of extra duty for our officers. I frequently pulled extra duty for him, allowing him to go home on weekends. Clearly, his burdens at home far exceeded mine. To this day I think of my men and their families whenever I focus on outreach programs for housing, health, and education.

Although my men may have been poor, they were rich in courage and fighting spirit. Many had little formal education but more than made up for it with street smarts and raw intelligence. At one point my unit was equipped with new Khalid/Shir I tanks, predecessors to the Challenger tanks from Britain. Boasting the latest in military technology, these fearsome vehicles were driven by a complex system of electronic wizardry. Yet in under a month my men were handling them as if they had been driving them for years.

Conditions were more basic than in the British army, but I liked our ways better. In the officers' mess at the 13th/18th Royal Hussars we came down to dinner in a coat and tie and ate off a table that had been captured from Napoleon in the battle of Waterloo. In the Jordanian mess we ate food that was sometimes well past its expiration date off plastic tables and chairs, but the true essence of an army is not its formal trappings and fancy weapons. It is the ability of its men to face the prospect of death without flinching. And my men were the most courageous soldiers I had ever met.

The 40th Armoured Brigade was commonly referred to as "God's Brigade," a reference to its historical role in defending Jerusalem in 1967 and its record of fighting to the last. The first occasion was in 1967 when, heading to cut off the Jenin-Nablus axis, it encountered two Israeli brigades advancing from the northern coastal plain. In 1970, against heavy odds, it took on better-equipped Syrian troops advancing into Irbid to support Palestinian guerrillas (by the end of that engagement, my unit, the brigade's 2nd Armoured Cavalry Regiment, had only three tanks left, but it stopped the Syrian invasion). In 1973 it fought the Israelis in the Golan Heights, launching an offensive up the slopes of Tal El Harra, a 3,000-foot volcanic mountain. It came under heavy Israeli fire from both flanks and had to withdraw. A motivation for my men was to one day reclaim land lost in 1948 and 1967. From the banks of the Dead Sea, we could see the walls of Jerusalem. Though the Israeli armed forces were much better equipped than us, my men never feared the prospect of facing a heavily armed enemy.

We would go on maneuvers and exercises all across the country, and it was then that I began to appreciate the extraordinary beauty and diversity of Jordan. Jordan is a small country, but in one day you could go from the mountains and pine forests of Ajloun in the north, down through the Roman ruins at Jerash to the Dead Sea, the lowest point on earth. Continuing south along the historic King's Highway, you pass the Crusader castles of Shobak and Kerak, the home of the French knight Raynald de Chatillon, who was beheaded by Salaheddin Al Ayyoubi (known in the West as Saladin) in the twelfth century. Stopping in Wadi Rum, one of the most beautiful desert valleys in the world, and at the ancient ruins of Petra, you would arrive at the beach resort town of Aqaba in the evening.

In the summer we sometimes went on exercises in the Jordan Valley, along the eastern bank of the river. To avoid the blazing heat and huge mosquitoes, we would get up at 4 a.m. and try to finish any strenuous tasks before the sun rose. The earth there is very fertile and reddish brown, and in the evening the setting sun glimmering off the rocks produces a range of brilliant red hues. Red has always been my favorite color: it is the color of the Hashemite flag, of the kouffiyeh, the traditional Jordanian headdress, and of the heart.

One afternoon I thought I would try out some of the new tactics I had learned at the armor school at Bovington, so we went out on an exercise. I had been taught how to perform a "fighting withdrawal"; that is, how to withdraw gradually when you are being attacked by a superior army, inflicting casualties as you retreat. After I had reconnoitered the first position with my noncommissioned officers (NCOs), we reconvened to discuss our approach to the battle. I said, "Right, let's go to the second position." One of my NCOs looked at me and said, "Sir, there's no need for a second position. This is where we are going to fight and die if necessary. We are not going to retreat!" I was impressed by his courage but a little startled by his tactics. He had been trained in the old school, where retreat meant dishonor. This fighting spirit had served Jordan well in 1948, when we preserved Arab control over East Jerusalem and the West Bank; in 1968, when we beat back an Israeli incursion at the battle of Karameh; and in 1970, when our army pushed back a Syrian invasion from the north. But with the increased firepower of modern weaponry, and the devastating combination of air strikes and long-range artillery, holding the line could be suicide.

I was determined to make my men more effective by supplementing their fierce courage with some tactical cunning. If we moved a few positions farther back, I argued, following standard NATO doctrine, we could kill more of the enemy as we retreated. The men looked at me quizzically and went into a huddle. Finally they emerged and said that killing the enemy was more important than holding the line; they agreed to retreat to the next position. That was my introduction to the fighting spirit of the Jordanian soldier. Nothing at Sandhurst had prepared me for this eagerness to die fighting. My men's passion reflected the temperament common in the dangerous neighborhood in which we lived. At that time, Jordan was still in a state of cold war with Israel, and although the shooting had stopped, we had to be ready to face a threat from our nuclear-armed neighbor at a moment's notice.

In March 1984, Queen Elizabeth II came to Jordan on a state visit. Security was extremely tight, as two days before the queen's arrival terrorists had set off a bomb at a hotel in Amman. My father asked me to serve as military equerry (a sort of aide-de-camp) to the queen and her husband, Prince Philip. It was an honor, and particularly exciting as I had fairly recently graduated from Sandhurst and served in the British army. Due to the security concerns, my father also asked me to be the queen's personal bodyguard. I went to Special Forces to receive extra training. As the day approached I asked my father: if somebody fires at me I'll fire back, but how far do you want me to go?

"If somebody fires at the queen," he said, "you will put yourself in the way. And if it means losing your life to protect our guest, you bloody well do it. Otherwise I'll shoot you myself!" I knew he was choosing his words for effect, but for my father, duty and honor came first, even before his own family.

I stayed by the queen's side for the duration of her five-day visit, and, thankfully, was not required to take a bullet for her. Although he could at times sound tough, my father and I bonded over our shared passion for the military. We enjoyed watching old movies together and often swapped notes on the latest military equipment produced in different countries and whether we should use it. It seemed that my military career earned me a newfound respect in my father's eyes as, slowly, he began to ask me to undertake extra duties and responsibilities.

Since the time of my great-grandfather, King Abdullah I, and the Arab Legion, the Jordanian army has been one of the best-trained, most disciplined, and most professional armies in the Middle East. But I was determined to make our army one of the best in the world. "Don't compare us to other armies in the region," I would argue, "compare us to NATO." To achieve this, I knew that we had to modernize. Although my soldiers were talented and courageous, they were being let down by a system that at times failed to provide advanced equipment. I learned to cope with what we had, to be resourceful, and to find innovative solutions. I would beg, borrow, or steal to get my men the equipment and supplies they needed.

Like all young men, I was impatient for change. But frustration mounted as I saw how far some of the most senior officers would go in defending the status quo.

# CHAPTER 7
## A SECRET MISSION

I was relaxing at my army base in Qatraneh one evening when the phone rang. My father asked me to come to Amman to see him immediately. I drove to meet him, wondering why he had to see me so late at night, and arrived around ten o'clock.

Pulling me to one side, my father told me he intended to go to Aqaba tomorrow night. From there, he would take a boat to meet with the Israelis to press them to agree to a solution that would end their occupation of the land they had seized in 1967 and bring peace to the region. "I want you to be my driver and bodyguard," he told me. Although Jordan shared a lengthy border with Israel, it was very foreign territory for us. To enter Israel would be like a West Berliner sneaking over the wall for a visit to East Berlin during the height of the cold war. I said it would be an honor to be at his side. He told me to meet him at the airport the next morning. Heading home, I felt excited, but also nervous. I was a captain in the army, and escorting my father on a secret mission into enemy territory was a weighty assignment. For the first time I would not just be an observer of Arab-Israeli history — I would play a small part in it myself.

I have decided to tell this personal story because it offers a glimpse of the huge risks my father would take for peace. With his passing, I feel it is important to describe how dedicated he was to bringing about a regional peace that would ensure an Israeli withdrawal from all occupied Arab territories, especially Jerusalem, which had a special place in his heart. He believed that peace was a right for all peoples of the region, Arabs and Israelis. You make peace with your enemies, not your friends, he would say. Nothing good would come of refusing to engage them. My father met many times with Israelis to discuss proposals, but he always held to the idea of full Israeli withdrawal from the West Bank, including East Jerusalem, as the basis of a solution. Jordan shared a 375-mile border with Israel and he felt discussions were needed to prevent war. We had already experienced one disaster in 1967 and needed to avoid another. One of my father's greatest virtues was that he was trusted and admired by everyone, even by those who disagreed with him. He was far too well-mannered to point out that many of the Arab leaders who criticized him publicly for engaging Israel were asking him in private to intercede on their behalf.

My father and I flew from Amman south to Aqaba, accompanied by the prime minister, Zaid Rifai, and by Sharif (later Prince) Zeid bin Shaker, the chief of the Royal Court. The plan was to take a clandestine nighttime trip in a small fishing boat across the Gulf of Aqaba into Israel. When we reached Aqaba we found our boat and waited for nightfall. Around 9 p.m. the four of us boarded the thirty-three-foot fishing boat and sailed out of the harbor. We headed for the border, then crossed into Israeli waters. Proceeding cautiously, we flashed a light from the bow of the boat and saw a light flash back. Out of the darkness came a small dinghy with Efraim Halevy, a member of the Mossad, the Israeli foreign intelligence service, onboard. Halevy, a British-born lawyer who would go on to head the Mossad, was not much for conversation that night, and beckoned for us to follow him. We began to pull in closer to Israel. A location for the meeting had been agreed, but the dinghy changed course. Sharif Zeid was very concerned. "This is not what we agreed on," he said. My father motioned for me to come with him to the top of the boat. When we were out of hearing, he said, "Well, what do you think?"

As a young man on his first secret mission, I urged my father to go ahead. He looked at me and smiled. We went back to the others and my father told Sharif Zeid, "It's okay, we're going to do this."

We went all the way to the Israeli city of Eilat, a short distance from Aqaba, and anchored in front of a naval hangar, some 325 yards from shore. My father, Zaid Rifai, and Sharif Zeid boarded the Israeli dinghy and went ashore, and I was left alone to guard the boat.

I turned off all the lights and scanned the beach with my binoculars, looking for Israeli soldiers. Everything seemed quiet. I saw a campfire and a couple of hippies sitting next to it, playing the guitar. I caught a glimpse of a glowing cigarette butt next to the hangar and focused on it with the binoculars. It was an Israeli sniper, watching me. I had no means of communicating with my father and realized how isolated I was, sitting alone on a fishing boat outside an Israeli port. So I took my hand grenades and rigged them up along the side of the boat with a pulley system. One pull of the string would set the whole lot off.

It must have been ten o'clock at night when we arrived, and hours went by while I waited for my father and the others to return. At one point I thought, "In about five hours, the sun will come up. I'm all alone on a boat in an Israeli harbor, loaded to the gills with guns and grenades, and nobody knows I'm here. If my father doesn't come back, what will I do?" Fortunately, I did not have to storm the beaches single-handedly or return to Jordan and explain how I had managed to misplace the king. Shortly before sunrise my father came back via that same small dinghy, and we all sailed back to Aqaba. Although my father never spoke of what had taken place that night, meetings such as this one laid the groundwork for the peace treaty that would eventually be signed between Jordan and Israel.

Over the years I progressed through the ranks, occasionally leaving Jordan for brief periods of training, then returning to the army. One memorable trip was a six-month company commander training course at Fort Knox, Kentucky, in the United States in 1985 to study armor strategy and tactics. Although we were closing the gap with the NATO armies, we still had a ways to go, particularly in obtaining the most advanced military equipment. One afternoon I was pulling on my kit when a colonel in the Israeli army who was attending the same course walked up next to me. Seeing the patch on my shoulder, he said, "40th Armoured Brigade, eh? You Jordanians are tough." He was obviously referring to the strong fight the brigade had put up against the Israeli army in the 1967 war.

When I returned to Jordan I was made a company commander in the 91st Armoured Brigade, which was based in Zarqa, to the northeast of Amman. The second largest city in Jordan, Zarqa was known for its military garrison, as well as for some heavy industry. Unlike towns with large military bases in England, such as Aldershot, where there could sometimes be tensions between the soldiers and the locals, in Zarqa the soldiers felt very much part of the community. People from all over Jordan serving in the army had moved there along with their families, so the inhabitants were diverse, with strong links to the military.

On the base, officers and soldiers would eat in separate mess halls, but once off base these distinctions disappeared. At that time there were very few restaurants in Zarqa, so my friends and colleagues would invite people to their houses to eat traditional Jordanian food. A particular delight was *mansaf*, boiled lamb served on a bed of rice, with a yogurt sauce garnished with roasted pine nuts. We would eat in the traditional way, using our hands.

One of the less pleasant aspects of life in Zarqa was the industrial pollution. There was an oil refinery to the north of town and a tannery to the south, neither of which was kept to modern environmental standards. When the wind blew in a certain direction, the fumes from the two factories mixed together, creating an unpleasant sulfuric smell. For a change of scene, we would sometimes head to the nearby town of Ruseifa, known for its gardens and citrus trees, to sit and eat in a restaurant, watching the world go by.

Although personally I was having a very good time, professionally it was tough. I still had not resolved my differences with some of the senior army officers who were determined to derail my career. Word had come down from the top brass to make life difficult for me, and during the year or so that I was in Zarqa my company was always getting extra duties and surprise inspections. I was friends with a group of other company commanders, with whom I would hang out to pass the time. I had a more formal relationship with another company commander, who was from a bedouin background and always respectful, but kept his distance.

Every year there was a general inspection, which required a lot of hard work and preparation. You had to lay out all your equipment, and the inspectors would go through the books to see if anything was missing. If you had lost even a spanner there would be big trouble, so all the companies would exchange notes and swap equipment before the big event. Normally the annual inspection was for the entire brigade, but one night the bedouin company commander came up to me and said, "They're going to have a surprise inspection tomorrow, just for your company. They want to catch you out, so they can send a bad report up to headquarters." This was unprecedented.

The other company commanders, whom I had thought were my friends, abandoned me and left me to my own devices, but the commander who had kept his distance said, "I'll give you anything you need." We worked together all night to make sure my company would be ready in the morning. I apologized to my soldiers, telling them that the extra scrutiny was imposed because of who I was, but that unfortunately we had no choice but to put up with it.

The battalion commander came in with his team the next morning and carried out the surprise inspection. We passed. But then an incident occurred the likes of which I have never seen before or since. The battalion commander walked up to my senior NCOs, who were standing in a line, and said, "Your boots are not good enough." My men had been up all night, and their boots were gleaming. While looking him straight in the eye, the battalion commander ground his boot into the sergeant major's. Another senior NCO did not answer a question fast enough, and the battalion commander, breaking all the rules, slapped him across the face, which in my culture is incredibly insulting.

At that point, I snapped. I followed the battalion commander back to his office and said, "If you ever touch another one of my soldiers again, I swear to God I'll shoot you." I think that got his attention. I am not someone who easily loses his temper, but his behavior toward my soldiers made me so angry. And although my outburst protected my company, that was not one of my proudest moments.

For the rest of my time in that company, which was around six months, I stayed in my room in the evenings. I never went back into the officers' mess. My fellow company commanders had let me down, and I elected to distance myself from them. This was the lowest point in my army career, and I gave serious thought to quitting. I badly wanted to talk about my problems with my father, but I didn't want to get special treatment. So I turned instead for advice to my uncle, Prince Hassan. After we discussed the difficulties I was facing, he suggested that I should wait out the end of my tour and see how I felt.

In 1987, I took a break from my military career and spent a year at Georgetown University in Washington as a mid-career fellow in the Master of Science in Foreign Service program. I studied international relations and got to know the U.S. capital well. When I got back from Georgetown, I again discussed my army career with my uncle, and said I was thinking about choosing a different career. Prince Hassan said, "Why give the bastards the satisfaction?" Although we did not always see eye to eye in later years, my uncle was a source of support and wise advice then, especially over problems that I felt I could not speak to my father about.

After leaving Zarqa, I continued in the armored corps and learned to fly attack helicopters.

■■■■

In the late 1980s I was invited by General Norman Schwarzkopf, who had recently taken over as commander in chief of U.S. Central Command, to spend a week on a training mission with the U.S. military in the Arabian Gulf. The Iran-Iraq war was drawing to a close, but oil tankers passing through the strategically important Strait of Hormuz would occasionally be attacked, so the U.S. Navy had extended its protection to all neutral ships. Special Forces troops, based on a floating barge in the Gulf, provided extra support, searching for hostile ships.

At that time, the Gulf was a very dangerous place to be. In May 1987 a friendly Iraqi F-1 jet fired two Exocet missiles at the U.S. frigate USS *Stark,* killing thirty-seven sailors and nearly sinking the ship. The Iraqis said that the attack was an accident. In April 1988 the frigate USS *Samuel B. Roberts* was badly damaged when it hit an Iranian mine; one American helicopter was lost in the U.S. response, and both of its crew members were killed. Then, on July 3, 1988, the American cruiser USS *Vincennes* mistook an Iranian civilian airliner as an attacking military aircraft. Tragically, the Iranian Airbus was shot down and all 290 civilians onboard died.

When I arrived in the Gulf, things were very tense, and the narrow waterways were crowded with American, Iranian, Iraqi, NATO, and even Soviet ships. Over the previous several decades control of the Gulf had been one of the major strategic issues in the Middle East. At Georgetown I had discussed such topics in abstract terms, analyzing the politics of the Middle East like a giant chessboard. But here the chess pieces had surface-to-air missiles and could fire back. I was seeing the larger political issues playing themselves out in real time and understanding both what it meant in practical terms to prevent the Iranians from blocking the Gulf and how small incidents had the potential to escalate quickly.

Although a civilian career has many strengths, some things you get only through serving in the military. If I had been a lawyer in Amman, I would have had a very different perspective of the conflict. But here I was, an army officer observing helicopter missions protecting neutral shipping. It gave me an up close and personal understanding of regional power struggles that would prove to be increasingly useful in the years to come.

I spent three days on the frigate USS *Elrod*.

Although I was well looked after, bunking in the captain's quarters, it did not make me want to join the navy. After three days, I transferred to a large barge called the *Hercules,* which was bustling with action. It was interesting to see so many different branches of the military — U.S. Delta Force teams, Navy SEALs (Sea, Air, and Land teams), and regular soldiers, sailors, and airmen — all working seamlessly together. The experience helped shape my enthusiasm later for creating our own Special Operations Command in Jordan.

Not long after that, in January 1990 and almost a year after I was promoted to the rank of major in February 1989, I returned to England for further military training. I spent nearly a year attending Staff College. It was next to Sandhurst, and as I drove through the ornate gates I remembered my time as a cadet, and my old color sergeant predicting that none of us would ever see the inside of the place. His taunt had worked.

As part of our introduction to international politics, we were scheduled to go on a trip to East Berlin, which was canceled at the last minute because of the dramatic changes then taking place. The previous November my fellow students and I had watched in amazement as the Berlin Wall fell and the old world order we had known was swept away. The confrontation between the West and the Soviet Union had divided the globe into two competing blocs. Old certainties would all too soon be replaced with new, shifting alliances.

In the Middle East, countries that had long looked to the Soviet Union as a patron were slow to adjust to a changed world, one in which there was now only one superpower. Opportunists and predators began to make different calculations about war and peace than when the region was divided into Soviet and Western spheres, and a small flashpoint could trigger a global conflict. What none of us at Staff College knew was how soon we would have to confront the new dangers of a changed world.

# CHAPTER 8
# "YOU GUYS DON'T STAND A CHANCE"

On my return from Camberley Staff College in October 1990, I rejoined the Jordanian army and became the representative of the armored corps in the office of the Inspector General. It was my job to ensure that there were common standards of training and equipment across all sectors of the Jordanian military. After Staff College, you are expected to serve at headquarters in a staff posting for at least a year, so I was posted to Amman.

Two months earlier, Iraq had invaded Kuwait. It was a terrible time for all of Iraq's neighbors. We share a long border with Iraq to the east, and we had to wonder whether Saddam Hussein would stop with Kuwait. My father was shocked at Saddam's action and had a tremendous sense of foreboding. As bad as the invasion was, he felt it was the beginning of something much worse. I was with my father at the offices of the Royal

Court, known as the Diwan, the day after the invasion. We listened together to the first reports of the Iraqi incursion.

That fall, Saddam Hussein became public enemy number one in the United States. But he had not always been regarded as a villain. A few years earlier he had been viewed as an ally against Iran. Although my father was no friend of Saddam, he had developed a close relationship with him in the 1980s, during the Iran-Iraq War, when Jordan was a transit point for Western weapons and intelligence to Baghdad.

Swept to power by the Iranian Revolution in 1979, Ayatollah Khomeini called for the overthrow of governments in the region and for their replacement by Islamic republics. Saddam Hussein feared the threat posed to the regional order by the new radical Iranian regime and believed that the Iranians were preparing to attack Iraq. In September 1980, just one year after he became president of Iraq, he launched a preemptive attack on Iran. But the new Islamic Republic fought back fiercely, and for eight years Iran and Iraq were embroiled in a bitter conflict.

Whatever the rationale behind the war, the United States, concerned about Iran's potential to destabilize the region and angered by the seizure in November 1979 of

American hostages at the U.S. embassy in Tehran, gave assistance to Saddam. Iraq, which already had the backing of the Soviet Union, was thus supported in its war effort by both superpowers. The United States covertly provided Iraq with satellite imagery of the movements of Iranian forces, which helped Iraqi military operations and ensured the success of Iraq's decisive 1988 offensive. By July 1988, Iran had accepted a cease-fire.

My father thought it was a good idea to expose younger members of the family to international diplomacy, so one morning over breakfast in the mid-1980s he announced that he would be making a visit to Iraq and he wanted some of us to accompany him. The next day my younger brother Feisal and I and two of our cousins, Talal and Ghazi, gathered at Nadwa Palace, a two-story building inside the Royal Court compound, and set out for Baghdad on my father's plane.

We landed at dusk and were met at the airport by Saddam Hussein, accompanied by his two sons, Uday and Qusay. Ever conscious of security, he had brought along several dummy convoys, all of which left in different directions as we made our way to Radwaniyah Palace, which was not far from the airport. My father's home, with its ten or so rooms, was decidedly modest by comparison. Radwaniyah was built on a grand scale, with hundreds of rooms paneled in ornate marble, gold faucets in every bathroom, and imitation Louis XIV furniture. This gaudy display was not what one would expect from the leader of a proud country that had given us the wonders of ancient Babylon and had once been the seat of the caliphate.

After pleasantries were exchanged, my father announced that we would stay the night. This was unplanned, a gesture of solidarity now that Iraq was mired in a long and bloody war. Saddam announced that, in that case, the next day the youngsters would all visit Habbaniyah, a large lake in Anbar Province, west of Baghdad, to go fishing and swimming. Saddam was ruthless but charismatic and radiated a strange kind of personal energy. He combined the impulses of a traditional tribal leader with street smarts. He was a fascinating character to observe.

Early the following morning we duly assembled in the palace lobby. "We'd love to go fishing," I said to Qusay, "but we didn't bring our swimsuits."

"Don't worry," he said. "We'll provide you with everything you need." We flew from Baghdad to Habbaniyah and went to a palace near the lake to get changed. In the dressing room, Talal, Ghazi, and I found garish Hawaiian shirts waiting for us. Although Iraq and Jordan shared a common language, we clearly did not share a common sense of fashion. We were guests and didn't have much choice, but our security detail burst out laughing when we walked out in our new costumes.

All six of us boarded a small motorboat, the type you might use to pull a water-skier, and headed out to the middle of the lake. At this point Feisal said, "Where are the rods?"

Uday smiled and pulled out a plastic bag filled with dynamite from the bottom of the boat. Grabbing a stick while puffing on a Cuban cigar, he drew a knife and began to cut slashes in the fuse. The idea was that, as the fuse burned down, it would fizz when it hit the knife marks, allowing you to see how close it was to exploding. Grinning, Uday raised the dynamite and lit the fuse with his cigar. The fuse began to sputter and then stopped. "Must be a dud," he grunted. He threw the stick into the bottom of the boat and grabbed another one.

Feisal and Ghazi were talking and looked on unconcerned, but Talal and I had handled explosives as part of our army training and knew this was beyond dangerous. Any professional soldier will tell you that even if a fuse seems to have gone out, it could still be burning. We pressed as far back into the boat as we could, our faces white as sheets, and prayed the "dud" would not go off.

The second stick did not work either. Finally Uday found one that did, and he hurled it into the lake. The idyllic scene was broken a second later by a huge explosion. "Okay, let's go get them," said Qusay, and he suggested that we dive into the water to collect the dead fish that were floating to the surface.

Talal laid his hand on my arm and whispered, "Let's let them get into the water first. Our family hasn't had the best of luck in Iraq." King Faisal II of Iraq and my father were first cousins. They had attended Harrow at the same time and were very close. In 1958, King Faisal was overthrown in a military coup and brutally executed together with the Regent, his uncle Prince Abdel Ilah, and all members of the Hashemite family who were in Iraq at the time. The attackers threw the body of the crown prince out of a window, at which point it was seized by an angry mob and dragged through the streets of Baghdad. The political instability triggered by the coup led to the rise of the Baath Party, and eventually to Saddam Hussein's ascent to power in 1979.

Finally, Qusay jumped overboard and

began grabbing fish and throwing them into the boat. On our return from our "fishing trip" we met my father at the palace. By then, he was ready to go home.

Back in Amman, Saddam's sons would from time to time send me requests through the Iraqi ambassador for the latest machine gun or rifle, knowing that my position as a Jordanian army officer gave me access to advanced weaponry. Usually I complied, as in Arab culture it is traditional to exchange weapons, and I could not easily refuse a request from another Arab leader's son. One time I got a request for a gun with a silencer attached. I politely refused, as by then I had heard rumors that Uday and Qusay would test their guns on unfortunate Iraqis in the basement of their palace. The last time I saw Uday he had recently emerged from prison for killing his father's valet. And the next time I would see Qusay was in Baghdad in January 1991, just before the beginning of the first Gulf War.

On August 2, 1990, after weeks of mounting tension, Saddam Hussein's army invaded Kuwait. Iraqi troops rampaged through Kuwait City, setting homes on fire, seizing goods, and attacking civilians. The emir's younger brother, Sheikh Fahad Al-Ahmad

Al-Jaber Al-Sabah, fought heroically in defense of his country before he was shot by Iraqi soldiers and his body was run over by a tank. Caught up in the turmoil were around four thousand Westerners, including thirteen hundred British citizens and nine hundred Americans. Some of the British and American hostages were used by Iraq as "human shields," held at strategic military sites across the country in the event of an attack. Sixteen days after it adopted Resolution 660, which demanded that Iraq withdraw from Kuwait, the United Nations Security Council passed Resolution 664 on August 18, calling for Iraq to let all third-state nationals leave Kuwait. It soon became clear that the United States was organizing a military response in the event that the Iraqi army refused to retreat.

Over a million people poured across our eastern border, fleeing the conflict. This was a massive influx for such a small country, around a quarter of our entire population at that time. People were camping out in downtown Amman. Jordanians responded with their customary hospitality, coming out onto the streets with gifts of food and clothing. Some even welcomed our unexpected visitors into their homes.

My father strongly opposed Iraq's invasion

and annexation of Kuwait, and reiterated Jordan's recognition of the government of the emir. But he thought this was an Arab problem and that it should be dealt with by the Arab states. Throughout the crisis he did his utmost to work for a diplomatic solution to end Iraq's occupation of Kuwait. A white paper subsequently published by the government in August 1991 highlighted those efforts in order to clarify Jordan's position, which was misinterpreted by some at the time.

Working in close coordination with King Fahd of Saudi Arabia and President Hosni Mubarak of Egypt, my father flew to Baghdad on August 3 to meet with Saddam Hussein. After heated discussions, he managed to persuade Saddam to attend a mini Arab summit in Jeddah on August 5 to solve the crisis within an Arab context. Saddam agreed to withdraw his troops from Kuwait on the condition that the Arab League did not condemn Iraq. He actually announced that Iraq would begin to pull back its troops from Kuwait on August 5. My father believed that he was about to succeed in brokering an Arab solution to the crisis within the forty-eight hours he had requested in his consultations with King Fahd and President Mubarak. But the Arab League rejected this proposal. That evening, the League passed a resolution condemning Iraq's aggression and calling for an unconditional withdrawal. My father's attempts at diplomacy collapsed.

While the Arabs were negotiating, U.S. rhetoric became increasingly belligerent. My father was troubled by the risk of internationalizing the crisis and by the senseless loss of life and destruction a new war would bring. He worried about the destabilizing impact of an invasion of a major Arab country by America and her allies, and of basing Western troops in the Arabian Peninsula and the Gulf. He foresaw that this would set in motion an unstoppable chain of events, leading to retaliation by radical groups and further wars in our region.

A few days after meeting with Saddam Hussein in Baghdad, my father traveled to the United States to speak to President George H. W. Bush at his vacation home in Kennebunkport, Maine. He firmly believed that the standoff could be resolved without war. "We can get Iraq out of Kuwait without violence," he said. He tried to explain the risks of a war in the Middle East, and detailed in sharp terms the destruction and misery it would cause, but President Bush would not listen. "I went to Kennebunkport as a friend!" my father would say in exasperation. "I told the president, I've got a commitment from Saddam to withdraw from Kuwait!" But the president had already made up his mind.

I was fiercely opposed to Iraq's invasion of Kuwait, but like my father I did not support a retaliatory war by the United States. My father had been placed in an impossible position and paid a heavy price for trying to arrange a peaceful withdrawal by Iraq from Kuwait. He felt his mediation efforts were willfully misinterpreted by the West, as he was accused of aligning himself with Saddam's camp. The attitudes of British prime minister Margaret Thatcher and President Bush were, to his mind, too black-and-white; there was no middle way. Most of his friends, including many in the Middle East, turned on him. One person who remained supportive was Prince Charles of Great Britain, who, standing out among all others, seemed to grasp that my father's efforts to slow down the rush to war was not a sign that he was backing Saddam.

In November, the UN Security Council passed Resolution 678 demanding Iraq's unconditional withdrawal from Kuwait by January 15, 1991. My father asked me in December to join him on a mission to Baghdad. This would be his third and last visit during the crisis. He had arranged to go with Yasser Arafat and the vice president of Yemen, Ali Salem al-Beidh, in an effort to negotiate the release of the Western hostages. We flew the five hundred miles from Amman to Baghdad on my father's plane in well under two hours, less time than it takes to fly from Washington, D.C., to Boston. Although Baghdad is close geographically, philosophically it was another world. While my father spoke with Saddam in the main hall of the Republican Palace, I waited outside in a courtyard with Qusay and his brother-in-law, Hussein Kamel. They were smoking and in high spirits. By then I was a major in the army. I told Qusay and Hussein Kamel that I had just completed Staff College in England and had a pretty good sense of how NATO armies operated, particularly with airpower. I said I did not think the Iraqis had the capability to stop the coalition forces and asked them how they would survive a multipronged attack. By then it was clear that most Arab leaders would join the international coalition that the United States and the UK were building to take on Iraq.

The Iraqi leadership was isolated from the wider world, and as can often be the case in dictatorships, nobody wanted to tell the leader that his ideas were faulty. So Saddam's sons had a greatly overinflated — and unrealistic — perception of their military strength.

"We can detect their stealth bombers!" Qusay said triumphantly. "Morale is very high; we want war." Both men went on to tell me about new types of artillery they had developed, secret radar systems and 20,000-pound bombs. None of it made much sense.

"I'm telling you," I said, "from what I learned in England, you guys don't stand a chance." They did not react. They had tremendous national pride but had badly underestimated the capabilities of their adversary. It was the kind of hubris that can (and soon did) cause the deaths of tens of thousands of people.

Shortly after our conversation, my father emerged from the conference hall looking upbeat, and we returned to Amman. The next day, on December 6, 1990, Saddam announced that he would free the hostages. But the preparations for war rumbled on.

Around the New Year, I regularly get together with a group of close friends from the United States and other countries — it has become an annual tradition. That year, given the likelihood of an imminent war on our border, I was not sure any of my friends from outside Jordan would want to come.

As my family and I tried to retain a semblance of normalcy, I could see that my father was exhausted; he was on the phone all day with the Americans, Saddam Hussein, and the Kuwaitis, trying desperately to talk them back from the brink. A few friends and I decided we would try to lift his spirits. We searched through my father's house at Hummar, and inside an old chest we found a collection of photographs of my father with Gamal Abdel Nasser, the British general Sir John Glubb, and many other historic figures. My father looked through the photos while the family gathered around. He gave us an impromptu history lesson, describing what was going on in Jordan at the time each photograph was taken and telling us about these historical figures, their personalities, and the various conflicts he had lived through.

On New Year's Eve that year I was in the Jordan Valley with my friend Gig, who came to visit along with some other American friends despite the protests at home. We talked about our families and the old days back at Deerfield, but most of our conversation focused on the impending war with Iraq and what it might mean for Jordan. If things went badly, would Jordan become the enemy in American eyes? The U.S. Army's 229th Squadron of the 101st Airborne Division, where I had learned to fly Cobra helicopters, had been deployed to Iraq, and it was shocking to think that we might soon be on opposite sides. I was a Jordanian and Gig was an American, but our friendship was stronger than politics.

By January 1991, over half a million troops from a coalition led by the United States and the UK, joined by some thirty other countries, were deployed in Saudi Arabia and the Arabian Gulf. Opposing them was Saddam's army, at around a million strong the largest in the region and the fourth largest in the world. Iraq had obtained weapon systems from all over the world and had been battle-hardened by its long war with Iran, so it was by no means sure that the impending conflict would be a walkover for the Americans.

We were concerned that we could be dragged into the war by either the Israelis or the Iraqis. It was possible that Israeli jets would try to fly over Jordanian airspace to attack Iraq, as Saddam had rhetorically tied his action to the support of Palestine, a common battle cry that still rings throughout the region today. It was equally possible that Iraqi troops would enter Jordan to attack Israel. My father told Saddam, "If one Iraqi soldier steps over the border, we are at war." He conveyed the same message to Israel: if one Israeli fighter flew across Jordanian territory to attack Iraq, it would mean war.

On January 16, 1991, the coalition war on Iraq started. As this was a time of national emergency, my father asked me to be on standby to deploy with the 2nd Battalion of the 40th Armoured Brigade near the border with Israel. A few nights before the fighting started, I was sent one evening to carry out an inspection of a unit keeping guard on the lower Jordan Valley border, down by the Dead Sea. It was the kind of night you find only out in the desert, with a faint light coming from the pale moon overhead. Because there is so little man-made light in the desert, you see many more stars than you do in a city. It feels like you are standing on the edge of the universe, looking in.

Suddenly the darkness was broken by a flash of light as an Iraqi Scud missile blazed across the sky, heading for Israel.

Our air force was on high alert. We worried that the Iraqi air force might try to flee to Jordan. As it turned out, they had gone to Iran to avoid the coalition fighters, and the Israelis held their fire.

Saddam's army was no match for the coalition forces, and six weeks after the war started it was over. From my knowledge of NATO tactics and of the firepower of the U.S. and British militaries, I knew there could be only one outcome, but even I was surprised at just how quickly the Iraqi army was defeated.

There was no love lost between my father and Saddam Hussein. My father was all too aware of the suffering Iraqi forces had imposed on Kuwaitis. But he also wanted to avoid what he believed to be the unnecessary suffering the war would inflict on the Iraqi people. Many Gulf states, including Kuwait, were unable to accept that my father was acting as a mediator seeking to avoid war, and they accused him of siding with Saddam. He was hurt by this. He felt his old allies should have trusted him more and appreciated that he was trying to act in everyone's best interests. Relations between Jordan and Kuwait remained strained for years, and our relations with other Gulf states deteriorated after the war. The resulting loss of financial assistance, of oil from Iraq, Jordan's main source of supply, and of remittances from Jordanians working in the Gulf, as many of them lost their jobs and were forced to return home, would together inflict severe harm on the economy.

All of us in the region were deeply saddened by the death and destruction that the Gulf War wrought. And perhaps that was a reason why some began to search more vigorously for peace with our other neighbor, Israel.

Following the end of the cold war and with Iraq out of Kuwait, the United States and the Soviet Union in October 1991 convened a peace conference in Madrid. The peace talks, which became known as the Madrid Peace Conference, represented a landmark breakthrough in the long history of efforts by moderate Arab states and the international community to resolve the wider Arab-Israeli conflict and negotiate an Israeli-Palestinian settlement. This was the first time that all Arab parties, including the Palestinians, had gathered to address their differences in a mediated forum. The Madrid process, in its bilateral and multilateral forums, revitalized the stalled peace efforts. As the Israelis said that they were not yet ready to negotiate directly with the Palestinians, Jordan offered a means for them to speak with the Israelis under a "Jordanian umbrella" in a joint Jordanian-Palestinian delegation. The goal of the process launched in Madrid was a comprehensive regional peace, and at the beginning of November, Israel began talks with its Arab neighbors on four separate bi-lateral tracks, with Jordan, the Palestinians, Lebanon, and Syria.

The implicit understanding among the Arab states was that they would maintain a united front to preserve the interests of the Palestinians, rather than each negotiating on the basis of its own interests. To do this, they agreed to coordinate their positions and keep each other informed of their progress.

But without my father's knowledge, Israel and the PLO began parallel secret talks in Oslo, Norway, and after eight months un-expectedly reached a historic breakthrough agreement that came to be known as the Oslo Accords. This agreement, which es-tablished mutual recognition between Israel and the PLO and self-government for the Palestinians in Gaza and Jericho, repre-sented a turning point in Israeli-Palestinian relations. It established the framework for a final peace agreement and set up stages for its implementation. The Declaration of Principles was signed in Washington in September 1993 by Israeli prime minister Yitzhak Rabin and PLO chairman Yasser Arafat in a ceremony at the White House hosted by President Bill Clinton.

My father was angered that Arafat had not informed him of the Oslo channel and that he had made a separate peace with Israel. "I can't believe they did this!" he said to me. He was also alarmed that the Syrians were more advanced in their talks than they had told us. Deeply disappointed that the Arabs had not been able to maintain their united front, my father focused more on Jordan's own peace negotiations with the Israelis.

Jordan had actually encouraged direct Israeli-Palestinian negotiations since 1988, when my father made the historic decision to sever Jordan's legal and administrative ties with the Israeli-occupied West Bank. When it was occupied by Israel in 1967, the West Bank was part of the Hashemite Kingdom of Jordan. Palestinians in the West Bank were Jordanian citizens and the government in Amman had remained responsible for their affairs and for sustaining Palestinian schools, the judiciary, and other institutions throughout the occupation. Civil servants in the West Bank were employees of the Jordanian government, even after 1967, and half of the seats in the parliament were allocated for the West Bank. The disengagement decision meant that Jordan would no longer be in charge of these institutions. Only its responsibility for the holy sites was excluded from the decision. My father felt that were he to relinquish his responsibility for the holy sites

151

in Jerusalem, a vacuum would be created that Israel would use to assume control of the sites. So he held on to this responsibility, which was later recognized by Israel in the peace treaty it signed with Jordan in 1994.

My father's formal break with the West Bank meant that the Palestinians could assume responsibility for their own political future in the Occupied Territories. In an address to the nation on July 31, he said that he believed this was the logical response to the conclusion of the Rabat Summit of 1974, when all Arab states had decided to designate the PLO as the sole legitimate representative of the Palestinian people. The decision was also prompted by many failed attempts to coordinate strategy with the PLO and by the outbreak in December 1987 of civil revolt in the West Bank and Gaza Strip against Israel's occupation — the first Palestinian intifada. Palestinians had made clear their intention to pursue their political aims independent of Jordan. My father was not going to stand in their way. His decision was crucial to Palestinian ambitions for statehood: the West Bank would now form the core of a future Palestinian state.

Another unintended consequence of the 1991 Gulf War was the flood of Iraqis into our country. Before, during, and after the war many hundreds of thousands of Iraqis and people from other countries who had been living in Iraq sought refuge in Jordan. Most Jordanian and Palestinian expatriates in Kuwait also made their way back to Jordan. And although I did not know it at the time, a chance meeting with one of them would soon change my life.

# CHAPTER 9
# A ROYAL WEDDING

In August 1992 I was a battalion commander
of the 2nd Armoured Cavalry Regiment. We
had been carrying out field exercises and
my men and I had been camped out in the
desert for two months straight, sleeping in
tents. Our accommodations were pretty
basic. To take a hot shower, I had rigged up
a contraption with a storage tank that heated
the water using the sun. The exercises went
well, so the brigade commander told me and
the other officers to take the night off.

I changed out of my army uniform, threw
on a T-shirt and sneakers, and drove to
Amman. I had just arrived home when my
sister Aisha called, saying, "I hear you're
in town, come over for dinner." I told her
I really just wanted a proper shower and a
comfy bed, but she had not seen me in some
time and promised the get-together was not
going to be anything fancy. I had been living
on beans and tinned spaghetti for the last

two months, so the prospect of a real dinner was too good to turn down.

I headed over to Aisha's house, my face like a lobster from weeks under the desert sun. Not realizing she was having guests over, I was still wearing the same clothes I had tossed on at the army camp. One of my sister's friends worked at Apple Computer in Amman, and he had brought along a colleague, Rania Al Yassin. As soon as I saw her, I thought, "Wow!"

Nearly twenty-two at the time, Rania had not been in Jordan for long. She came from a Jordanian family of Palestinian origin and had grown up in Kuwait. She and her family had moved to Jordan during the Gulf War. Her father had long planned to retire in Jordan and had built a house in Amman, but the war sped up the family's plans.

After studying business at the American University in Cairo, Rania had worked at Citibank in Amman, and then at Apple, where she met my sister's friend. We spoke only briefly at the dinner, but I was struck by how poised, elegant, and intelligent she was. I was smitten and knew I had to see her again. It took me a little while to track her down, but I finally managed to get her number, and I called her at work. I introduced myself and said that I was hoping to

155

see her again. "I've heard things about you," she said. She did not finish the sentence, but the implication was that what she had heard was not entirely favorable. "I'm no angel," I replied, "but at least half the things you hear are just idle gossip." She was not convinced and said she would need to think about it.

I would not be so easily dissuaded. I got a mutual friend, Tawfiq Kawar, to stop by her office and assure her of my good intentions. Rania was still not convinced; she thought he was not objective. Tawfiq returned from his mission saying that he had not secured a date for me, but he had found out that Rania liked chocolate. So I sent him back bearing a box of Belgian chocolates. After that, she accepted my invitation to dinner. It was November by the time she came to my house, and I decided to surprise her and cook.

I first learned to cook out of necessity in the army, but later I came to enjoy it. I find it a great way to relax and unwind. I had a Japanese teppanyaki table made locally, and an iron griddle on which I prepared traditional Japanese dishes of chicken, shrimp, and beef in the style of a Benihana restaurant. The meal went well, and we saw each other once or twice more before the end of the year, and talked many more times by phone. We had to be discreet. Amman is a town that loves to gossip, and neither one of us wanted to be the source of speculation.

Just after the beginning of the new year, I met up with Gig. By then I could no longer contain my excitement. I told him that I had met an amazing woman in Amman, and I thought she was the one.

My birthday was on January 30, and I invited Rania to the celebration. My father sat himself down next to her and they began to talk. He was stunned by her intelligence, charm, and beauty and did not take long to uncover our secret. After the guests had left, Rania and I were sitting in my house when the phone rang. It was my father, who loved to play matchmaker. "So," he said, "when can I meet her parents?"

I used to do a lot of rally driving, including competing in professional events, and my co-driver Ali Bilbeisi and I even managed to take third place in the Jordan International Rally in 1986 and again in 1988. One of my favorite places was Tal Al Rumman, a mountain outside Amman where my father and some of his Lebanese friends in 1962 started a hill climb that is today one of the Middle East's longest-standing sporting events. I asked Rania if she would like to go for a drive with me, and we drove up to the top of the hill. I had hoped for a much more romantic proposal, but as we stood outside the car talking, I told her I thought our relationship was getting serious, and I could see us getting married. Rania looked back at me, smiled, and said nothing. Taking her silence as assent, I told my father about our conversation, and things began to move quickly after that.

A couple of weeks later we arranged for my father to visit her parents' house. I had been traveling on army business, and as I stepped off the plane at Queen Alia International Airport in Amman, I saw my father standing at the gate. It was the first time I remember his meeting me at the airport. I think he just wanted to make sure I didn't get cold feet! Very much the romantic, he had for many years wanted me to marry and settle down.

In our culture, when a man wants to ask a woman to marry him, he gets the most powerful and influential members of his family or tribe to assure the intended bride's family that their daughter will be welcomed and well cared for. What better spokesman could you have to make your case than the King of Jordan? On the way to Rania's house, my father took a detour to his office, where he had some papers to sign. He kept me waiting for a good forty-five minutes. I was sweating, afraid we would be late.

When we arrived at the house, Rania's parents were expecting a casual meeting. They had no idea that my father intended to ask that day for their daughter's hand in marriage for me. They were gracious hosts, and her mother had prepared cookies, tea, and coffee. When she offered my father a cup of coffee, he took the cup, but did not drink it. In Jordan, when a man intends to ask for a woman's hand in marriage, it is traditional for the woman's family to offer a cup of Arabic coffee and for the man's family to refuse to drink it until the family has accepted the proposal. If her family turns down the marriage proposal, then that slight to the family honor is thought to be matched by the slight of not drinking the coffee. These days this is a ritual that is performed with everyone knowing their role. But in all of the rush, and even though Rania and I had spoken of marriage since I proposed to her, I had forgotten to inform her of the plan.

When my father refused to drink the coffee, Rania began to realize what was happening. But her poor mother had no idea what was wrong. She began urging my father to eat and drink. Finally, my father turned to Rania's father and made his case for why Rania and I would be a good match. I was so nervous that I can't remember much of what he said. But he must have been persuasive. Much to my relief, Rania's parents agreed, and finally my father drank their coffee. About a week later, on February 22, 1993, Rania and I formally announced our engagement.

That same month, I moved from commanding a battalion in the Armoured Corps, where I had spent most of my military career, to becoming deputy commander of Special Forces. In common with other elite army regiments like the U.S. Delta Force and the British Special Air Service, the Jordanian Special Forces had responsibility for counterterrorism operations and were trained to operate by land, air, and sea. One personal benefit of the move was that it was a headquarters appointment, so I was able to move from an army base to the family house in Amman. With our wedding fast approaching, I had little time to settle in.

My father wanted a grand occasion. He went so far as to fly in from London one of the organizers of the Royal Tournament, an annual military pageant that was at that time one of the largest in the world. Rania and I wanted a small wedding, so I began negotiating with my father. He was so excited that I knew I could never dissuade him. In the end, we agreed that he would arrange the formal event in the daytime and we would organize the evening entertainment.

June 10, 1993, was a sunny day in Amman, and crowds lined the streets, waving and throwing flowers. I wore my black military dress uniform, and Rania was resplendent in a flowing white satin dress with gold embroidery and a white veil. We were married in a simple ceremony in the afternoon at Zahran Palace in downtown Amman in front of family and a few friends. Zahran, which in Arabic means "blooming flower," was the home of my grandmother Queen Zein.

After the ceremony we drove through the streets of Amman in an open-top cream 1961 Lincoln convertible bedecked with white flowers, waving to the crowds. We drove slowly through town to Raghadan Palace, seat of the Royal Court, where my father had arranged the formal reception. Built by my great-grandfather King Abdullah I, the founder of modern Jordan, on a hill overlooking Amman, Raghadan contains the throne room and is often used for formal state occasions.

That afternoon the atmosphere was anything but formal as around two thousand festive guests spilled out of the palace and into the tree-lined grounds. As well as friends and family from Jordan, we had invited friends from overseas, including Gig Faux, Perry Vella, and several others from Deerfield. Some of my Deerfield teachers came too, including Jim Smith, and one of my old bodyguards. There were friends from Sandhurst, other friends from England, and Rania's friends and family came from Kuwait and from Cairo. The Crown Prince of Morocco was there, as was General Joseph Hoar, the head of U.S. Central Command. Queen Sofia of Spain also came, as my father was very close to the Spanish royal family. (This connection had developed in a roundabout way. One of my father's classmates at Victoria College in Egypt was the exiled King Simeon II of Bulgaria, who introduced him to other European royal families, including the Spanish. In a quirk of fate, King Simeon returned to Bulgaria after the collapse of the communist government, formed a new political party, won a majority in the 2001 Bulgarian elections, and was sworn in as prime minister.)

The highlight of the reception was the surprise arrival of my old jumpmaster, Samih Janakat. As befits a Special Forces officer, he arrived by parachute, jumping into the palace grounds after dusk. Managing to avoid the nearby trees, buildings, and fountain, he landed perfectly in front of the assembled guests and presented Rania and me with a sword that we used to cut the wedding cake.

After the formal reception in the palace grounds, family and close friends retired for dinner at my mother's house in the hills above Amman, where we ate, talked, and danced next to a swimming pool. Finally, at around two in the morning, Rania and I said good night. The next morning we set out for America on our honeymoon, eager to begin our new life together.

As a wedding gift, my father paid for a first-class flight via London to San Francisco, but once we were there we bought a Visit USA Air Pass, which allowed us a month of unlimited economy-class travel. Rania had visited the United States a few times before, but I was eager to show her more. We flew first to Hawaii, detoured to Tahiti and Bora Bora, and then traveled to the East Coast, visiting New York and Washington, D.C. Occasionally, when they heard we were honeymooners, the check-in staff would upgrade us to business class.

After we returned from America, Rania and I were looking for a house to buy together when my father said he would give us a place on the outskirts of Amman that he had bought previously and intended to renovate. The renovations were fairly extensive and took us about a year. In the meantime, we lived in a small guesthouse, part of my father's house that he would use to accommodate visitors. Living next door to my father meant that we saw him a lot, and allowed Rania and him to get to know one another better. We would often sit together for breakfast, or watch television together in the evenings. This time also served as Rania's introduction to the other side of royalty. Such proximity to the king caused some people to become envious, and she had to be extremely diplomatic. I commuted from Amman to the Special Forces headquarters in Zarqa, about an hour away. For the first time in many years I was not living on an army base. Our home was far from a palace — just a living room, dining room, and two bedrooms — but we were very, very happy. Our happiness was made even greater by the constant presence of my father in our lives. In later years we would look back and realize just how precious that time was.

Rania had left her job at Apple. Initially we had thought that she would get our household set up and spend some time getting accustomed to being a member of the royal family. But she was a career woman and had far too much energy to sit around at home all day. Being a housewife was not the future that she had envisioned for herself. Our relationship had always been an equal partnership. I could tell that she wanted to return to work, but as part of the royal family, it would not have been appropriate for her to go back to her old job at Apple, or to work for another commercial enterprise. We decided together that the ideal way for her to use her vision, talent, and intelligence would be within the public sector. I went to my father and asked him if he could suggest a suitable role for Rania. Knowing of her background in the commercial sector, he suggested that she work at the Jordan Export Development and Commercial Centers Corporation, helping to promote Jordanian companies in foreign markets.

Although he could be conservative about some things, my father believed women should play a public role, which was unusual for a man of his generation in the region. In the 1970s, at a time when the wives of many Arab leaders were rarely seen in public, my father insisted that his wife, Queen Alia, accompany him to public functions and meetings with heads of state, both in the region and overseas. He was also very supportive of my sister Aisha's desire to go into the military.

Always a bit of a tomboy, Aisha was very tough, as we found out when we were children. If Feisal or I ever tried to tease her, she would give as good as she got. Aisha left for the United States at the age of eight, where she attended school in Washington before moving to Dana Hall High School in Wellesley, Massachusetts. One summer, when she was back in Amman on holiday, she asked me if I would take her parachute jumping. I said I would, but we would have to keep it secret from my father, who was not very keen on the idea. She was not yet sixteen and so light that we had to put weights and rocks in her webbing. I landed first, and because of her weight, she drifted away from the landing zone and ended up in a nearby field. I sprinted across the rocky ground, and as I drew near I found her lying on the ground, not moving. Alarmed, I ran up alongside her. Flat on her back, she was singing with happiness! That summer I took her up several more times, and she became the first woman in Jordan to complete five parachute jumps and receive her wings.

At this point, we decided we would have to let my father know. He was traveling, so I called him up and said, "By the way, Father,

I have Aisha next to me, and I wanted to say congratulations. Your daughter has earned her jump wings." There was a moment of stunned silence on the other end, and then my father proceeded to ask me exactly what I thought I was doing. He pretended to be angry, but we all knew that once he had recovered from the shock he would be tremendously proud. Coming from a military family herself, my mother was also extremely supportive of Aisha's interest in the armed forces. Their pride grew even greater when in 1987 Aisha became the first woman from the Middle East to graduate from Sandhurst. She is currently a brigadier general and is serving as a military attaché to the Jordanian embassy in Washington, D.C., the first female officer ever to hold such a post. She believes that women should play a greater role in the armed forces and is a powerful advocate on the subject.

It is women like Aisha, with her active role in the armed forces, and Rania, with her leadership positions in philanthropic and charitable organizations, who are showing that the potential for women in our country is unlimited.

In the summer of 2009, I was on holiday in Arizona with my son Hussein and Aisha's son, Aoun, when we went to a flight school and the boys asked if they could go parachute jumping. "Please don't let my mother know," Aoun said to me. "She'd kill you!" Knowing my sister, this was no idle threat. After the boys jumped, I called Aisha and said, "I have your son standing next to me, and I just wanted to say congratulations, he's done his first parachute jump."

I have always loved parachuting, and when Rania and I were newly married I would get up before dawn two or three times a week to go and jump. The thrill of jumping from a plane thousands of feet in the air, feeling the wind rushing past my face, and seeing the ground below rushing up would keep me on a high for days afterward. For Rania, who had very little previous interaction with the military, this took a bit of getting used to. She would insist that each time I jumped, somebody phone to tell her I had landed safely. No matter how early I left, she would stay awake by the phone until she had received that call. As I progressed through the army, my other responsibilities began to increase and I had fewer and fewer opportunities to go parachuting. My father began to ask me to travel more, representing Jordan internationally, conducting informal diplomacy, and assessing foreign military equipment. I accepted gladly, as I wanted our Special Forces to have the best, most advanced equipment and training available anywhere. And at times he would ask me to go to some very out-of-the way places.

# CHAPTER 10
## LESSONS IN DIPLOMACY

In late 1993 my father was scheduled to travel to Asia for a visit to Singapore, Japan, China, and North Korea. At that time, the United States was engaged in a political confrontation with North Korea, which had recently successfully tested a Nodong-1 ballistic missile in the Sea of Japan and had threatened to pull out of the Nuclear Non-Proliferation Treaty (NPT). My father felt that a formal visit to North Korea from a head of state might be perceived by the United States as undermining its efforts at tough diplomacy, so he canceled his trip and asked me to go in his place. He asked me to apologize to President Kim Il-sung, whom Koreans called "the Great Leader," that he could not come in person.

At the end of November I set out for Singapore, where I met with senior leaders and bought some light weapons. I continued on to Japan, where we discussed assistance to the Jordanian police, as the Japanese were then helping us with training in bomb disposal. After Tokyo I went to China, where I met with senior members of the People's Liberation Army in China. The meetings went well, and my delegation and I prepared to travel on to Pyongyang. But getting there would prove to be an adventure in itself.

One of the world's least modern airlines, Air Koryo, the North Korean state airline, is currently banned from operating in the European Union due to its poor safety record. The plane looked like a Russian copy of a Boeing 727, and inside the "first class" section, rather than rows of seats we found a couple of couches. To reach the bathroom you would have to make your way past boxes and crates stuffed into the back of the plane. We landed at Sunan International Airport late in the evening and taxied along the runway in the dark for what felt like half an hour. The airport was blacked out, perhaps because the North Korean authorities feared an escalation in the standoff with the United States.

Finally the plane came to a stop and my delegation and I headed down the steps and onto the tarmac. We were met by a group of soldiers, one of whom said something in Korean, which I believe meant "Welcome."

We were escorted to the side of the tarmac and lined up against a wall when suddenly a bright spotlight came on. While blinking in the sudden glare, I thought, "Oh no, we're going to be shot!"

As it turned out, our hosts were filming our arrival. They showed us to an official guesthouse and led us into a large dining room with 1970s décor where some twenty generals, marshals, and assorted army officers were waiting. The dinner was very stiff and formal, and near the end of the meal one of the officers leaned over to me and asked, "What gifts are you going to give the Great Leader?"

I said, "I have brought a clock, a traditional Jordanian dagger, and a gift box from my wedding." The general nodded his approval. We finished the meal and then headed to our guesthouse.

Not long after midnight, as I was about to fall asleep, there was a knock on my door. I got up from bed and found my protocol officer, Faisal Fayez, at the door. Faisal said the generals were outside and they wanted an explanation of the significance of my gifts. I headed back to the dining room and found the twenty officers waiting for me, all in full uniform, holding notepads. The lead general asked me what the meaning of my gifts was, and I replied that they were gifts of friendship. He was not satisfied and pressed for more detail on each specific present.

"What is the meaning of the clock?" the general continued. I was stumped. But as it was nearly one in the morning and I was keen to get to bed, I remembered one of the basic rules of international diplomacy and started making stuff up.

"The clock," I said, "signifies the precious time my father and the Great Leader spent together at Tito's funeral, and the time that has passed since then." The generals nodded in unison and began scribbling furiously in their notebooks. Getting into the spirit, I continued, "The dagger is a gift from one warrior to another."

The general asked, "And the wedding box?" I said, "I look on the Great Leader as a father, and so this is a gift from my recent wedding, from a grateful son." The generals nodded and continued writing. After they had finished, Faisal and I retired, eager to get some rest.

The next day we were taken to see the village where the North Korean president had lived as a young man, then on to lunch with the Great Leader himself. Kim Il-sung was dressed in a two-piece safari outfit and greeted us warmly. He was in good spirits, and his view on the mounting crisis between North Korea and the United States was that it was not too serious. In common with isolated dictators across the world, Kim Il-sung had an unrealistic belief in the strength of his own military and a lack of understanding of the power and technological prowess of Western forces. "I've beaten the Americans once and I can do it again!" he said in an apparent reference to the Korean War, when he was prime minister. His rhetoric reminded me of the language used by Saddam's sons, Uday and Qusay, before the Gulf War in 1991.

After lunch he took us to a side room where our gifts and his were laid out on a table. Then one of the generals from the previous night appeared, holding his notepad, and said, "Please explain to the Great Leader the significance of your gifts." I began to sweat, struggling to remember what I had said the night before.

Thankfully, I remembered the gist of it, and Kim Il-sung seemed satisfied by my explanation. He pointed to a silver soup pot and said, "I hope you get the chance to try this traditional dish before you leave." I thanked the Great Leader for his hospitality and went to visit a North Korean Special

Forces base, where I was treated to one of the most impressive demonstrations I have ever seen. They performed a live-fire exercise in which soldiers would run, jump into the air, somersault, and while in midair fire and knock down the targets. We discussed Kim Il-sung's offer to send North Korean Special Forces to Jordan to build a new military base and train our soldiers, and then we said good-bye. In the car heading back to the guesthouse, one of the generals leaned over to me and said, "What did you think of our Great Leader?"

"He is a very charismatic man," I replied. The general whipped out his notepad and, pencil at the ready, asked, "What do you mean by 'charismatic'?"

I leaned over to my protocol officer, Faisal, and quietly said, "See if you can get us on an earlier flight."

Faisal had us on a flight leaving early the next morning, and after writing a formal letter of thanks to the Great Leader for his hospitality, I headed to bed. At about 4:30 a.m. there was another knock at my door and Faisal appeared with a look of astonishment on his face, saying, "You're not going to believe this . . ."

Waiting for me in the guest room were the same twenty generals, accompanied by a steaming pot of traditional sweet-and-sour North Korean soup. Apparently they were serious about having me try it before I left. I took a sip and said, "It's very good." One of the generals looked at me and said, "What do you mean by 'very good'?" as the rest of the group raised their notepads.

We made it onto our flight that morning without any further delays and headed to Russia for the final leg of our trip. We flew on a Russian-made airplane that was similar to a TriStar, and a couple of hours into the flight I happened to look up at the cockpit. The crew were sitting on the floor playing cards and the copilot was asleep with his feet up on the dashboard. They carried on like this for most of the fourteen-hour flight. After experiencing the best of Pyongyang's hospitality, Moscow felt almost like home, and I was happy to meet friends from the Russian army who were at the airport to receive me.

In June 1994, shortly after Rania and I moved into our new house, our first child, a boy, was born. We named him Hussein, in honor of my father. In Arab culture, when a man has a son, close friends and relatives often stop calling him by his own name and refer to him as the father of his son. So many people began to refer to me as "Abu Hussein," which means "Father of Hussein." It is hard to express how proud I was — and still am — to hear that phrase.

Not long after that, Rania left the Jordan Export Development and Commercial Centers Corporation (now Jordan Enterprise Development Corporation), where she had worked since 1993, to set up the Jordan River Foundation, a nonprofit organization devoted to tackling tough social issues. She decided to focus on speaking out against child abuse, which is a taboo subject in much of the Arab world, and on empowering Jordanian women by encouraging entrepreneurship. Some of the foundation's first projects sponsored training, offered funding for craft-making programs, and helped teach women how to set up new businesses. Once a woman starts to bring in money, she is empowered in the household, because she is also a breadwinner. If her husband wants to try to keep her down, she can demand respect by pointing out that she is contributing to the family finances. So opportunities for women to work or become entrepreneurs can have a sizable social impact.

My father was very supportive of Rania's work. He had encouraged Jordanian women to enter professions typically regarded as male bastions, and had even sponsored women's motor-racing teams. On his recommendation, Royal Jordanian was the first airline in the Middle East to have female pilots.

A few months before Rania began setting up her foundation, I became commander of Special Forces. I had been promoted to colonel in late January 1993 and had finally managed to persuade the army's senior brass that I was there to stay. We trained hard, aware of the many enemies threatening Jordan, including terrorist fighters returning from the wars in Afghanistan, Bosnia, and Chechnya; smugglers; and spies. This was my chance to put into practice some of the lessons I had learned at Sandhurst and serving in the British army. The first thing I did was to insist that all of our officers lead from the front.

One morning I was at an airbase watching the men prepare for a parachute jump. Airborne operations are a crucial part of Special Forces tactics, as they allow troops to penetrate far into enemy territory. The air was thick with the smell of aviation fuel and the noise of C-130 transport plane engines. Smiling at the chance to get a parachute jump, which were rare by that time, I began to suit up. One of the young captains came up to me, grinning, and said, "This is the first time we've ever seen an officer above the rank of major jump with us."

I realized then that a lot of officers were wearing jump wings on their uniforms but not necessarily carrying out the regular jumps needed to keep their parachute qualification current. I decided that in order to shape this unit into what I wanted it to become, I would need to ensure that the senior officers shared the same dangers and hardships as their men. That evening in the officers' mess I rose to make an announcement. "From now on, anybody who wants to wear the jump wings of Special Forces has to regularly do parachute jumps," I said. For the rest of the meeting, some of my officers were very quiet. I went on to train as a jumpmaster, somebody who supervises the paratroopers jumping out of the airplanes, and ran regular jumps for my men.

Parachute jumps were not just useful in training for war, but also turned out to have a valuable role to play in international diplomacy. During World War II, C Company of 156th Para, a parachute regiment of the British army, was stationed in what at the time was Transjordan. They arranged an exercise to demonstrate their capabilities to the ruler of Transjordan, my great-grandfather

Abdullah. The British troops parachuted into an empty fort at Shouneh, a mile east of the River Jordan, and took it from its imaginary defenders, capturing the flag in the process. My great-grandfather was so impressed with their maneuvers that he let them keep the flag to fly in place of their regimental standard. C Company subsequently fought their way across North Africa and Europe and suffered heavy losses at the battle of Arnhem in the Netherlands in 1944, when the British paratroopers attempted to capture a bridge over the Rhine. C Company carried the Transjordan flag into battle, but was overwhelmed by the German forces. The company adjutant stashed the flag under his clothing, kept it hidden through several years in a German prisoner-of-war camp, and brought it back safely to Britain after the war ended. I was extremely touched when I watched a dramatization of that battle in the movie *A Bridge Too Far,* as I remembered the story of how C Company raised the flag over the divisional headquarters at the town of Oosterbeek to denote its position.

Five decades later, to mark the historical connection between Jordan and the British parachute regiment, I jumped out of a Douglas Dakota aircraft in the Netherlands as part of the proceedings commemorating the fiftieth anniversary of the battle of Arnhem. I landed and presented a new Jordanian flag to Prince Charles, who in turn gave it to the successor of that regiment, C Company of 1 Para. We had been celebrating the end of a historical war. But it wasn't long before we would have the chance to celebrate a new peace.

On July 25, 1994, on a sunny morning in Washington, D.C., some six hundred journalists, foreign dignitaries, and U.S. government officials waited patiently in front of a raised dais on the South Lawn of the White House. Behind the stage were the flags of Jordan, Israel, and the United States. The guests clapped as my father and Rabin stepped onto the dais, accompanied by President Bill Clinton. This was the first time the two men had met publicly, although they had done so privately many times. They had both come to the White House to end the state of belligerency that had existed between Israel and Jordan for forty-six years, since 1948.

The signing of the Oslo Accords had allowed Jordan to focus on its own peace negotiations with Israel. My father was now determined to secure the peace he had long sought. On many occasions, when we spoke of his negotiations with the Israelis, he would point out how difficult they were. But he believed a breakthrough was possible.

Although initially wary of each other, over time my father and Rabin had become close. They were both military men and heavy smokers. Once my father found out that Rabin smoked almost as much as he did, they were always passing cigarettes back and forth. They met many times in secret, in both Jordan and Israel. Once they had bonded, they sat around the table as two friends, trying to see things from each other's perspective and to work out a common ground for peace. My father did not need to see a document signed. He felt that as long as Rabin said it was going to happen, it was going to happen.

Before signing the document, known as the Washington Declaration, which formally terminated the state of belligerency between their two states and recognized Jordan's special role in protecting the Muslim holy shrines in Jerusalem, my father said, "For many, many years, and with every prayer, I have asked God, the Almighty, to help me be a part of forging peace between the children of Abraham. . . . Out of all the days of my life, I do not believe there is one such as this." He continued, "This is a dream that those before me had — my dead grandfather, and now I. . . . This is a day of commitment, and this day is a day of hope and vision."

Rabin also addressed the gathering. "It is dusk at our homes in the Middle East," he said. "Soon darkness will prevail. But the citizens of Israel and Jordan will see a great light."

After the ceremony, my father and Rabin were Clinton's guests at a White House dinner, and the next day they addressed a joint session of the U.S. Congress. My father told Congress that "the state of war between Israel and Jordan is over."

Three months later, on October 26, 1994, my father and Rabin met again, accompanied by President Clinton, at the border crossing at Wadi Araba in southern Jordan for the signing ceremony of the formal peace treaty between Jordan and Israel. It was a historic moment. Jordan became only the second Arab country, after Egypt fifteen years earlier, to make peace with Israel. Two years after signing the treaty in 1979, Egyptian president Anwar Sadat was assassinated by an Egyptian radical. We all anxiously hoped my father would not pay the same price for peace.

Initially, Jordanians and Israelis had high hopes for the fruits of peace. Jordan had regained all of the territory in the East Bank that had been occupied by Israel and its fair share of water rights. The urgent need to end the occupation of the West Bank, including East Jerusalem and Gaza, was being addressed in direct negotiations between the Israelis and Palestinians. Thanks to its peace treaty with Israel, Jordan would now be able to help advance these negotiations.

For the first time, Jordanian planes were allowed to fly over Israel and the occupied Palestinian territories, and flights from Amman to Europe would thus go over Jerusalem. Although I had visited Jerusalem as a young child, I have not been back since it was occupied by the Israelis in 1967. But on a clear day, sitting on the left side of a passenger plane, I could now look down and see the sun glinting off the golden Dome of the Rock. One of the three holiest sites in Islam, the ancient shrine of Al Aqsa is also the site from where the Prophet Mohammad first ascended to heaven — in the miracle of Isra and Miraj — when the angel Gabriel took him from Mecca to Jerusalem.

Jordan's treaty with Israel opened the way to increased political and economic cooperation, and a wave of Israeli tourists washed into Jordan, visiting Aqaba and historic sights like Petra and Wadi Rum. An equally curious group of Jordanians began making their way to Israel, many visiting for the first time this neighbor who had played such a large role in our history.

But, like many things in the region, this initial optimism would soon be marred by tragedy.

On November 4, 1995, Israeli prime minister Rabin was assassinated by a Jewish extremist at a peace rally in Tel Aviv. The murderer was opposed to the 1993 Oslo Accords and their follow-up, Oslo II, signed at the White House in September 1995, which gave the Palestinians partial control of over 40 percent of the West Bank. Like many from Israel's extreme right, he opposed the withdrawal from the West Bank on religious grounds and decided to take matters into his own hands.

My father would devote the rest of his life to working for a peaceful settlement of the Israeli-Palestinian conflict, but the only time after 1967 that he visited Jerusalem was for Rabin's funeral. The ruthless warrior of the 1967 war had in later decades been transformed into a soldier for peace. My father believed that had Rabin lived longer, they would have made even greater strides together in bringing about a comprehensive Arab-Israeli settlement.

At Rabin's funeral, he spoke to honor his friend and former foe, saying:

Never in all my thoughts would it have occurred to me that my first visit to Jerusalem and response to your invitation, the invitation of the Speaker of the Knesset, the invitation of the President of Israel, would be on such an occasion. . . . We are not ashamed, nor are we afraid, nor are we anything but determined to fulfill the legacy for which my friend fell, as did my grandfather in this very city when I was with him and but a young boy.

Rabin's tragic death meant that we lost a true partner for peace. And in the years after his death, no Israeli leader would follow his example and succeed in the hardest challenge of all, that of achieving a lasting peace between Israel and the Palestinians.

That year, much of our attention was focused on Israel, our neighbor to the west, but we could never forget about our neighbor to the east. In August 1995, Hussein Kamel, one of the most powerful men in the Iraqi government, defected to Jordan following a clash with Uday. His wife, Saddam Hussein's daughter Raghad, came with him, along with her sister Rana and Rana's husband, Saddam Kamel, a senior officer in the Republican Guard and Hussein Kamel's brother. The two families drove five hundred miles from Baghdad to Amman, ostensibly to catch a flight to Sofia for an official visit to Bulgaria. Iraq was then under United Nations sanctions, so there were no international flights out of Baghdad. Once in Amman, they met with my father, who granted them asylum.

Hussein Kamel was responsible for overseeing Iraq's chemical and biological weapons program — and its nuclear program. He was the most senior member of Saddam's regime to defect. My father arranged for him to be debriefed by the United Nations weapons inspectors, and he decided to house the Kamel brothers and their families in the Hashemiyah Palace, a modern palace frequently used to host visiting heads of state and other dignitaries.

The night they arrived, my father called me and said, "Could you please go over and say hello to them and tell them that their safety is guaranteed? Just make them feel at home." So I went and greeted the Kamels. I introduced myself, saying that I was the Special Forces commander and that one of my units was protecting them. They were our guests.

But from what I had seen on my visits to Baghdad I knew what type of people these men were, and I kept my distance. Although we were neighbors — at the time Rania and I were living nearby in our new house — I probably saw Hussein Kamel and Saddam's two daughters only three times while they were living in Amman. I believe Hussein Kamel thought he would be embraced by the West, and that the United States would use its power to install him as the leader of Iraq. Clearly he was delusional.

Six months later, in February 1996, Saddam sent a message to Hussein Kamel and his brother that if they returned to Iraq all would be forgiven. Tired of their relative lack of status in Jordan, and proving conclusively that their judgment was fatally flawed, they decided to believe their father-in-law and return, along with their families. My father gave orders that they were to be escorted to the Iraqi border. A Jordanian military convoy drove them east through the desert, while one of my sniper teams watched the handover from afar, in case of trouble.

When the Kamels arrived at the border, Qusay and Uday were at the other side, waiting to meet them. The sniper team reported that Uday shook hands with both of the brothers, and then Iraqi soldiers grabbed them. As the soldiers hustled the Kamels into a waiting car, Uday and Qusay turned and knelt on the ground in prayer. When I heard this, I called my father and said, "The Kamels are as good as dead." Three days later Hussein and Saddam Kamel were killed by Saddam's men. Both his daughters, Raghad and Rana, lost their husbands, and his grandchildren their fathers.

The disregard for rules I had witnessed in Uday and Qusay on our fishing expedition in the 1980s had by then begun to mutate into something much darker. The wife of a friend, an Iraqi woman who grew up in Baghdad, told Rania and me that when she was at university, Uday would burst into class, surrounded by armed guards, scan the female students, and when he found one to his liking, he would arrange for his men to take her back to his palace. I heard that he kept lions and cheetahs in the basement of his palace, and had garages filled with luxury cars, including a pink Rolls-Royce. The luxurious lifestyles of Saddam's family were in shocking contrast to the misery suffered by ordinary Iraqis as sanctions imposed by the West in the wake of the 1991 Gulf War took their toll.

We had our own problems with Uday. He was in charge of the Iraqi national football (soccer) team, and at times Jordan would play Iraq. If we defeated the Iraqi team, Uday would arrange to have the Iraqi players beaten on return. Although his brother, Qusay, was quieter and less flamboyant, he was the smarter and, I suspected, more dangerous of the two.

After the U.S. invasion of Iraq, Saddam's daughters asked if they could come and live in Jordan, to escape the chaos and danger of Baghdad. We agreed, and they came to live, for the second time, in Amman. One subsequently left Jordan and went to live in Qatar.

Over time, as some senior officers began to retire, I found the army brass becoming more supportive of my drive to modernize, and I decided that I would make my life in the army. After almost a year as deputy commander of Special Forces, I was promoted to commander and immediately pushed the idea of restructuring our Special Forces along the lines of other leading nations. In November 1996 I created Special Operations Command (SOCOM), based on the model adopted by the French and the Americans. Reporting directly to the chief of staff of the armed forces, Field Marshal Abdul Hafez Kaabneh, SOCOM brought together under one roof Special Forces and a number of elite specialist brigades from throughout the army. We had a unit similar to the British Special Air Service (SAS) or the U.S. Delta Force, a dedicated counter-terrorist unit, and two airborne battalions similar to the British paratroopers.

That year we put our parachuting skills in the service of international diplomacy. I had been approached by a group of international Special Forces veterans who wanted to carry out a parachute jump in Jordan. There is an everlasting brotherhood among Special Forces soldiers, and I readily agreed. So in mid-June 1996, a C-130J transport aircraft took off from Zarqa filled with veterans of every war imaginable, including two German soldiers in their eighties who had parachuted into Crete during World War II. I acted as the jumpmaster. The men were lined up in rows of eight, and as they reached the rear door, I slapped each man on the back, sending him out of the plane.

Colonel Shaul Dori, a retired Israeli Special Forces officer, stepped forward. "Go!" I shouted over the roar of the engines, and slapped him on the back. Smiling, he jumped out of the plane, and became the first Israeli soldier to jump with the Jordanian army.

"If someone had told me back in 1973, while I was fighting along the Suez Canal, that one day Israeli paratroopers would be jumping with the Jordanians," said another of the Israeli veterans who jumped with us that day, "I'd have told him to get his head examined." The jump was a great success and reminded all the men, fierce fighters and veterans of countless wars, how much they shared in common. Although today the relationship between Jordan and Israel is strained, at that time there was a sense of a new beginning. We hoped that the peace treaty between the two countries would lead to a comprehensive regional peace and that we were entering a new phase in Middle Eastern politics. There was so much optimism that I can't help but look back on those years with great fondness, as well as with some bitterness at the opportunities that have been squandered.

I asked the French Special Forces and the British Parachute Regiment to come out and train my men. We made quite a few changes. One was to introduce live-fire exercises and to ban the use of blanks. I remembered from Sandhurst how using real bullets increases one's concentration. We have been fortunate that only one soldier has been wounded in the years since we started live-ammunition exercises.

We had a chance to demonstrate our capabilities to our neighbor in 1997, when the Israeli defense minister, Yitzhak Mordechai, visited Jordan. My father asked me to put on a demonstration exercise in Zarqa, and we happily obliged. We began with basic trench work, in which you assault a fortified position. The soldiers ran toward the trenches, firing as they went, using live ammunition. Then they threw grenades and blasted their way across the barriers. The second exercise involved fighting in built-up areas. My troops assaulted a series of buildings using flamethrowers and Bangalore torpedoes, long tubes with explosives inside that cut through barbed wire. The men cleared a path up to the buildings, tossed grenades through the windows, and then stormed inside.

When they had finished, Mordechai turned to me and said, "I'm very glad your father decided to make peace with us!"

Live-fire exercises were nothing compared to actual missions. Due to the nature of Special Operations, many of our activities remain confidential. One particular mission, however, stands out in my mind.

# CHAPTER 11
# VERY SPECIAL OPERATIONS

In 1997, Special Operations Command (SOCOM) was deployed to eastern Jordan to help the police combat drug smugglers on the Iraqi border. The smugglers were looking to transit Jordan to access lucrative markets in Saudi Arabia and Egypt. One of Saddam's sons, Qusay, ran a drug-smuggling operation from Baghdad, but the problem was not all foreign — people on the Jordanian side were also known to be involved.

The last Jordanian town before the Iraqi border, Rweished, was a small town with little industry. Most people made their money from trade across the border, both legal and illegal. From there to the Iraqi border was fifty miles of completely flat ground. The smugglers had souped-up General Motors trucks, with the exhausts pointed down so that they would kick up a dust cloud as they drove to prevent identification. They had secure communications, night-vision capabilities, and heavy machine guns mounted on the back of their trucks.

The desert police patrolled at night in old jeeps and didn't have anything like night-vision equipment. The smugglers would roar past at full speed and disappear into a network of tents and buildings on the outskirts of town. It was a bit like facing a well-equipped foreign army, and the police were outgunned. When a policeman was killed while trying to tackle the smugglers, my father asked army headquarters to send me in. Although they were directed from Qusay's headquarters in Baghdad, the smugglers had a long reach. Just how long, I had discovered to my discomfort a few weeks earlier.

Rania and I were living in the Hashemiyah district of Amman, and I would leave for work early in the morning. One day I noticed a pickup truck parked by the side of the road, with a man sitting in it. When I returned from work that evening, he was still there. I noticed him the next day, still sitting there, watching. Worried that he was carrying out surveillance for a terrorist attack, I alerted my guards. The next morning, as I pulled out of the driveway, the watcher gunned his engine and the truck screamed toward me. Thinking it was an ambush, we drew our guns and rushed out of the car, preparing to shoot.

The man jumped out of his truck shouting, "No, no, no!" and brandishing a briefcase. When he reached me, he said, "I know you're going to get the order to go out to the border. Here's one hundred thousand dollars to look the other way." My heart was pounding. I asked the fellow if he knew who he was talking to, and he replied that I was the commander of Special Operations.

"But do you know I'm the son of the king?"

The man, a Jordanian, said, "Yeah, here's one hundred thousand dollars."

I was shocked by his audacity. My father was renowned for his transparency and open governance, and here was this fellow thinking he could just bribe the king's son and have me look the other way. I had him arrested on the spot. The army can be a little isolated from wider society, and this was my first introduction to the scope of narco-terrorism and the corrupting influence of large sums of money. It is straightforward to guard the border and defend Jordan from our enemies, but this was a much more complex situation. This border operation had suddenly become personal.

We had been there a year before with our regular equipment — pistols, rifles, and machine guns — and could do very little.

I went back to my father and said, "Please untie my hands." I asked him for permission to deploy heavier weapons from the Special Operations arsenal. He agreed, and now we were returning with the firepower we needed to tackle the smugglers head-on. I deployed my troops three days earlier than planned, because I was worried that the smugglers would find out the timing of our operation. The troops were armed with artillery and some anti-aircraft weapons.

That evening, my soldiers took up positions in trenches near the border and waited. It was quiet until about eleven at night, when they saw an Iraqi car at the border, flashing its headlights. About two miles away, inside Jordan, several cars flashed their lights back. The smugglers were using their headlights to communicate. Soldiers heard the roar of a truck engine and saw a convoy heading across the border. They opened fire. Then all hell broke loose. The smugglers began shooting back, using automatic weapons, and there were firefights up and down the border. The first few nights my battalion must have fired ten thousand rounds of amunition. The smugglers did not want to leave men or machinery behind for us to capture, so when we knocked out one of their trucks, others came with grappling hooks to drag the burning wreck across the Iraqi border.

A few days later, the smugglers stopped trying to sneak goods past us and focused on killing my soldiers. Although they were unsuccessful, at that point I lost patience. I joined the troops and decided to deploy the heavy guns. I brought out the M61 Vulcan 20mm cannon, which is capable of firing six thousand rounds per minute. A company closer to the border was engaged in heavy fire with the smugglers. My brother Feisal, who at the time was in the air force, commanded a squadron of fighters in support of our operation. As F-5 fighters flew past dropping flares, I gave the order to fire. My men opened up with artillery and our Vulcan anti-aircraft guns. Originally designed for use against Soviet jets, these were also pretty devastating on the ground. You could hear a "brrrrrrrrrrrp, brrrrrrrrrrp" as a wall of bullets descended, and see the explosions up and down the border.

After that we had few problems with the smugglers. But as we would soon find out, smugglers were not the only threats to Jordan.

May 25, 1998, was a pleasant spring morning. As it was a public holiday — Jordanian

Independence Day — I was at home, working out on the treadmill, when the telephone rang. It was my uncle, Prince Hassan, calling from the Police Crisis Management Center. "How good are you at taking terrorists alive?" he asked. "Not very," I said. "My unit is trained to kill them." "Well, we have a major problem in Sahab," he said, referring to a small town outside Amman. "It's either you or the police." I threw on my uniform and headed for the door.

Early that year, Jordan had been terrorized by a series of brutal murders in wealthy neighborhoods of Amman. In January, eight Iraqis had been killed at a villa in Rabia, and in April three Jordanians had been killed in Shmeisani. A prominent doctor had been killed simply because he showed up at the wrong house when one of these murders was taking place. Rumor varied as to whether the murders were the work of terrorists, drug gangs, or petty criminals. The police had tracked down two of the members of the gang they thought responsible, a hit man and his accomplice, and had them trapped in a house in Sahab. Senior officials thought it was important to capture these men alive. They wanted to know for certain whether the murders were inspired by foreign sources and to assure a frightened and skeptical public that they had caught the killers. The previous night the police had gone up to the house at 1 a.m. They knocked on the door, and the criminals opened fire, wounding a policeman. The police fired back, and in the exchange of bullets that followed, the hit man's accomplice was killed. Since then the police had kept him trapped in the house.

I activated the 71st Battalion, which was highly trained in counterterrorism operations, and within minutes they were suited up and ready to go. I was accompanied by my aide-de-camp, Nathem Rawashdeh, an officer from the town of Kerak, about ninety miles south of Amman. As the battalion did not have enough body armor, Nathem and I stopped by the office to pick up some newly arrived samples of Russian-made body armor, and then drove at full speed to rejoin our unit. We met up with the rest of the battalion at a roundabout on the outskirts of town and headed into the center. The tires of the jeep screeched as we skidded around the final corner and stopped in the town square, which was crowded with people.

As my troops were piling out of their vans and assembling their guns and equipment, I asked who was in charge. A short policeman, who was quite aggressive, told me that this was his operation. "Look," I said, "I've been sent by Prince Hassan with orders to take over this operation. He told me I'm to take the terrorist alive. So please stand down." After a heated argument, he finally gave way, and I was now in charge.

Standard operating procedure would have been for the police to clear the area and create a secure cordon even if we were in the middle of a town, surrounded by panicked people and curious onlookers. But this was not done, and I had no choice but to make the best of a messy situation.

"So," I said at last, "how far up the street is this man?" The policeman pointed to a house no more than ten yards away on the other side of the street. There is no way we should have been standing unprotected this close to a known killer. We all scrambled for cover in a sewing shop across the street. It had a large glass window looking out over the square that made us quite vulnerable. One of my men, Jamal Shawabkeh, who later headed Special Operations Command, was leading the assault team. He lived in Sahab and had been one of the first on the scene. After briefing me on the situation, Jamal said, "Now that we're in charge, let's storm the building and kill him. It will take five minutes." I told him no, that we had to take the man alive. I explained that those were my orders, so that he could stand trial for his crimes. We would have to try to capture him alive, even if it meant some of us getting killed. This was a very difficult order to give, but Jamal accepted it without missing a beat. "Well then," he said, "I'll be the first man through the door."

One policeman, overhearing our planning session, came up to me and said, "I don't think you should use explosives to blow the side wall or windows out. He's got explosives in there." At that moment, looking out the window of the sewing shop, I saw that there were policemen standing all over the roof of the house and, exasperated, I said, "Then bloody well get those men off the roof!"

We resumed planning the assault. A middle-aged man in civilian clothes stood next to me. I thought he was a plainclothes intelligence officer. When I caught his eye he said, "Would anybody like tea?" It turned out he was an enterprising falafel seller who had left his cart out in the street and come in to see what was going on. It was a surreal moment. Here we were in a life-and-death situation — with bystanders taking it all in like a soccer match. Although it seemed comic, we knew that at any moment the situation could turn into a tragedy.

The police were failing to keep a secure

area around the building. "We've got to get some order here! Throw this guy out and cordon off the street," I told Nathem, but the general chaos continued.

Once we had blocked off the area, I told Jamal to lead the assault. He readied his team of crack operatives, including a huge Special Forces officer by the name of Abu Khasheb, who was a real character. Special Forces used to test new equipment like Tasers and pepper spray on him to make sure they worked. Neither one could stop him, so he was the ideal man to assault a hardened killer. Onlookers held their breath as Jamal walked through the square and made his way to the house. He pushed the door open and poked his head through.

"Keep out!" shouted the hit man. "If you come in, I'll take as many of you with me as I can."

"Listen," said Jamal in a low voice, "we're not the police. We're Special Forces. You know what that means. Either you give up or I'm going to roll a grenade into the room and that will be the end of you." Then Jamal sprinted back across the square to brief me. "If we're going in, it has to be now," he said.

I gave the order for Jamal to lead the assault. He went back to the front door at the same time as an assault team crept around the side of the house. Then he stepped inside and confronted the terrorist one-on-one without raising his weapon, distracting him while the rest of the team stormed into the house through a side window.

Seven minutes later, there was a commotion inside the house. Jamal came back out the door, followed by Abu Khasheb, who was carrying the hit man. Running over, I said, "What happened?"

"I walked through the door slowly," Jamal said, "so he could see I was dressed in civilian clothes. He pointed his gun straight between my eyes. I told him not to be stupid and said we weren't going to kill him, he would get a fair trial." Breathing heavily, Jamal continued, "Then the team burst into the rooms and rushed him." He looked sheepish and apologized for the blood running down the man's face. Considering the fact that Jamal had stared this vicious killer down, I felt that a few scrapes were more than acceptable!

When the crowd understood what had happened it rushed into the square — policemen, civilians, falafel sellers — and everyone began to shout, "Special Forces! God is great!" Many tried to attack our man, so we had to get him into a van and out of there quickly. Not wanting to take credit, I asked the officials on the scene to tell everybody it was a police operation, and that they should receive the plaudits.

The police later rounded up four other accomplices, but one escaped and fled to Europe. In total, there were seven members of this gang. They turned out to be criminals who were targeting wealthy businessmen for extortion.

The next morning, as I walked into my office, I saw a couple of my men shaking their heads and smiling. I had not realized it at the time, but television cameras had captured the whole thing. The story had made headlines on the next morning's news, and my team and I found our names plastered across the front page of the newspapers. So much for my attempts to keep the whole thing quiet.

My father had been advised that the operation was taking place, but he had not been briefed in detail, so he was quite surprised to see me on the morning news. I was summoned to the palace. When I arrived, my father was standing by the breakfast table, frowning. Picking up a copy of a newspaper and waving it at me, he said, "What on earth were you doing yesterday? You put your life in danger." I explained that although I had commanded the operation, the media had exaggerated my role. "Jamal and his people went into the house. They're the ones who took the risks," I said. "Well," he said, "don't let me catch you pulling a stunt like that again!" Although he pretended to be angry, I later learned from family members that he was very proud of my role in the operation.

My military training had prepared me for being shot at. What it had not prepared me for was a life in politics. When people are shooting at you, it is evident who the enemy is. This is not so clear when they are smiling and paying compliments.

*Developing an early love of cars with my parents at Marka Airport, where my father would sometimes speed-test his Porsche 911.*
(PERSONAL ARCHIVE)

*With my father, King Hussein, in my early days as crown prince. This picture was taken for the December 1964 issue of* National Geographic. (LUIS MARDEN / *NATIONAL GEOGRAPHIC*)

*Like most boys, my brother Feisal and I loved to play with planes and guns. In this picture I am on the right playing with a plane and Feisal is clutching a gun, though Feisal would later join the air force and I'd opt for the army.* (Personal Archive)

*At four, in military gear. My mother's father was a British military officer, and my father went to Sandhurst right before he became king.* (Albert Flouti / Royal Hashemite Court)

*Standing next to a portrait of my great-grandfather King Abdullah I, the founder of the Hashemite Kingdom of Jordan. He was assassinated in Jerusalem in 1951 by a Palestinian extremist.*
(PERSONAL ARCHIVE)

*At Eaglebrook School in western Massachusetts, with my brother Feisal (right), on the day of my graduation from the ninth grade.* (EAGLEBROOK SCHOOL)

*On an exercise at Sandhurst, the British military academy.* (Royal Military Academy Sandhurst [RMAS])

*Surveying the terrain as a new platoon commander in the 2nd Armoured Cavalry Regiment in Qatraneh in the early 1980s.*
(Zohrab Markerian / Royal Hashemite Court)

*Speaking to my father and commander in chief following a military exercise in the early 1980s.* (ZOHRAB MARKERIAN / ROYAL HASHEMITE COURT)

*Learning to fly helicopters in Jordan in 1985.* (ZOHRAB MARKERIAN / ROYAL HASHEMITE COURT)

*With my brothers Ali (far right) and Hamzah (second from left) and my cousins Talal (far left) and Rashid (third from left), preparing for a jump.* (JORDAN ARMED FORCES)

*With my cousin Talal during a training session with the Special Forces in 1986. Seven years later, I became commander of the Special Forces.* (ZOHRAB MARKERIAN / ROYAL HASHEMITE COURT)

*With Rania on our wedding day in Amman, June 10, 1993. We wanted a small affair, but my father insisted on a big party; he even persuaded my old jumpmaster to parachute onto the grounds with the knife we used to cut the wedding cake.*

*Presenting President Kim Il-sung of North Korea with gifts of a dagger, a clock, and photographs from our wedding. The gentlemen in the back would come to my room at midnight and ask me to explain the significance of these gifts. I had to improvise on the spot.* (Royal Hashemite Court)

*My uncle Prince Hassan handing me the standard of the crown prince the night my father changed the line of succession in January 1999. I asked my uncle to keep the standard.* (MELIDOS YAQUENIAN / ROYAL HASHEMITE COURT)

*Saluting the portrait of my father in 1999, prior to taking the constitutional oath.* (YOUSEF ALLAN / ASSOCIATED PRESS)

At my father's funeral in February 1999, when friends and onetime foes gathered to pay their last respects at what was called the "funeral of the century." President Clinton and Jacques Chirac came, as did Palestinian president Yasser Arafat, Khaled Meshaal of Hamas, Benjamin Netanyahu of Israel, and Hafez al-Assad of Syria. Egyptian president Hosni Mubarak and Moroccan crown prince (now king) Mohammed VI, who appear in this picture, were also among the many heads of state and officials who attended the funeral. (COURTESY OF AGENCE FRANCE-PRESSE [AFP])

*With Palestinian president Yasser Arafat, inspecting the honor guard upon arrival in Gaza in May 1999. My father had a difficult relationship with Arafat. Some PLO factions tried to assassinate him and topple his government in the 1970s, but my father's relations with Arafat improved in the 1980s and '90s. By the time of his death, Arafat was a potent symbol of Palestinian aspirations and frustrations.* (MELIDOS YAQUENIAN / ROYAL HASHEMITE COURT)

*Acting as jumpmaster for my sister Iman in 2000. She later graduated from Sandhurst.* (JORDAN ARMED FORCES)

■■■■

# Part III

■■■■

# PART III

# CHAPTER 12
# IN THE FOOTSTEPS
## OF A LEGEND

As King Hussein's firstborn son, I started out life as the crown prince, but in 1965, when I was just three, my father decided to remove me from the line of succession. There had already been some eighteen documented assassination attempts on his life, most during the turbulent 1950s, when radical Arab nationalism was on the rise, and it seemed unlikely that he would survive long enough to see me reach adulthood. My father asked parliament to amend the Constitution, and named his brother, Prince Hassan, as his new heir.

As a young man I believed my mission in life was to be a soldier, acting as my father's shield and sword. But there was one attacker from which I was powerless to protect him. In the summer of 1992 he went to the Mayo Clinic in Rochester, Minnesota, and was diagnosed with cancer. He underwent surgery and the operation was successful. The family, and the nation, breathed a sigh of relief. But in July 1998 he again began to feel unwell, and he returned to the United States for medical evaluation.

At the time, I was attending a short course at the Naval Postgraduate School in Monterey, California. With me on the course was Abdul Razaq, a Jordanian general who had been my battalion commander in my first army posting. He was a great mentor to a young second lieutenant still trying to learn the ropes. He had heard the news of my father's return to Mayo, and in a quiet moment between classes he took me aside and said, "Without your father, Jordan will not survive."

The graduation ceremony was the day after my father's arrival at Mayo. As soon as it ended, I went straight to Minnesota with Rania and the children to be by his side. My son Hussein was very close to his grandfather. Sharing more than a name, they both had a deep love of aircraft. After work, my father would often stop by our house. He would ask me if Hussein was in the house, and if Hussein was not, he would not even come in. "Okay, bye," he would say in a rush, before heading off on his way. From the age of two, Hussein began to memorize the names of various types of planes, and my father delighted in showing him small Corgi models and hearing his little voice cry out "Stuka" or "Jumbo." Once, when we traveled to London, my father flew his TriStar himself and called Hussein, then two and a half, into the cockpit as he landed at Heathrow. To the amazement of the crew and my father's delight, he correctly identified a Concorde and a Boeing 747 sitting on the tarmac as we came in to land.

After the laughter and joy of our little family reunion in Minnesota, my father asked to speak to me alone. Placing his hand on my arm, he said, "The cancer has come back." I had never given serious consideration to the possibility that my father might die. I thought he would defeat his cancer, as he had done before. But something about his tone of voice told me this time might be different.

We stayed two more days, and then he asked me to go back to Jordan and carry on my army duties. In 1996 I had been promoted from leading Special Forces to heading Special Operations Command (SOCOM), and I was focused on modernizing our tactics, facilities, and equipment. But I would soon have much more to think about than military training.

In late July 1998, my father released a televised public statement from the Mayo Clinic saying that his cancer had returned and that he was undergoing chemotherapy. That summer in Amman was hot and tense. The air was thick with rumors and gossip. It was then that Crown Prince Hassan inadvertently added fuel to the fire.

I was at my brigade headquarters, sitting at a long oak table with some army officers discussing the weekly training program, when I was told that the crown prince would join our meeting. Prince Hassan was acting as regent in my father's absence. We all stood when he entered the room. Motioning us to sit, he asked us what we were working on and, after I had explained, said that there was an urgent matter he needed to discuss. He then began telling us how he had just heard that King Hussein was in dire straits and didn't have long to live. "It is irreversible, just a matter of time," he said. We sat in stunned silence. It is a harsh moment when a son is told that he may soon lose his father. And it is sobering for a soldier to be told he may soon lose his king and commander in chief. A hundred thoughts were going through my mind about what I had just heard and what the terrible news, if true, could mean for my country and my family.

After my uncle left, the other officers and I looked at one another in confusion. We did not know whether the news could possibly be true. But if it were, it would mean a change of king, with a possible shake-up of the army to follow. Still reeling from my uncle's visit, I headed off to a previously scheduled lunch in Amman. At the lunch were General Samih Battikhi, the head of the General Intelligence Department (GID), responsible for both internal and external security, and Field Marshal Abdul Hafez Kaabneh, chairman of the Joint Chiefs of Staff of the Armed Forces. They had both also just been told by the Crown Prince that my father was terminally ill, and they looked pale, concerned for my father and uncertain as to what exactly was going on. I told them I would call my father to find out the truth.

After lunch I spoke to my father's aide-de-camp, Colonel Hussein Majali, who was with my father at the Mayo Clinic. I asked him if the news was true. He did not answer my question directly but said he would have my father call me back. Two long hours later, my father called and angrily asked me who was spreading this rumor. I told him that the crown prince had told me and a few others that his condition had deteriorated.

"Well," he said, "it is not true at all. I've got better things to do over here than worry about this nonsense. But thank you for letting me know."

Our conversation put my mind at rest. He sounded like the same upbeat fighter I had always known. But rumors and speculation continued to abound, strengthened by my uncle's statement.

Prince Hassan had served loyally as crown prince for more than three decades and believed he had earned the right to be king, as did those around him. But some in the country had begun to believe that my father, in his last days, would name somebody else as crown prince. And there were those who had a candidate in mind. A group of people, including my father's head of security, the chief of protocol, and the head of the GID, were pushing for Prince Hamzah, the king's eldest son by his fourth wife, Queen Noor, to head the line of succession. Only eighteen at the time, and a cadet at the Royal Military Academy Sandhurst, Hamzah was innocent of the plotting going on around him. He and I were very close, as I was with all four of my brothers. Sensing an opportunity, the two groups competed behind the scenes to promote their candidate and discredit the other. Rumors in Amman were rife.

Adding to the gossip was Crown Prince Hassan's decision not to visit my father in America. His supporters argued that he was just doing his job as regent, providing much-needed stability in the country at an uncertain time. But Field Marshal Kaabneh later told me that while my father was in the hospital Prince Hassan gave orders for some officers to be given early retirement and others to be promoted. Kaabneh refused. Prince Hassan had said, "I am the supreme commander now."

"No, sir," was Kaabneh's reply. "Nobody has told me that. I only take my orders from His Majesty King Hussein. The king is in America, but we can call him at any time." The crown prince was insistent, but Kaabneh stood his ground. Military affairs were strictly under the control of the king, and it was unprecedented and unconstitutional for the crown prince to issue orders directly to the military. Prince Hassan may well have had good intentions, hoping to provide leadership and continuity in the face of a growing power vacuum and to quell the many rumors flying around Amman. But his attempt to bypass institutional structures only added to the mounting apprehension.

I still hoped for the best, and prayed that my father would win his struggle.

In early October I took time off and went back to the Mayo Clinic to visit my father. He loved Japanese food, so as a treat I had some Kobe beef flown in fresh from Japan. I reached the clinic in the evening and met up with my sisters Aisha and Zein, who had also come to visit. We found him watching *Patton,* one of his favorite movies (he was a big fan of movies and would watch one every night if he could). The opening scene always brought a gleam to his eye. Patton addresses his men under a huge American flag, saying as he sends them off, "Now, I want you to remember that no bastard ever won a war by dying for his country. He won it by making the other poor dumb bastard die for his country."

While my father, sisters, and other family members watched the film, I prepared the Kobe beef teppanyaki style, one of his favorites. The conversation turned to the situation back in Jordan, and some family members started repeating a few of the rumors circulating in Amman. At this point I lost my temper and asked to speak with them outside. "Listen," I said, "we're here to keep his morale up, not to sit around and peddle nasty gossip." Going back inside, we enjoyed the meal and watched the rest of the movie before retiring for the evening.

The next morning I came back early to apologize to my father for losing my temper. He told me to sit down, and we had a long personal talk that lasted almost three hours. Although we talked often, we mostly spoke about affairs of state, military matters, the family, cars, and motorbikes — rarely about personal feelings. Educated at boarding schools in Egypt and England, he could be reserved, and he encouraged his children to act the same way. But this conversation was different.

He told me he was really proud of the work I had done in the military, and said he was proud of me as his son. He told me that although I may have felt at times that he was neglecting me, in fact it was the opposite. He had been watching my career very closely. He had wanted me to make my own way in the military. So he had withheld his support many times, hoping that I would overcome challenges on my own. But, he conceded, he might have gone too far. "I feel I've let you down as a father," he said, "because at many times during your military career I knew that you were getting the short end of the stick, and I didn't step in. You must be angry that you didn't get your father's support."

With a smile I told him that, frankly, there were a couple of times over the previous twenty years when I could have done with some help. But in hindsight, I could not thank him enough, because it was during the hardest times that I had learned the most. Then he went on to say that he was expecting a lot from me, and that when he got back to Jordan he had some major changes he wanted to make. I thought he was talking about changes in the government, or a new approach to jump-starting the economy, which had been slowing in part because of the king's deteriorating health. I still hoped and prayed that he would have many years left ahead of him. Was my father telling me that he was dying? If so, I was not ready to face that possibility.

Two years earlier, in May 1996, the Likud leader Benjamin Netanyahu had assumed power in Israel. Netanyahu was no supporter of the Oslo Accords, which the Palestinians had signed in 1993 with his Labor predecessors, Shimon Peres and Yitzhak Rabin. A few months after Netanyahu came to power, the opening of a tunnel in Jerusalem in the vicinity of Al Haram Al Sharif triggered Arab anger and violent protests in the

West Bank. It also ran counter to the peace treaty Israel had signed with Jordan in 1994, which included a clause recognizing Jordan's special role in overseeing Jerusalem's holy shrines. Relations between Israel and the Palestinians deteriorated precipitously after that. Against this backdrop of tension, U.S. president Clinton invited Prime Minister Netanyahu and Palestinian president Yasser Arafat to join him on October 15, 1998, for a four-day summit at the Wye River Plantation, a compound on Maryland's eastern shore. The talks were going badly, and on October 18 Clinton asked my father to come and energize both parties. Two days later the sight of my father, gaunt and nearly bald, having painfully risen from his hospital bed to plead for peace, helped inspire the feuding parties to resolve their differences. After days of prolonged negotiations, the two delegations endorsed a breakthrough land-for-peace agreement under which Israel would redeploy from a further 13 percent of the West Bank. Although they were thrilled that their king had come to fight for peace, many Jordanians watching the proceedings on television were shocked to see the change in his condition. Two months before, he had been much sturdier; by now he had lost weight and looked very frail. His rapid deterioration fueled speculation in Amman that perhaps my father was sicker than people had realized, and that the country might soon need to prepare for a new king.

The Wye River Memorandum, signed on October 23 at the White House, restarted the peace process between the Israelis and Palestinians that had been stalled for a year and a half. In exchange for control over additional land in the West Bank, the Palestinians agreed to prevent "acts of terrorism, crime and hostilities" against Israel and to amend the Palestinian National Charter, removing provisions calling for the elimination of the state of Israel. In return, the Israelis agreed to release hundreds of Palestinian prisoners, open the Gaza airport, and provide safe passage for Palestinians moving from Gaza to the West Bank. Both sides, it seemed, were at last moving toward tackling the most difficult final status issues, including political control of Jerusalem, the return of refugees from the 1948 and 1967 wars, and the final borders of a Palestinian state.

My father asked me to come and be with him in America, so I flew to Washington, D.C., from Jordan on October 22, the day before the signing ceremony. I arrived in the evening and received word on arrival that my father wanted to see me. From the airport I jumped into a waiting car. Driving to my father's home in Maryland, I watched the sun glinting on the Potomac River and wondered what was in store. When I arrived, my father called for me to join him in the study. I stood at attention until he motioned for me to sit. I never lost sight of the fact that although he was my father, he was also my king. I was a bit shocked to see how frail and thin he had become, but I found that he still had that reassuring look of strength in his eyes.

He told me he had missed me and said he had heard good things about me since we had last met. It was clear he had heard about a lot of the intrigue going on back home, and he knew I was not part of it. Then, in a low voice, he described his anger at hearing reports that Prince Hassan had attempted to bypass the military chain of command and issued orders to the chairman of the Joint Chiefs of Staff. I told him that the chief of staff was holding the armed forces in complete and utter loyalty to him. He would have resigned rather than follow orders given by anyone but the king.

My father told me that he had been thinking about the matter a lot. Then he said, "I have decided to change the line of succession." I nodded, and he continued, "I hope you understand that this will be difficult for many in Amman, but I believe you will be up to the task. I will be expecting things from you." He didn't specify who he intended to choose, and I didn't press him. My father was tired from his treatments, and this was clearly a very difficult conversation for him. He left it at that and said, "Why don't you go out and have a good time."

My head was spinning as I headed to Morton's restaurant in Georgetown with a family friend for a steak. Perhaps my uncle's prediction was about to come true. If my father intended to change the line of succession, then clearly my uncle would not become king. But then who? If he was planning to make Hamzah crown prince, why hadn't he told me? I was not yet ready to accept that my father was dying, let alone that he might intend to choose me as his successor.

The signing ceremony between Israeli prime minister Benjamin Netanyahu and Palestinian president Yasser Arafat was scheduled at the White House late in the afternoon of the next day. My father spoke a few words at the ceremony.

"We quarrel, we agree; we are friendly, we are not friendly," he said. "But we have no right to dictate through irresponsible action or narrow-mindedness the future of our children and their children's children. There has been enough destruction, enough death, enough waste. It is time that, together, we occupy a place beyond ourselves, our peoples, that is worthy of them under the sun . . . the descendants of the children of Abraham."

After the event, I waited for my father at our embassy in Washington, where he would soon begin to receive senior members of the Jordanian government who were visiting. Usually he saw such delegations at his house, but by holding the meetings at the embassy he was making a public statement. He held a series of private meetings with visiting dignitaries, including the chairman of the Joint Chiefs of Staff of the Armed Forces, a delegation from Crown Prince Hassan's office, and two former prime ministers. All of the visitors were sitting together in the waiting room outside the ambassador's office. My father walked into the waiting room and, in front of everybody, embraced one of the former prime ministers, Abdul Karim Kabariti, who was known to be opposed to Prince Hassan. My father then met with each delegation individually in the ambassador's office. In every meeting, I later learned, he said that he planned to make "major changes" when he returned to Jordan — a message he would reiterate in public for the first time in late November.

That fall, the speculation surrounding the succession intensified, and the gossip was no longer confined to Amman. "Jordan's Feuding Queens Fight Over Succession," proclaimed a headline in the London *Sunday Times*. "King Hussein Ails; His Brother Waits," said the *New York Times*. Papers all over the world joined the game. In Canada the *Calgary Herald* ran a story headlined "Princes Jostle for Hussein's Crown," which alleged a feud between Queen Noor and Crown Prince Hassan's wife, Princess Sarvath, accusing both women of trying to manipulate the succession. It was very painful to read all of this in the press and to see details of my father's illness and our family dynamics debated openly in public. I was dismayed to see our private grief splashed over the front pages.

A rare spot of good news came in late November, when we heard that my father had been nominated for the Nobel Peace Prize. In a curious anomaly, Egyptian president Anwar Sadat and Israeli prime minister Menachem Begin had received the Peace Prize in 1978 for ending the state of war between Egypt and Israel, and President

Yasser Arafat, Israeli prime minister Yitzhak Rabin, and Israeli foreign minister Shimon Peres had shared the prize in 1994 for their work on the peace process. But my father and Yitzhak Rabin would not be similarly honored for signing a peace treaty between Israel and Jordan that same year.

In early January 1999 my father left the United States for London. On January 7, I landed at Heathrow and drove through the freezing rain to his house near Ascot, some fifteen miles southwest of the airport. The house was bustling with family. I could tell he wanted to speak to me privately, but it was hard to find a quiet moment. Every time I went to see him another family member would show up. Even so, we had that comfortable feeling that fathers and sons have when not saying much and just enjoying the closeness of each other's company. On my last day in London I had hoped at last to speak to him privately, but my uncle Crown Prince Hassan paid a surprise visit. He had been facing quite a bit of criticism back home for not visiting my father at the Mayo Clinic. Although my father was still seething about Prince Hassan's army overreach, he managed to hide his anger during the visit. I finally succeeded in finding a few moments alone with him that night. "Stay here for a couple of days," he said. "Sir," I said — I never stopped calling him that — "I have really got to get back to Jordan." I told him that I was in charge of a major element of security for his arrival. He sighed and said we would catch up in Amman.

Back in Jordan I began making arrangements for my father's return. He had been away from the country for almost six months, and hundreds of thousands of Jordanians wanted to welcome him home following what they believed was a successful cancer treatment. The plan was for him to travel by car from the airport through the streets of Amman to his home in the Hummar district, northwest of the city. His house was called Bab Al Salam, which means "gate of peace" in Arabic. It was named after one of the entrances to the Grand Mosque in Mecca, which my family had ruled for many generations, until Abdulaziz bin Abdulrahman Al Saud of the Nejd took over the Hijaz in 1924 and went on to found present-day Saudi Arabia.

Over the next ten days speculation continued to mount that my father had decided to change the line of succession. Several people came up to me and hinted conspiratorially that I was a candidate. I really felt it was none of their business. Over the years I had avoided meddling in politics and had devoted myself to my military career. I was not about to change that now.

On January 19, 1999, my father landed at Marka airport near Amman. He had flown his aircraft, a Gulfstream IV, all the way from London. Dressed in a dark suit and wearing the kouffiyeh, the traditional Jordanian red-checkered head scarf, he stepped out of the plane. The scene on the tarmac was emotional, with hundreds of people gathered to welcome my father and thousands more lining the streets of Amman. The night back in July when he had told me his cancer had recurred, I had a dream that he would return to his country and our people would turn out in the thousands, as they had in 1992 after his first illness. That dream came true, but in real life there would not be a happy ending.

There were tears streaming down my wife Rania's face, and I was trying as best I could to keep my emotions in check. But not all emotions on display that day were genuine, as family members, politicians, and members of the Royal Court lined up to welcome their king home. The way my father handled the welcoming line was a quiet lesson in statecraft. Some people he kissed, some he hugged, some he shook hands with, and some he walked straight past, not even acknowledging. He knew who had been loyal while he was away — and who had not. One family member tried to kiss him as they shook hands, and my father pushed him away. Realizing my father knew of his hypocrisy, the man broke down in tears.

When he reached me, my father completely ignored me. He did not even look me in the eye. He just shook my hand and walked straight past. Oddly, that was when it hit me. He did not want to focus attention on me because he wanted to make me crown prince. If he had given me a more effusive greeting, the watching courtiers would have taken it as a sign that I had risen in his favor, and would accordingly have begun jostling for influence. And those with ill intentions would have begun working against me.

The next day the crown prince of Dubai, Sheikh Mohammad Bin Rashid Al Maktoum, and the crown prince of Abu Dhabi, Sheikh Mohammed Bin Zayed Al Nahyan, came to pay their respects. My father ordered me to go and meet them at the airport. Normal protocol demanded that the crown prince greet them, but my father said, "I want you to meet these two. They are your friends, and you should bring them in." I welcomed the two guests, drove them to meet my father, and then took them back to the airport.

A few days later, on January 22, my father called the house and said, "I want to see you." I immediately drove out to Hummar, winding up the steep hill that rises above Amman. I found my father waiting in the dining room and shut the door behind me. He looked a lot worse than he had in London. I had heard from the guards that he had had several blood transfusions, and I was scared for him. He took my hand and said, "I want to make you crown prince. This is your right. You are the most capable, and you are the one out of all of them who can take the country forward." I sat in stunned silence. Then, finally, I said, "What about my uncle, Prince Hassan?"

He said that one of the reasons he had chosen me was that I always thought about everybody else, and he knew that I had the ability to lead the country and to keep the family together through this difficult time. At the end of the day, Hassan was still his brother and my uncle. My eyes misted up as I realized that my father was telling me he was dying. He would be heading back to the United States in a few days, he said, to try a bone marrow transplant. It was his last chance. The strength in his eyes seemed to dim a bit with that, and a cold sensation crept into my stomach. I think that was the first instant I truly felt alone. I felt like breaking down in tears and telling him how much he meant to me, but I knew that was not my father's way. The best way I could show my love and affection was to focus on the consequences of his decision and to take my new responsibility seriously. So although it was an emotional conversation, we continued to talk about practical matters.

The most immediate question was whom I should name as crown prince. According to the Constitution, the succession would pass to my son Hussein, but he was only five. I asked my father for his advice. "It is up to you who you choose as your crown prince," he said. Overtaken by emotion, he paused. At this point, the tone of his voice changed. "For your own safety, I'd advise you to make Hamzah crown prince," he said in a low voice, "but in the end it is up to you. Be very careful." It was then that I realized just how aware my father had been of the political intrigues back in Amman.

After we finished speaking I went home, struggling to control my sadness. When

I walked through the front door I found Rania sitting on the floor of the living room surrounded by a pile of photos. We had a cupboard full of family pictures that she had been saying for years needed to be organized, and she had decided to go ahead and get started. I looked down at my wife, surrounded by pictures of happy family moments, and told her my father was making me crown prince. "His health is really, really bad," I said. "I don't think he has long left." She looked at me with an expression of fear and sadness, tinged with foreboding. All too soon we would be thrust into the spotlight in a way neither one of us could ever have imagined. And there were a lot of wolves out there, waiting for us to stumble.

The morning of January 25, I was sitting at home when the phone rang. It was the chief of protocol, who let me know that King Hussein wanted me and my uncle to come to the palace that afternoon at four o'clock. So this was the transition, I thought. It was still early, so I went to my mother's house in the hills outside Amman to wait. I walked across the walled lawn where I had played as a child and where I had watched Israeli jets flying overhead during the 1967 war. Inside the house my family was waiting, gathered to help support each other. My brother Feisal was there, my older half sister Alia, my younger sisters Zein and Aisha, my cousins Talal and Ghazi, and my mother. We talked about happier times, sharing memories of our father. I waited until four o'clock, but just as I was about to leave I was told that there had been a delay. I later learned that my father was struggling to finish the final draft of a letter to Prince Hassan about his decision. Late in the evening, the phone rang again. The chief of protocol asked me to come immediately.

When I arrived at my father's house, Bab Al Salam, I was brought into his office, where my father and Prince Hassan were waiting. My father told Prince Hassan that he had decided to change the line of succession, and that I would now assume the responsibility of crown prince. Prince Hassan handled the situation with great grace and dignity. He handed me his personal flag, the standard of the crown prince. Passing it back to him, I said, "Please, Uncle, keep it. It is your flag." We went outside after that and stood in front of the waiting cameras, the three of us shaking hands, while my father announced the news to the nation.

That same day my father made public a strongly worded letter to Prince Hassan in which he was sharply critical of his brother, and in particular of the political infighting in Jordan, saying:

I have lived through many experiences and I noticed at an early age how some climbers climb onto the branch to ruin the relation between brothers and between father and son, and I swore to myself that this would not happen here in my lifetime. But surely, this has become the objective of every declared or hidden enemy, and all of those have used all means at their disposal to weaken confidence between leadership and people, but they have not succeeded.

Their plan at this stage, together with those who want to destroy Jordan, was to instigate infighting in the ranks of the leadership after they failed to dismantle the base, and they find in my being alive an impediment to all their designs, forgetting that Al Hussein has lived only to gain the blessings of God, to have a clear conscience and to achieve the best for all his people, regardless of their origins, who cooperate in holding the banner high and carrying the message of Jordan with their heads held high, not bowing except before God.

My father then referred specifically to Prince Hassan's attempts to interfere with the army, saying, "I have intervened from my sickbed to prevent meddling in the affairs of the Arab Army. This meddling seemed to be meant to settle scores, and included retiring efficient officers known for their allegiance and whose history and bright records are beyond reproach."

Many in Jordan were stunned by the letter's tone. But they trusted their king implicitly and knew him as a wise and insightful ruler. If King Hussein had taken the decision to change the line of succession, Jordanians knew there were good reasons. For his part Prince Hassan wrote a letter on January 28, replying to some parts of the king's letter and asserting his unwavering loyalty to his brother and king and his full support and backing for me as the new crown prince.

The next day, Rania and I drove my father to the airport. He was headed back to the Mayo Clinic for further treatment. My father and I sat in the front, with Queen Noor and Rania in the back. My father had bad hiccups as a result of his illness, and was extremely jaundiced so that even his eyes were yellow. I tried to make light conversation but failed dismally. As we drove out of Amman, he stared at the countryside as if for the last time. I placed my hand on top of his, and we drove the rest of the way in silence.

At the airport we found a receiving line of relatives waiting to say farewell. I struggled to keep my composure, and for a brief moment lost control of my emotions. I felt a hand on my arm. "Get a grip on yourself," one of my aunts whispered. "People will be looking at you." It was a sharp reminder of how much my life was about to change. I had never been so miserable or felt so alone in my life. Jordanians do not like to see grown men cry, and from then on my face remained a mask. I walked onto the airplane with my father, doing my best to assume an air of military correctness, and when he turned around our eyes met in silence. He too was having a hard time controlling his emotions. Before I could hug him good-bye, he gave me a nod, turned, and continued down the aisle into the plane. That was the last time I saw him conscious.

The week after my father's departure was very tense. I had been thrust unexpectedly into the very center of Jordanian politics and had to begin operating in my new role. I had had very few contacts with senior Jordanian political and private-sector figures and was moving into uncharted territory. Some of the existing leaders, including the prime minister and the chief of the Royal Court, had been appointed by Prince Hassan. Others, including the chief of protocol and the chief of royal security, were quite close to Queen Noor. There were a lot of people who hoped I would stumble, so I fell back on those closest to me, my colleagues in the army and in Special Operations.

Prince Hassan had been reaching out to several of his constituencies, and reports reached me that he had invited many senior political leaders to his house, including some of the senior tribal leaders. Wanting to get a better understanding of the situation, I asked Mohammad Majed, who was my number two in Special Operations, to gather some of my key officers at my house that evening. These were men I trusted implicitly. When the group had assembled, around 7 p.m., I told them that I had heard reports that Prince Hassan was being very active. I did not want to get blindsided by something stupid, however unlikely. My time in the military had taught me to protect my flanks. It would be prudent, I told them, to put some units on alert, just in case. As I was speaking, some of my commanders began to chuckle. Annoyed and tired, I said that this was serious and asked them what they thought was so funny. They told me that they had placed Special Operations Command on alert days before. They had already been in touch with the 3rd Division, and both the 40th and 60th Brigade commanders and their units were on standby. I looked into the faces of my unit commanders, and for the first time in a week I felt confident that things would turn out well.

Just over a week later we got word that my father's treatment had failed. He would return to Jordan to die in the land he loved. He landed on February 5, 1999, and was brought out of the airplane on a stretcher, unconscious and on life support. The family met him at the airport and accompanied him to the King Hussein Medical Center. Thousands of people from all across the country had gathered outside, praying, crying, and lighting candles. They waited in the street all night, saying their last good-bye. Senior Jordanian officials, old warriors, were weeping, and many were looking to me to see how I would handle it. "We always believed he was bigger than Jordan," one said to me. "We thought he would be here forever." At the hospital we spent the night taking turns standing by my father's bed. Only the immediate family was there: Noor, my mother, my wife, my brothers and sisters, and some of our cousins.

The following evening, with the family still gathered around, one of the doctors asked to speak to me privately. The cancer had spread much more quickly than anybody had expected, and there was nothing further anybody could do for him. For a second I broke down, overcome by grief. Then I walked back into the room and informed the family, and together we said good-bye to a brave man with an extraordinary force of will whom we loved so much. The doctors said the end would come that evening, but he lasted until late the next morning. Everyone had always remarked on what a great heart my father had, and it was the last part of him to give up, still beating strong as the rest of his body failed.

The funeral was the next day, on February 8, 1999. It was an overcast day and a light rain began to fall. People said that even the sky was crying for King Hussein. Most Jordanians had known no other king, so for the country his death was intensely personal, more like losing a member of their family than a head of state. Hundreds of thousands of distraught mourners lined the streets as an armored car carried his coffin, surrounded by flowers and covered by the Jordanian flag, to Raghadan Palace, his final resting place. As the car passed by, people surged forward, sobbing and wailing, trying vainly to seize a last glimpse of my father or to touch his coffin. The car was followed by an honor guard and a man leading my father's favorite white horse. Out of respect for my father, the horse, named Amr, would never be ridden again.

In the palace grounds an extraordinary collection of world leaders had come to pay their respects. Dubbed the "funeral of the century" by one observer, it brought together perhaps one of the most disparate groups of world leaders ever assembled. Some of the mourners were at war with each other, and one or two had even tried to kill each other in the past. But they were all united by their shared respect and admiration for my father. President Hosni Mubarak of Egypt, Crown Prince Abdullah of Saudi Arabia, and President Hafez al-Assad of Syria had come, joined by Crown Prince Mohammed of Morocco, President Yasser Arafat, and Saif al-Islam, the son of the Libyan leader Muammar Qadhafi. There were President Clinton and three former U.S. presidents, George H. W. Bush, Jimmy Carter, and Gerald Ford. Russian president Boris Yeltsin was there, as were Prince Charles and the British prime minister, Tony Blair. Prime

Minister Benjamin Netanyahu of Israel had come, as had Khaled Meshaal, a leader of Hamas, whom Netanyahu had tried to assassinate the year before. In all, representatives of some seventy-five countries came to Amman to honor my father. Inside the palace, my father lay in state, watched over by the Royal Guard. The Circassians, a Muslim people from the Caucasus who immigrated to Amman in the nineteenth century, provide the Royal Guard for Jordan's kings. They had served my father loyally for many years. Now they stood by him as he took his final journey.

My brothers and I carried my father's coffin from the Royal Guards Mosque to his grave in the palace burial ground, next to the graves of his father, King Talal, and his grandfather, King Abdullah I. My brothers and I stood at attention while a trumpeter played the last post. The Royal Guard fired a fifteen-gun salute as my father was lowered to his final resting place.

Although it was a day of great sadness, Jordanians felt a sense of pride that the whole world had come to pay its respects to their king. There was also a sense of determination as many realized that they needed to be strong to keep the country together. Many Jordanians fondly referred to their king as

Abu Abdullah, "father of Abdullah," as is common in the Arab world. In the weeks and months to come, I would benefit more times than I could count from Jordanians' love for my father and from their determination to help his son succeed.

After the funeral I headed to Parliament, to be sworn in as king. I had asked the chief of protocol to get a portrait of my father for the ceremony. As I walked in, I saw a huge picture of my father on the podium, dominating the room. I stood to attention. I felt his kind gaze looking down on me, and my eyes began to mist. Struggling to keep control, I stood motionless for several seconds, maintaining my salute. Then I went to swear the constitutional oath: "I swear by God that I will respect the Constitution and remain faithful to the nation." The president of the senate replied, "May God protect His Majesty King Abdullah and give him success. May Jordan live long, as His Majesty King Hussein intended."

After the ceremony was finished, an aide came up to me and said, "Your Majesty, this way." Out of habit, I looked around for my father, and saw his portrait looking down at me. For nearly half a century my father had ruled Jordan, sometimes fighting wars, sometimes negotiating peace treaties, and always encouraging others to lay down their weapons and place hope above fear. Now it would be my job to manage these conflicts and warring parties on Jordan's borders, and to honor my father's memory by continuing his ceaseless quest for peace.

# CHAPTER 13
# BECOMING KING

The days and weeks after my father's death were an extraordinarily sad time. The nation mourned its king, the only leader most Jordanians had ever known, and I grappled with the loss of my father, who had always been such a firm and guiding presence in my life. But I had little time for personal grief. The night before his funeral I went to bed with a family of four, and I woke up the next morning with a family of five million. If there was one thing that my father had taught me, it was that a king must not command so much as watch over his people.

After being sworn in, one of my first acts as king was to issue a decree naming my brother Hamzah the crown prince. Five years later, I relieved him of this responsibility. Although the months before my father's death had been tense, our family gathered together to support one another, and our shared grief brought many of us closer. I was very grateful for their love and support, but I knew that there were many outside the country, and some inside, who were watching and waiting for me to falter. As the rumors continued to circulate in the salons of West Amman, I heard that some people whom I had thought of as good friends were saying, "He won't last more than three months."

While I was awed by the task before me, it slowly dawned on me that my father had been preparing me for this all along. Although for most of my life I was not the crown prince, my father had taken me along with him on countless state visits, important foreign policy missions, and on trips to every corner of Jordan. Without the public scrutiny of being the heir apparent, I was given a golden opportunity to watch him as he navigated the perilous waters of international diplomacy. Plucked from my army postings for short trips with my father, I sometimes felt that I was present when history was being made.

Just three weeks after my father's funeral, I received one of my first official visitors, Prime Minister Benjamin Netanyahu of Israel, accompanied by his foreign minister, Ariel Sharon. Interactions between our countries were tense at that time, and this particular prime minister had sometimes stretched the relationship to the breaking point.

In 1996, the year after Yitzhak Rabin's assassination, Benjamin Netanyahu was elected prime minister of Israel on the heels of a wave of suicide bombings, believed to be the work of Hamas (the Palestinian Islamic Resistance Movement), which killed some sixty Israelis. On September 25 the following year he hit back at a Hamas leader then residing in Jordan.

Hamas had agreed that they would not conduct any political or military activity from Jordan and would only establish a media relations office. Over time, they went back on their commitment. Khaled Meshaal, a senior member of the political wing of Hamas, was walking toward his office in Amman one morning when Israeli intelligence agents leaped out of their car and squirted a mysterious substance into his ear. Meshaal suddenly became deathly ill. Two of the Mossad agents were chased across Amman by one of Meshaal's bodyguards and eventually captured by police. Four other members of the assassination squad made a dash for the Israeli embassy, while two others hid out at the InterContinental Hotel.

At this point Netanyahu called my father to say, "We have a problem." He sent his chief of intelligence, Danni Yatom, to explain what had happened and to ask that the Mossad agents be released. Although Yatom did not say so, we later learned that the assassination attempt had been personally approved by Netanyahu. In a déjà vu, a Hamas leader was assassinated in Dubai in January 2010, in what is believed to have been a Mossad operation that involved agents traveling with fake passports. And Netanyahu is again prime minister of Israel.

My father was livid. He had been working night and day to try to advance the cause of peace in the region. The previous January he had played an important role in facilitating the Hebron agreement, whereby Israel agreed to redeploy its soldiers from the city of Hebron in implementation of the Oslo process. A few days before the assassination attempt, he had discreetly passed to the Israelis a proposal from Hamas for a thirty-year cease-fire. And here Netanyahu was trying to assassinate one of Hamas's leaders on the streets of our capital!

Jordanian doctors struggled to save Meshaal's life. They were fighting a losing battle, because they could not identify the poison that had been used. My father demanded that the Israelis identify the poison at once and provide its antidote.

Yatom said Meshaal had been injected

with a complex chemical compound, and that he would die within twenty-four hours. My father told him that if Meshaal died, he would cancel the peace treaty and break off diplomatic relations with Israel. Finally, after stepping out of the meeting to call Netanyahu, Yatom told my father that there was another member of the Mossad team, a female doctor, staying at the InterContinental Hotel, and she had the antidote with her.

The Jordanian and Palestinian people were outraged at Israel's brazen act. Even if we managed to save Meshaal's life, we still had the dilemma of what to do about the two detained Mossad agents and those holed up in the Israeli embassy in Amman. All had entered our country using fake Canadian passports and had been involved in an assassination attempt. They did not have diplomatic immunity, but the Israelis refused to turn over the four accomplices who had sought refuge in the embassy. Jordanian security forces surrounded the embassy to make sure that they did not slip away. At the time, I was commander of Special Operations, and I can say it was a very tense period.

That evening, Meshaal, whose medical condition was rapidly deteriorating, was taken to King Hussein Medical Center and tended to in the Queen Alia Heart Institute, one of the country's leading medical facilities. The Mossad doctor, who had by then moved to another hotel, was found and brought to the hospital, carrying a vial of the antidote with her. But senior members of Hamas were suspicious and refused to let anyone inject anything further into the sleeping Meshaal without knowing what it was. They demanded the chemical formula for the antidote.

My father called President Clinton, urgently seeking his help. He asked Clinton to demand that America's close ally undo the damage it had done. Clinton complied, and finally Netanyahu relented and told us that the antidote was naloxone, a drug used to counter the effects of an opiate overdose.

We later learned that the poison was a chemically enhanced version of the painkiller fentanyl, which would kill without a trace in forty-eight hours. It had been hidden in a modified camera that had a long, retractable needle instead of a lens, which one of the assassins had jabbed into Meshaal's ear. Once they knew the antidote, a team of Jordanian doctors was able to administer it and save his life.

Khaled Meshaal's life was spared, but relations between Jordan and Israel were in critical condition. My father insisted that the

Israelis pay a high political price for their actions, and that they release from jail Sheikh Ahmed Yassin, the blind and wheelchair-bound spiritual leader of Hamas, who was one of the organization's founders. Yassin had served eight years of a life sentence for allegedly conspiring to kidnap Israeli soldiers. Eventually, a negotiated solution was reached: the Mossad agents were allowed to leave the country in exchange for the release of scores of Palestinians held in Israeli jails — including Sheikh Yassin. At 1:30 a.m. on September 29, 1997, as part of the agreement, Israeli prime minister Netanyahu flew to Amman to make a formal public apology.

Fast forward two years. I unexpectedly find myself as my father's successor, the new King of Jordan. Benjamin Netanyahu is still prime minister of Israel, and Khaled Meshaal, now fully recovered, has broken his agreement to restrict Hamas's activities in Jordan to media outreach. In the last year of his life, my father told me that he was very unhappy with Meshaal's continued political activity in Jordan — trying to smuggle weapons across the border into the West Bank and interfering in Jordanian politics. He felt that Meshaal, and the rest of the Hamas leaders in Amman, were taking advantage of Jordan's hospitality.

In countless negotiations and meetings Meshaal and other Hamas leaders residing in Jordan were repeatedly asked to stop activities that violated the conditions they had accepted for their stay in the country. But to no avail. They were obstinate, and wanted to operate with impunity. The government finally asked Meshaal to leave Jordan in August 1999. The Qatari government stepped forward and seemed eager to host him, so Meshaal and other Hamas leaders left for Doha.

A few days before our scheduled meeting, Benjamin Netanyahu made an inflammatory speech at Bar-Ilan University, near Tel Aviv. In his remarks he accused my father of siding with Iraq in the 1991 Gulf War, implied that Jordan might ally with Saddam Hussein in the future, and conjured the image of the Iraqi menace reaching the Israeli border through Jordan.

The speech was widely criticized in the region, and even inside Israel. Ehud Barak, the Israeli opposition leader, said, "There is no pit into which the prime minister has not fallen. The problem is he drags along the entire country into the pit with him. Even during the mourning period for King Hussein, Netanyahu found it fitting to endanger the few achievements of peace left."

Our meeting was not memorable. In a two-hour session over lunch we discussed the peace process and water rights. But Netanyahu's mischaracterization of my father's role in the Gulf War in order to score a few political points had left a bad taste in my mouth. My father did not side with Saddam — he tried to prevent a war that he saw as serving no one's interests. I came away from the meeting with the sense that getting the peace process back on track was going to be a long, hard slog.

In a country like Jordan, outside pressures force you to focus on foreign policy, but I had some critical domestic issues on my plate. One of my first decisions as king was whether to appoint a new prime minister. Jordan has a parliamentary system of government with a hereditary monarchy. Under the Constitution, Parliament's upper house, the Senate, is appointed by the king and made up of Jordanians who have distinguished themselves through public service, such as former prime ministers, ambassadors, and senior military officers. The lower house, the Chamber of Deputies, is chosen by a general election every four years. The king, as head of state, appoints the prime minister, who then selects cabinet ministers to form a government. Cabinet ministers could be selected from among members of Parliament or from outside it. This government must then win a vote of confidence in the Chamber of Deputies. If it does not, the government is disbanded and the process begins again.

Separate from the parliamentary system is the Royal Court, or Diwan. Every Jordanian citizen has the right to petition the king directly, on any matter of concern, and these petitions are presented to the Diwan, which people refer to as "the house for all Jordanians."

A petition can be on any topic, ranging from "I'm broke" or "I have a loan I can't pay" to "I can't educate my children," "I have a health issue," or "I can't find a job." Part of the role of the chief of the Royal Court is to meet everyone, listen to their petitions, and transmit their requests to the king. This system, based on tradition, was created when Jordan was a much smaller country. Now, with a population of nearly six million, it is not possible for the chief of the Royal Court to meet everybody personally, so various departments have been set up to address different topics. People of prominence, however, still see the chief of the Royal Court in person. And when I visit rural areas of the country, people will frequently come up to me directly and hand me a piece of paper with their petition written on it.

Although it is not formally called for in the Constitution, in Jordan it is traditional for the existing government to resign following the proclamation of a new king. Of course, this tradition had not been exercised in some time, since my father had ruled for nearly half a century. In my early dealings with government officials, they would tell me of their grand plans for improvements. But when I asked the simple question "When?" I rarely got a satisfactory answer. This was my first indication that a government does not run like an army.

When changes are made at a high level, Jordanians often assume that it is personal and that the official being replaced somehow got into my bad books. But that has never been the case. What I look for in all my advisers is the ability to implement my program and to get things done expeditiously. If the advisers do not get results, they will be replaced. In the end, we are all working for the people of Jordan, and they deserve the very best.

In early March 1999, I requested and received the existing government's resignation and asked Abdul Raouf Rawabdeh, an experienced parliamentarian and administrator, to be the new prime minister, and Abdul Karim Kabariti, a loyal confidant of my father's who had been prime minister from 1996 to 1997, to be the new chief of the Royal Court. That first decision, to change the government, was one of the most stressful that I have ever had to make. It does not really get any easier, but the first time was particularly difficult. I remember being in Basman Palace, in the Royal Court compound, preparing to retire the old government and to bring the new one in, wondering whether I was doing the right thing. Abdul Raouf was not somebody widely expected to be nominated as prime minister, and I knew I would come in for criticism whatever decision I made.

I was standing in a room off the main hall in the Diwan, when, deep in thought, I glanced up and saw a picture of my father in military uniform, looking down at me and smiling. I took that as a sign that I was doing the right thing. My father trusted me enough to make me king; now I had to trust my own instincts. I announced the changes and held my breath.

A couple of weeks later, as the forty-day mourning period for my father came to an end, I had to make another sensitive decision. I knew that Jordan would benefit from my wife's energy, intelligence, and compassion, and so I decided to give her the title of queen. But I was also sensitive to the impact that this might have on Noor, my father's widow, who had been queen for two decades. So I went to meet with her in private. She was understanding, and said that it was time for a new generation to take over. She also said that, although he may have been reserved at times, my father would constantly tell her how much he loved me, how proud he was of my achievements in the army, and how he thought that I would be the best person to lead the country when he was gone. I thanked her for her kindness and said I appreciated her support.

On March 21, 1999, Rania was proclaimed queen. I sent her a public letter announcing that fact, saying, "Over the past years, you shared with me the blessings bestowed upon us under the great father, my father, and the father of all Jordanians. . . . Now that I have been destined by God to shoulder the number one responsibility in Jordan, I decided, especially since you are my life companion and mother of Hussein, that you will become Her Majesty Queen Rania Al Abdullah as of today." As we were all still mourning the loss of my father, we postponed the formal enthronement ceremony, which took place a few months later. The following day, Queen Noor was heading to the United States with her children Hashim, Iman, and Raiyah to take them back to school in America. Rania and I offered to drive her to the airport. In the days following my father's death, our relationship had been stronger than ever, but as we drove I could sense that something had changed. Noor was polite but very formal and reserved, and it was an uncomfortable trip. Our relationship has been cold since then.

One of my top priorities was to carry out a broad program of social reforms, and in particular to provide more support for the weakest members of our society. My new government and I began to look at ways of protecting women and children, and to talk publicly about topics that had previously been taboo, such as domestic violence and child abuse.

One of the biggest taboos was the issue of so-called honor killings, which I had first encountered as a young officer in the army. Women are sometimes murdered by members of their own family, frequently fathers or brothers, when these men feel that they have dishonored the family by indulging in inappropriate relationships. One of my men had killed his female cousin with a knife, and then turned himself over to me as his superior officer. His family had gathered together and debated the issue, and he had been selected to carry out the murder. This soldier was one of my best tank commanders, and he was pressured to fulfill a distorted concept of "honor" that robbed a young woman of her life. I handed him over to the military police, regretting this terrible loss of two young lives, and he was subsequently convicted of murder and sent to prison.

At the time, I had thought it was a senseless waste. Now that I was in a position to influence public policy, I was determined to act. I could not change people's mindset overnight, but I could do something about how these crimes were investigated and prosecuted, and how they would be treated by society.

I attacked on several fronts. We began an awareness campaign, stressing that such murders were morally wrong and went against the teachings of Islam, and tackled the penal code and judiciary. Rania was an outspoken critic of "honor" killings, and she joined a demonstration march to Parliament against them. We began to provide institutional support to women suffering from domestic violence, and set up shelters for battered women.

One of our biggest problems was that the victim's family would often not come forward and press charges. Added to that, many judges treated "honor" killings as crimes of passion rather than murders, and the typical sentence handed down was between six months and two years. Now all such crimes are considered murders; special courts have been set up to address these cases and they are taking a harsher view. The penal code was amended to ensure that the perpetrators receive no leniency.

Over time, our efforts began to show fruit. Sentences became harsher, and cases became less frequent. The number of "honor" crimes dropped from thirteen in 2008 to ten in 2009. The murderers whose trials ended in 2009 were sentenced to ten years in prison, compared to sentences that ranged between six months' to two years' imprisonment before the law was amended. But to my mind, even one such killing is a stain on the honor of all Jordanians, and I will not rest until such a barbaric view of justice no longer has a place in our country.

One of the more frustrating misconceptions in the West is that all Arab women are oppressed, illiterate, kept at home to look after children, and forced to wear the veil when they venture out of the house. Many women across Jordan and the Arab world, like my wife, go to university and then achieve great things in their professional careers. Statistics for the school system in Jordan show that every single year the highest grades in high school exams are achieved by girls. Our modern, educated, successful professional women have more in common with professional women in London, New York, or Paris than with the oppressed prisoners of Western imagination. Some of these women choose to cover their hair with a head scarf, while others, like Rania, do not. But this tells you nothing about their abilities or professional achievements. The traditionally dressed Jordanian woman wearing a head scarf may have a PhD from MIT or Harvard. As Rania likes to say, "We should judge women according to what's going on in their heads rather than what's on top of their heads."

But it is a sad fact that there is more than a grain of truth to the stereotype. Many Arab men are extremely prejudiced and believe that women should either stay at home and raise children or be restricted to certain professions. Even in my own family, some of my brothers and cousins were against my sisters, Aisha and Iman, going to Sandhurst — although no one dared to try to stop them. Somewhere along the line you need more women like them to stand up and say, "Let me lead my life as I want to lead it!"

Rania has worked hard to address misperceptions about women in Arab societies. She has been an outspoken champion of women's rights, and in recent years she has adopted the most modern communications tools — such as YouTube, Facebook, and Twitter — to make her case. She quickly realized that, in a globally connected world, the Internet allows us Jordanians to speak beyond our borders, making our country's small size and lack of resources irrelevant. By going online, she could be heard around the world.

Technology is in many ways an equalizer, and it means that the first lady of even a small country like Jordan can have a prominent voice on the international stage. But the question then is, how do you make sure that what you have to say is interesting? How do you make sure that you use this tool in the most effective, creative, fun way that will just keep people engaged to hear your message? And it is here that Rania has done some terrific work, using technology to communicate her messages on the importance of education and to challenge misconceptions about Islam and the Arab world. Her most important work has been improving the educational standards for children across Jordan.

In April 2008, Rania launched the Madrasati ("My School") initiative, a groundbreaking program to improve the quality of education in five hundred disadvantaged public schools throughout the Kingdom. At the heart of Madrasati is a simple concept: we all share responsibility for our children's education. Madrasati brings together businesses, nongovernmental organizations, communities, and the Ministry of Education with parents, teachers, and pupils in pursuit of one common goal: rejuvenating schools in need. Since its 2008 launch, over three hundred public schools have been revitalized, lifting the lives of more than 110,000 students. The initiative has significantly enhanced the infrastructure of those schools and has introduced a series of programs that improve the educational experience, such as health awareness, access to technology and medical services, and teacher training.

Alarmed by the deteriorating conditions of schools in East Jerusalem and the dangerous implications of the increasing school drop-out rate for a population that not only prizes education but needs it for its survival, Rania launched Madrasati Palestine in 2010. The initiative will build on the experience in Jordan while trying to address the specific needs of the 94,000 school-aged Palestinian children in East Jerusalem. It hopes to reintegrate some of the 10,000 children who are now out of school in the city, and to improve graduation rates, especially among boys, who are now dropping out at a rate of over 50 percent.

In early March 1999 we restored diplomatic relations with Kuwait, suspended since the first Gulf War. Feelings among Kuwaitis had been raw, because some people mistakenly believed that my father's attempts to prevent the war meant that he had sided with Saddam. That Rania had grown up in Kuwait proved helpful in putting all of that baggage behind us. Later that month, I met with Yasser Arafat, chairman of the PLO and then president of the Palestinian National Authority, who visited me in Amman for the first time since I had become king. We discussed the lack of progress in the peace process and Arafat's upcoming visit to Washington. Although Arafat had a long history of jousting with my father, I sensed that he respected him. He had been quite emotional when he bowed before my father's coffin at the funeral. I was prepared to listen to him and to help where I could.

Two weeks later, to mark the end of the forty-day mourning period for my father, some of my advisers suggested that we grant amnesty for certain prisoners, as was the tradition with the accession of a new ruler. I agreed, on condition that we not release anyone accused of a very serious crime, such as murder or rape. My advisers came up with a list of seven hundred people who, they said, had been very carefully vetted, and I gave my approval for their release. Both houses of Parliament voted to approve the amnesty, and a few days later the first of the prisoners walked free. One of them, Ahmed Fadil Khalayleh, a man now notoriously known as Abu Musab al-Zarqawi, should never have been allowed out of jail. I would later bitterly regret that his name was on the list.

Some leaders, such as Netanyahu and Arafat, had come to visit me. But others were waiting for me to visit them. It was a delicate time. My fellow Arab rulers had all known my father and my uncle, in many cases for decades, and I would have to work hard to earn their respect as a peer. Some had fought with my father, and even tried to kill him. In those instances, I could use the fact that I was new to the job to start over with a clean slate.

# CHAPTER 14
## FRIENDS AND NEIGHBORS

One thing that is not well understood in the West is the diversity of the Middle East. Even though the countries of Europe share a common religion and political structure, there are tremendous cultural and social differences between a Swede and a Greek, a German and a Spaniard. Even European countries that speak the same language, such as Ireland, England, Scotland, and Wales, have fiercely defended their cultural and historical identities. So it makes little sense to talk about a "European"; most citizens of Europe will define themselves by their national identity.

There is a similar level of diversity in the Middle East. A Moroccan is quite different from a Jordanian or a Yemeni. Even though most Arab countries share a common religion, Islam, and a common language, Arabic, there are important cultural and historical differences between them, and they are also home to significant religious minorities. The Egyptians trace their history back to the ancient civilization of the Pharaohs, while the Gulf states have a bedouin desert tradition. Turks and Iranians speak different languages and have their own histories and cultures. So it makes as little sense to make sweeping generalizations about all "Arabs" as it does with all "Europeans."

Even though I had met my counterparts around the region with my father, no one was going to go easy on me just because I was my father's son. I live in a tough neighborhood. And as the new King of Jordan, I was about to find out just how tough it really was. To the west were Palestine as well as Israel, the region's only nuclear power. To the east was Baathist Iraq, ruled by Saddam Hussein, who had fought wars with two of his other neighbors and had a million men under arms. To the north was Syria, ruled by Hafez al-Assad, an astute leader who had been in office for around three decades. And to the south was Saudi Arabia, home to the holy cities of Mecca and Medina, where Crown Prince Abdullah bin Abdulaziz was assuming wider responsibilities due to the illness of his brother, King Fahd. Just over the horizon in Egypt was Hosni Mubarak, an experienced leader with whom my father had developed a strong friendship. And farther afield were Libya, the Gulf states — Bahrain, Kuwait, Qatar, the United Arab Emirates, and Oman — and, across the Arabian Gulf, Iran. Many leaders of those countries had been in power for decades and would likely remain there for years to come. The presidents were often in office longer than the kings.

My father had known all of these leaders personally and, as one of the world's longest-serving heads of state, many of their predecessors too. He had taught me that Jordan had to maintain a delicate balance in regional politics. Relations with our neighbors had sometimes been turbulent. A few of them during the 1950s and 1960s, when Arab nationalism was pervasive, had even tried to overthrow or assassinate my father. But all had come to pay their respects at his funeral and mourned his passing. Now I would have to form my own relationships with them. And from my father's experience I knew it would be hard to predict when they would be supportive and when they would not.

One leader I knew I would not be too close to was Saddam Hussein. Once I became king, I had very little direct contact with him. I chose not to visit Baghdad, but Iraq was not so easily avoided. It continued to be a source of concern, as many in the international community were worried about the possibility that Iraq would again attack one of its neighbors and suspected that Saddam had restarted his biological and nuclear weapons programs.

Tensions between Baghdad and the United States had been building steadily in the last year of my father's life. In September 1998 the Iraq Liberation Act was introduced in the U.S. Congress, stipulating, "It should be the policy of the United States to support efforts to remove the regime headed by Saddam Hussein from power in Iraq and to promote the emergence of a democratic government to replace that regime." President Clinton signed the act into law on October 31, 1998, at which point "regime change" became official U.S. policy. The next day, Saddam threw the UN weapons inspectors out of the country. Six weeks later, Clinton launched four days of air strikes against Iraqi weapons facilities from carriers in the Arabian Gulf, with British forces also joining in the attack.

This was a period of intense domestic pressure for Clinton. Throughout 1998 his affair with a White House intern had been under investigation, and the president had been forced to testify before a grand jury. On the last day of the air strikes, December 19, he was impeached by the U.S. House of Representatives for perjury. He was acquitted by the Senate the following February, but that did not signal the end of his woes.

The relentless legal assault on the U.S. president made my father furious. Whatever Clinton's personal failings, my father knew him as a firm friend of Jordan and a strong supporter of the peace process, and it was his nature to always come to the defense of friends. My father was a great admirer of America's democratic traditions, but on occasion he believed things could go too far. He thought the whole investigation into Clinton's personal life was like a soap opera, and he was really upset that people were attacking the president in such a vicious way. I remember watching television with him at the Mayo Clinic when Ken Starr, who was leading the investigation, came on the news. My father blew up and forcefully expressed his disapproval of how Starr was handling the investigation. "If I ever met that man, I would give him a piece of my mind," he burst out — and that was not all he said. I left Mayo that night pleased that his morale was high and he still had his fighting spirit.

■■■■

One difference between politics in the Middle East and in Europe and America is its deeply personal nature. In the West, international affairs tend to be conducted through institutions and permanent cadres of civil servants who provide policy continuity as political leaders step on and off the stage. Personal relations tend to be less important than the correct set of talking points.

But in my part of the world, people like to get to know one another face-to-face. We pride ourselves on our culture of hospitality, which often means a lot of eating and socializing. In the West, it is perfectly acceptable to meet with a head of state for twenty minutes, conduct some business, and move on. But in the Arab world it is considered rude to visit for a short time. The appropriate way to host honored guests is to invite them to a grand dinner. The real work gets done in informal conversations after the dinner, not in official meetings.

I knew I would have to build personal relationships with my fellow Arab leaders. The centers of power in the Middle East are Egypt, Saudi Arabia, Syria, and Iraq, due to their size and historical importance, and the Gulf countries, because of their wealth and influence. I would need to meet the leaders of all of these nations to establish good relations. So in late March 1999 I began a whirlwind tour of the region, stopping first in Egypt, where I met President Hosni Mubarak.

Egypt has for centuries been a major center of regional power due to its size, history, and religious institutions. Cairo is home to Al Azhar University, which at over a thousand years old is one of the world's most ancient, and Egyptians fondly refer to their country in Arabic as *um al dunya* — "mother of the world."

The Mubaraks have been family friends since the early 1980s, and I knew Hosni Mubarak and his son Gamal well. Mubarak was extremely warm when he greeted me. We talked about some of the challenges we were both facing, and in particular about the difficulty of providing jobs and opportunities for a young population facing terrible poverty and unemployment. Mubarak mentioned how much the region had suffered from Rabin's assassination a few years earlier. Rabin had been prepared to make considerable sacrifices for peace, and we both reflected on how the entire Middle East would have benefited from his forceful determination to come to terms with the Palestinians. Looking across our borders into Israel, neither of us saw a leader with the strength to bring his countrymen along with him as Rabin could have done. The stalled peace process and how to reinvigorate it were, and would be in every other meeting we would later have, major items on our agenda. We talked about the need to push for a breakthrough that would put the region back on track toward a settlement on the basis of the two-state solution.

Not long after that, in early April, I paid a visit to King Fahd bin Abdulaziz Al Saud and his brother Crown Prince Abdullah in Jeddah. Crown Prince Abdullah had assumed a great deal of responsibility for ruling Saudi Arabia in recent years due to King Fahd's failing health. I first met Prince Abdullah in the late 1970s when, on holiday from Deerfield, I went with my father and Feisal to Taif, a mountain town that is the summer seat of the Saudi Royal Court. I sat next to him at a dinner and remember reflecting on the fact that this man, almost forty years older than me, and I shared the same name. He had been a crack shot and told me stories about putting out cigarettes with his pistol. He was also a keen rider and regaled me with accounts of his horses.

But although Crown Prince Abdullah and

I had a good personal rapport, the relationship between Jordan and Saudi Arabia had historically been a delicate one. The Hashemite family originally came from the Hijaz and had ruled over the holy cities of Mecca and Medina for more than seven hundred years, until 1925, when the Hashemites lost the area to Ibn Saud, who founded the modern Kingdom of Saudi Arabia. My father's relationship with the Saudis had been very strong, but it was damaged by the position he had taken in the Gulf War in 1991. Never one to let politics trump personal friendship, however, Crown Prince Abdullah visited my father at his house in Washington in the last months of his life and brought him Zamzam water, which comes from a well in the holy city of Mecca. He poured the water for him as a good omen, and also brought a copy of the Holy Quran, a gesture that deeply touched my father, who spoke of it more than once with warm appreciation in the days that followed.

I had been to Saudi Arabia several times during my days in Special Forces and had gotten to know some of the younger generation, including two of Crown Prince Abdullah's sons, Mutaib and Abdulaziz. We had spoken about the historic clashes between our two families and how we should put history to one side and focus on strengthening our relationship.

Abdullah, who succeeded King Fahd in 2005, is a rare mix of traditional and modern leader. He is a leader with an instinctive understanding of what makes people tick in our region. With values firmly rooted in his country's heritage and culture, he has a far-reaching vision for the future of his people. Saudi Arabia is a conservative society that has traditionally enforced a strict segregation between men and women. But on September 5, 2009, the King Abdullah University of Science and Technology, Saudi Arabia's first coeducational university, located on the Red Sea near Jeddah, opened its doors. And when a senior Saudi cleric criticized the coed nature of the university, King Abdullah removed him from his post. Under his reign, Saudi Arabia has witnessed tremendous development in education, telecommunications, and infrastructure. His policies have led to significant diversification of the economy and facilitated the growth of the private sector. King Abdullah initiated major reforms in the judicial system, restructuring courts and introducing a supreme court of justice to achieve uniformity in rulings. For the first time in the country's history, a woman was appointed as a deputy minister in the cabinet.

King Abdullah is the kind of man it takes a while to get to know, but once you have built a relationship, it is generally very strong. He likes to watch the news while he eats, and it is a sign that you are an honored guest if he feels relaxed enough in your company to host you in a more informal setting with the TV on. He is a very gracious host, and at state dinners when I came to visit he would sometimes walk beside me, surveying the various traditional dishes of rice, lamb, and pastries, pause beside a particularly appetizing dish, taste it, then put a little on my plate. He has been a close friend, and a strong supporter of Jordan.

Later that month I went to Oman, where I met with Sultan Qaboos Bin Said Al Said in the desert near Nizwa, a town some 120 miles southwest of the capital, Muscat. Every year, the sultan goes for a three-month tour through the different regions of Oman, accompanied by his government ministers. A fellow Sandhurst graduate, the sultan is a modest and meticulous man who is always immaculately groomed. He pays close attention to the way his country is run, and moved Oman from the twelfth to the twenty-first century without losing sight of its rich heritage as a seafaring country. (Tradition has it that Sinbad the Sailor was born in a small fishing village northwest of Muscat.)

The sultan of Oman has remarkably few enemies. A testament to his evenhandedness and diplomatic skill is his ability to stay on friendly terms with both the Iranians and the Americans. His relationship with my father was very strong, in part because my father sent Jordanian troops to help defeat the rebels who led an insurgency against him in the 1960s and 1970s. The Dhofar rebellion began as a protest against the rule of the sultan's father, Said Bin Taimur, but by 1970, when the current sultan gained power, the rebels had embraced Marxism and were supported by China and the Soviet Union. The rebellion was finally defeated in 1975, and Sultan Qaboos began to modernize his country after that.

Focusing on education, the role of women, and political stability, he took pains to ensure that his country developed efficient institutions and was forward-looking. His government always has a five-year plan and Oman has set aside funds for the day its oil runs out. The sultan plays a discreet role on the world stage, but his standing in the region is extremely high. The Western leaders who know him always pay careful attention to his words. When my father passed away, one of the people who was most supportive and helpful to me was the sultan. He always gives wise advice and often has a completely original way of looking at a situation. In my early years as king especially, I benefited greatly from his counsel.

I continued on to the United Arab Emirates, meeting with Sheikh Zayed Bin Sultan Al Nahyan, the emir of Abu Dhabi and president of the UAE. A traditional ruler, Sheikh Zayed, who by then was in his early eighties, had a disarming personal manner. He presided over Abu Dhabi's and the rest of the UAE's amazing transformation into one of the Arab world's most modern countries, with vibrant business, cultural, and educational centers. When he died in 2004, the region lost a great leader, known for his wisdom, vision, and compassion. His successor, Sheikh Khalifa, has carried on his father's tradition of ruling with tolerance and wisdom. Sheikh Zayed was very supportive of Jordan and was always there if I needed help. I am close friends with his son Mohammed Bin Zayed Al Nahyan.

Next, I went to Sirte, a coastal town 250 miles east of Tripoli, in Libya, to meet Colonel Muammar Qadhafi. When he took power in a military coup in 1969, Qadhafi allied himself with various radical factions across the region. In 1982, he devised a plan to smuggle ground-to-air missiles into Jordan and to position them at the Amman and Aqaba airports to shoot down my father's plane. The man entrusted by Qadhafi with carrying out the plot, the Libyan ambassador to Jordan, was horrified. Knowing he would be put in jail or worse if he refused, he pretended to carry out his orders. But as the day of the plot approached, he defected to Jordan and told my father about it.

The next year, to the astonishment of many Westerners, my father invited Colonel Qadhafi to come to Amman for a public reconciliation. On June 10, 1983, a jet plane landed at Amman's military airport, and Qadhafi descended from the plane accompanied by a group of female bodyguards, young women wearing Cuban-style combat shorts with safari vests, sporting small peaked caps over afro hairdos, and carrying guns. After two hours of talks, my father invited Qadhafi to spend the night in Jordan before continuing on his journey to Syria. To an outsider, this might seem like an odd way to treat a man who the year before had tried to kill you. But my father always believed in keeping one's friends close and one's enemies even closer.

He knew that the Middle East was a crowded neighborhood, and his three decades as king had taught him that today's enemy may be tomorrow's friend. There was no sense in bearing grudges. Like members of an extended family, the leaders of the twenty-two Arab countries were going to be dealing with one another for many years to come. Over time, my father and Qadhafi became closer, to the point where, when I was commander of Special Operations, he would send me to Libya to discuss military cooperation. On these trips I got to know Qadhafi's sons.

My father took an equally enlightened approach in his handling of domestic opponents. Jordan is a small country, and he knew he would have to live with the people he disciplined and their families, too. The traditional punishment in the Middle East for plotting to overthrow a government is execution. But my father would often exile the people who plotted against him for a few years and then welcome them back to Jordan. He would sometimes even offer the returning plotter a job in government. It was his way of showing forgiveness and inspiring loyalty. The next time they might think twice before seeking to undermine the man who had shown them such kindness. I had learned much from watching my father lead our country, but I knew that with his passing I would have to find my own approach.

In late April I visited Syria. Relations between Syria and Jordan had been strained since my father had signed a peace treaty with Israel in 1994. Hafez al-Assad was furious that Jordan had not waited for him to conclude his own negotiations with the Israelis over the Golan Heights, which had been seized by the Israeli army in 1967. Assad would not visit Amman after the treaty until my father's funeral. So my visit to Damascus was a chance to recalibrate relations.

I knew a little about Assad and what kind of man he was. In the late 1980s, when tensions between him and Saddam Hussein were running high — Saddam was entrenched in a lengthy, violent war with Iran, and Assad was siding with the Iranians — my father, working through back channels, persuaded the two men to meet, following Winston Churchill's advice that "to jaw jaw is always better than to war war." The site he chose was Al Jafr, a remote desert village about 140 miles south of Amman. At that time, I was a military officer flying Cobra helicopters and my unit was part of the aerial security. The Royal Guard cordoned off the meeting site, stationing armed troops along the perimeter and around the landing strip. We separated the compound into two halves, one side for the Syrians and the other for the Iraqis, and prepared accommodations.

Once preparations were completed, my father beckoned me to join him. "Stay with me and watch what happens," he said. Looking back, I realize that he wanted me to have a glimpse into international diplomacy, a world far removed from my duties as an army officer.

Both Syria and Iraq were then ruled by the Baath Party, which espoused a form of secular Arab socialism. In the late 1960s, the Baath Party, which was formed in Syria, split. The party's founders were driven into exile — moving to Iraq, where they soon drew a following and took over the government in 1968. Relations between Baathist Syria and Iraq fluctuated over the years between high tension and collaboration, and by the mid-1980s, when my father brought them together, these two strong military powers were jockeying for regional primacy.

Late in the afternoon of the appointed day, the sound of an aircraft engine floated across the desert, and then several jets with Syrian flags on their tails landed and taxied down the makeshift runway. Accompanied by around fifty soldiers carrying AK-47 assault rifles, Hafez al-Assad emerged from his plane. My father greeted him and escorted him and his delegation to the Syrian half of the compound.

About half an hour later several more planes landed, this time bearing Iraqi colors. Saddam Hussein marched out of the lead plane, accompanied by some fifty heavily armed Iraqi soldiers. My father welcomed Saddam and showed him to the Iraqi delegation's area.

I watched the proceedings with Dr. Samir Farraj, my father's personal physician. As dusk fell, our soldiers set up bright spotlights to illuminate the whole area like daylight. We did not want any confusion caused by shadows in the night.

Saddam and Assad went into the meeting room my father had prepared, while my father waited outside with the rest of us. Several hours passed, during which he kept sending in more coffee and food. Finally, in the early hours of the morning, the meeting ended. My father took Saddam to one side and asked how it had gone. Saddam wearily said that he had spoken for no more than fifteen minutes during the whole time. Relegating someone with Saddam's massive ego almost entirely to listening was not a good idea. Despite all my father's efforts, he could not persuade the two men to reconcile, and they left the desert meeting still on hostile terms. But both leaders respected my father's attempt to act as a peacemaker. And I had learned a valuable lesson about the need for patience in diplomacy.

I had been invited to visit President Clinton in Washington in May, and when I saw President Assad in Damascus, he asked me to relay a message to Clinton. He said he was ready to talk to the Americans. I told him I would convey his message and we discussed the peace process and water rights. We also talked about his son, Bashar, whom I met on the visit. We got along well. Hafez al-Assad was nearing seventy, and I think he was excited by the prospect of his son and me becoming friends.

President Assad died unexpectedly just over a year after my visit and was succeeded by his son. Though Bashar and I do not agree on every aspect of regional politics, our countries are collaborating more than ever before. We consult on the peace process, and are expanding our cooperation in many areas, including regional energy projects. We are encouraging the private sectors to forge stronger links. Even our young children have established ties. When we first visited, all the children were very shy, but it didn't take them long to discover a common interest in Super Mario Brothers — and now they get along well.

The last stop on my tour of the neighborhood was Gaza, where I had my first official meeting with Arafat in my role as king. Arafat had come to Amman for my father's funeral, but we did not have any discussions then.

My father and Arafat had become closer toward the end of their lives. I would sometimes attend their meetings and my father would laugh, watching me standing helpless while Arafat showered me with kisses. By then, having won the Nobel Peace Prize together with Yitzhak Rabin and Shimon Peres in 1994, he had taken on the role of elder statesman.

As we gathered for lunch, each accompanied by our respective delegations, Arafat said, "The Palestinian people of the West Bank and the East Bank welcome you to Gaza!" My people bristled, as Arafat was implying that he still retained some political influence in Jordan, the "East Bank," invoking memories of his failed attempt to overthrow my father in 1970.

Arafat was also referring to the large number of Jordanians of Palestinian origin. He never gave up his claim to represent all Palestinians who had been chased from their homes in Israel or forced to flee during the wars. During and after the 1948 Arab-Israeli war, a wave of refugees from Palestine crossed into Jordan, significantly increasing Jordan's then population of 433,000. These refugees were given Jordanian citizenship. A second wave of Palestinians crossed the River Jordan after the 1967 war — they already had Jordanian nationality as they mostly lived in the West Bank, which belonged to Jordan. In 1999, around 43 percent of Jordan's population was of Palestinian origin.

I let his curious comment pass, but later, in a tête-à-tête, I spoke my mind. "The Palestinian people will always have 110 percent of my support in the search for a Palestinian state," I said. "And once the Palestinians achieve their right to statehood, Jordanians of Palestinian origin will at last have the right to choose where they want to live. Those who want to be Palestinian citizens and move to Palestine will be free to do so, and all of our citizens who choose to stay in Jordan, whatever their background or origin, will remain Jordanian citizens. Their loyalty will be to the Jordanian flag, not the Palestinian, which for some is not the case today."

I saw a flicker of a smile pass across the old freedom fighter's lips. He had been testing my authority with his reference to the "East Bank," and my vigorous response I think surprised him.

We moved from discussing inter-Arab politics to the attempt to revive the Wye Accords and the implications of Ehud Barak's election as prime minister of Israel. Arafat and I both agreed that it was important for the Arabs to maintain a united front in any negotiations with the Israelis. We discussed the possibility that the new Israeli prime minister would try to split the Arabs by opening peace negotiations with Syria. Arafat, who was curious about my conversation with Assad, worried that the Syrian leader would respond positively to any overtures by the Israelis, at the expense of the Palestinians. I told him that I did not believe Assad would accept such a deal. I returned to Jordan curious to see whether Barak would live up to our hopes and expectations.

# CHAPTER 15
# TRANSFORMING JORDAN

When I became king in February 1999, my first challenge was not war or a terrorist attack. It was how to pull Jordan's economy out of a short-term crisis and put it onto a path of strong and resilient growth.

My father had left the country a rich inheritance of peace, political stability, and a strong international standing, but economically Jordan was struggling. Throughout the 1990s the economy had suffered from the fallout of Iraq's invasion of Kuwait. Most Gulf countries had perceived his efforts to stop the war as siding with Saddam, and as a result they dramatically cut back on their aid, loans, and investments in Jordan. The return of large numbers of expatriate Jordanian workers from Gulf countries, mainly from Kuwait and Saudi Arabia, meant that we no longer benefited from their remittances, and the imposition of sanctions on Iraq hit us particularly hard, since Iraq had been our main trading partner and the principal source of our oil, supplied on concessional terms.

Economic growth slowed, and the government had to rely on foreign borrowing to underpin its spending. By the end of 1998, foreign debt had risen to over 100 percent of GDP. We would soon be unable to service the debt. Jordan turned to the International Monetary Fund, as it had done in the previous debt crisis in 1989, and in the month after I became king we secured new financial support from the IMF, which was followed by a rescheduling of our debt to the Paris Club of international creditors.

The immediate difficulty was resolved, but we needed more than a quick patch. From my time in the army, speaking to soldiers, traveling to their villages, and meeting their families, I knew that many of our people were struggling financially. My priority was, and remains, to secure a decent living for Jordan's citizens. I set for my government the goal of laying the foundation for the strong and stable economic growth that would make this possible.

This was not an easy task for a small, vulnerable economy. Jordan has no oil and its other natural resources are limited. Both water and agricultural land are scarce. Its industrial base has never been very strong, and with a population of only four and a half million in 1999, it was unlikely to become an economic powerhouse. We would have to learn to compete more efficiently in this new era of globalization, as dismantling the barriers to trade and investment had exposed countries to ever fiercer competition for markets and investment.

I assembled a team of talented economic advisers, including Bassem Awadallah, a former investment banker and economist with a PhD from the London School of Economics, and Samir Rifai, a Harvard and Cambridge graduate and the son of my father's trusted adviser Zaid Rifai, and asked them to come up with bold, innovative ideas to jump-start Jordan's economic recovery. "We don't have time for complex theories and debate," I told them. "I just want to know the right thing to do." They came back with a host of proposals that built on the measures the IMF's structural adjustment program had introduced at the end of the 1980s: privatize state enterprises, downsize the state bureaucracy, end subsidies, improve education, promote innovative industries, remove trade barriers, and get the public and private sectors to work together to promote industries like information technology, pharmaceuticals, and new media.

We had a basic problem. Much of what we would do was going to be very painful in the short term. Many of the benefits would take years to be felt. And we knew all too well that the previous set of structural adjustment measures had triggered riots. Comfortable with the old ways, many people would resist change — or claim that it could not be attained.

The top priority, my advisers all agreed, was for Jordan to gain admittance to the World Trade Organization (WTO), an international organization formed in 1995 to promote free trade between countries by reducing tariffs on imports and exports. By joining, Jordan would be able to export to over one hundred countries and enjoy greatly reduced tariffs. In return, the other WTO members would be able to export to Jordan on the same terms. Jordan had begun its application in 1995, but the process was stalled. I agreed to do everything I could to get it moving again.

In mid-May 1999, just three months after I became king, I made my first visit to the United States in my new role. My father and President Clinton had been very close. Before the trip I wrote the president a letter, telling him how much my father had valued their friendship. I do not know whether it was the letter or his fond feelings for my father, but when we met at the White House, Clinton was in an expansive mood. "What can I do to help Jordan?" he asked with a broad smile.

"Help us become a member of the World Trade Organization," I said quickly. I do not think he was expecting this at all. Usually countries in dire financial straits simply ask for more direct aid. But I did not want handouts. I wanted us to have a chance to help ourselves. Clinton took note of my request but gave no immediate answer. We continued our discussions of the subject with the U.S. government, which finally supported our application. Eleven months later, in April 2000, Jordan became a member of the WTO.

Switching from economics to regional politics, I told the president about my recent trip to Damascus and of President Hafez al-Assad's desire to meet with him. Clinton smiled, thanked me for passing on the message, and said he would see what he could do. True to his word, he met Assad for the first time in Geneva the following year. Syrian-Israeli peace was the main subject of the meeting, which failed to achieve any breakthroughs. Assad insisted on full Israeli withdrawal from the Golan Heights to the borders of June 4, 1967. Israel, in previous talks with the Syrians, had demanded alterations to this border. Clinton's attempts to change Assad's position failed and the stalemate persisted.

The U.S. government was a gracious host, but the contrast to my previous visits was striking. I could no longer slip out to catch a movie with a couple of friends. Instead, as I found out when I went to see *The Matrix,* I would have a six-car Secret Service motorcade in tow, sirens blaring. If I wanted a quiet night at the movies, I would have to shed my security detail and go in secret.

Some Middle Eastern leaders think that dealing with the United States is just about one's relationship with the president. In our neighborhood, it is essential to know the heads of state personally, as power tends to be highly centralized. If the top man says he wants something, it gets done. But in the United States, political power is much more dispersed. In my time at Deerfield and Georgetown, I had learned a lot about the complexities of the American political system.

I was in the United States on a military course in 1985 when my father met with

President Ronald Reagan. I saw him right after the meeting and he was elated, because Reagan had agreed to provide extensive support for Jordan in the form of a defensive arms package. I warned my father that such a proposal was unlikely to get through Congress. But he thought Reagan's personal agreement would be enough. "I have the word of the president of the United States!" he told me. But the truth was that without the consent of Congress, even the word of the president will not get things done.

A visit to America, done right, takes at least a week. First, you have to meet with the president and vice president, then with the secretary of state, the secretary of defense, and, ideally, the national security adviser. Next come senior intelligence officials and military officers. Finally, on the political side, you also have to engage both the Senate and the House of Representatives. I typically spend two long days in Congress, meeting with members of up to ten different Senate and House committees, both Republicans and Democrats. In America, you have got to work the system. It is not just about getting the green light from the White House. The challenge is to have the support of both the White House and Capitol Hill.

■ ■ ■ ■

Back in Jordan there were many pressing domestic problems to deal with. I was eager to improve the lives of Jordanians, but I suspected that privatizing state-owned industries and holding officials and civil servants accountable to more vigorous sets of performance measures would not sit well with them. First I would try to make more tangible improvements that they could see and understand.

One example of the magnitude of the challenges we faced was the Al Bashir Hospital in Amman. As the largest state-run public hospital in the capital, it was in great demand. But when I visited the hospital in April, it was in an awful state. The wards were crowded and dirty, and none of the elevators in the building worked. Doctors had long lines of patients waiting for them and very little support. I was appalled and told the health minister to fix the situation — quickly.

In the army, when you say do something, it gets done. But dealing with the civilian government ministries, I was learning, required a different approach. First of all, armies march in time, so everything happens on a fixed schedule: you attack at a certain time, you wake up at a certain time, and you expect something to be done by a certain time. With the government, that is not necessarily the case.

I made a follow-up visit a couple of weeks later, and nothing had been done. The elevators were still broken, and the place was still deeply unhygienic. I told the health minister that I was serious about seeing improvements, and made a third visit after that, on returning from my trip to the United States.

With my third visit the hospital management began to get the message, and conditions started to improve. But inefficient public services were a challenge across the whole country, not just in Amman. A lot of information had started to come in to the Royal Court about other problems. To my frustration, many times when I raised these issues with the relevant ministers, they would tell me that the reports were exaggerated and that everything was fine. I quickly understood that I would need to see with my own eyes what was going on.

My father used to tell me how when he wanted to take the pulse of the country, he would wrap a traditional checkered head scarf around his face and drive round Amman at night in a battered old taxi, picking people up. He would ask every new passenger, "How's the economy going? What do you think of the Palestinian-Israeli situation? What do you think of the king's new policy?" One time, in order to provoke conversation, my father told his passenger, "You know, this king is rubbish." The man pulled a knife on him and said, "Listen, you speak badly about the king and I'm going to cut your throat right here!" He was only able to calm the man down by pulling off his head scarf and revealing his true identity.

I decided I would find a way of visiting government institutions discreetly to see what was really going on. I had several disguises made, which, because I still use them, I will not describe in detail here. But suffice it to say that anybody who met me in one of my disguises would never mistake me for a king.

I went to government offices and facilities across the country, from the north to the south, incognito. Accompanied only by a skeleton security detail, I visited hospitals, tax offices, police stations, and many other parts of the bureaucracy. Occasionally my secret visits were discovered by the public, but more often they were not. If I found people were being treated badly, I would raise the matter with the relevant minister back in Amman, and now I knew when they were not telling me the whole story.

One time I visited a tax office that was in complete shambles. People's records were lying around everywhere in boxes on the floor. Wanting to see what would happen, I walked over to a box, grabbed a handful of files, and headed for the door. Sure enough, nobody stopped me. I don't think any of the civil servants even noticed.

The next day I called the ministry and demanded to know why it was handling people's confidential information in such a sloppy way. One of the bureaucrats argued that I was misinformed. When I pulled out the tax records I had taken, he turned white and went very quiet. That visit was made public. For one thing, I had to return the tax records. And I wanted everyone to know that I was pushing hard for reform. Government employees sometimes get complacent if they feel nobody is watching them. My military training had taught me that expecting a lot from people delivers the best results.

Over time, my penchant for secret visits resulted in "Elvis" sightings. For each visit I actually made, there were reports that I had been spotted in another thirty or forty places. We heard of one such sighting at a tomato-packing plant up in the north of Jordan. A long line of farmers were waiting in their trucks for the plant to process their cargo, which might spoil in the sun. One farmer, as he pulled in to the gate, said he thought he had seen the king in disguise, waiting in one of the trucks. Whether he actually thought he had seen me or was just being cunning, no one will ever know, but the effect was the same. Pretty soon the line started moving at top speed.

Across the country civil servants started panicking. If the next person in line could be the king, they figured, they had better treat everyone like royalty. The message to the bureaucrats was: you are there to serve the people, not the other way around. One newspaper ran a cartoon showing me dressed as a road sweeper, a prisoner, a beggar, and so on. The secret visits were popular with many Jordanians, but I knew that I could not end all inefficiencies and make the kind of changes Jordan needed by myself. The private and public sectors would have to begin working together.

On November 26, 1999, we held our first National Economic Forum, a two-day conference at the Mövenpick Hotel, on the shores of the Dead Sea. Newly opened that year, the Mövenpick had a spa with impressive health facilities, but the delegates had little time for relaxing. They were too busy arguing. We'd invited about 160 representatives from the government and every part of Jordan's private sector: industrial farmers, IT companies, pharmaceutical companies, and many others. What the business community was asking for from the government seemed like common sense, but when the meetings expanded to include civil servants, the two groups started shouting at each other.

Halfway through the first day, it was clear that this approach wasn't working. So I tried a different approach. I let the delegates know that nobody would be leaving until they came up with some solutions. I would lock the door and throw away the key until they sorted things out. When they realized that I was serious, and that they would be stuck there for the next two days unless they came to terms, the delegates put aside their differences and started coming up with a plan that would benefit all of Jordan. There was no press, so everybody could speak openly.

The ideas ranged from the simple to the ambitious. One of the simplest was to introduce a two-day weekend. At that time, everyone in Jordan worked a six-day week, with Friday as a holiday. But the question being debated was, if we went to a two-day weekend like most of the world, what should the extra day off be? The Islamic holy day is Friday, so a lot of people wanted Thursday and Friday as the weekend. But many of the businessmen worked with companies in the West, so they wanted the weekend to be Friday and Saturday. After a healthy debate, the delegates settled on Friday and Saturday.

We were not the only ones looking to move our economy more into line with international markets. Four years later, in July 2003, Qatar followed suit, shifting to a Friday-Saturday weekend. They were followed by the UAE, including Dubai and Abu Dhabi, Bahrain in 2006, and Kuwait in 2007.

The delegates discussed more ambitious goals, including building on the success of Qualifying Industrial Zones (QIZs). Formed by the U.S. government in 1996, two years after the Jordan-Israel peace treaty was signed, these were manufacturing zones from which the products could enter the United States duty-free so long as at least 20 percent of the content was produced in either Israel or Jordan. The zones supplied U.S. companies such as Gap, JCPenney, and Levi Strauss. Exports from Jordan to the United States had shot up from virtually nothing to $18 million in 1998, and the delegates wondered how we could raise them still further.

By the end of the conference the delegates had agreed on an ambitious economic development plan, including changing laws to make things easier for private companies and encouraging investment, privatization, and educational reform. They also agreed to set up the Economic Consultative Council, which would have representatives from both government and the private sector, to continue the debate and to implement reforms. Unlike many countries in the Middle East, Jordan has no oil and comparatively few natural resources. So the delegates knew that we would have to develop the true wealth of Jordan — our people — if we want to prosper in a competitive global economy.

Two days after the conference ended, the World Trade Organization held its annual meeting in Seattle. While protesters raged outside, tossing insults and brickbats at baton-wielding riot police, inside the convention center the Jordanian delegation lobbied hard to be allowed to join. While some in America were violently rejecting globalization, we were rushing to embrace it. The next month, WTO members voted on our application, and Jordan joined on April 11, 2000. Our efforts to modernize our economy were gaining momentum.

■ ■ ■ ■

In January 2000, I went to Davos, Switzerland, for a meeting of the World Economic Forum, the yearly get-together of leading businessmen, politicians, academics, charity workers, and international bureaucrats. This was the first time I had attended the forum, and I had invited some young Jordanian businessmen and -women to travel with my delegation, hoping they would be able to benefit from the connections they were sure to make among the three thousand delegates.

The guest list was as refined as the mountain air. President Clinton and UK prime minister Tony Blair were there, as well as South African president Thabo Mbeki and the leaders of some thirty other countries. There were leaders from the business world too, such as Microsoft chairman Bill Gates; John Chambers, chairman and CEO of Cisco Systems; and AOL chief executive Steve Case.

I hosted a breakfast meeting on Sunday, January 30, with some of the leading technology executives present, and also met privately with Bill Gates, whom I invited to visit Jordan. At a session later in the day I spoke about the challenges facing the Middle East, the terrible pressure of unemployment, and how technology could help. Even in the Swiss Alps I couldn't escape neighborhood politics. Yasser Arafat was there, meeting on the side with President Clinton. And two Iranian exiles were arrested for throwing paint bombs at the Iranian foreign minister. In 2003, Jordan hosted the World Economic Forum on the Middle East, a regional meeting that we have since hosted every other year in the summer. And that year, Rania was invited to join the board of the World Economic Forum Foundation, as the only member from the Arab world.

Davos was a beautiful place in which to carry out the important task of persuading global executives to consider investing in Jordan. But not all my work that first year took place in such elegant settings. A few months after becoming king, I paid a visit to Sudan. It was quite a contrast.

As we were about to touch down at Khartoum airport, I looked down from the plane and could not see any welcoming committee. But out of the corner of one eye I caught a glimpse of an old T-55 tank rumbling toward us with soldiers clinging to its side. I was momentarily alarmed until we landed and saw the welcoming committee and I realized that this was the presidential guard, sent to patrol the area and ensure security. President Omar Al-Bashir invited us to join him in an aged Mercedes saloon car. I sat in the back with the president, the faded leather seat covered by polished wooden beads, and my brother Ali, at the time the head of my personal security detail, sat in the front, next to the driver. As we sped off to the heart of Khartoum, Ali pointed to two bullet holes in the passenger window and asked the driver what they were from. "Ah, that's from the last assassination attempt," he replied. He did not elaborate.

The Sudanese were gracious hosts, and on my return to Jordan I sent them an official gift: a new armored car. A few days later I got a message from the royal protocol staff that the Sudanese had sent a present of their own: a C-130 transport aircraft had landed at Amman's airport with two lion cubs inside. They also had sent a warden, who explained how to care for the animals and then went back to Khartoum.

Valuing the symbolism of the gift but not quite knowing what to do with the animals, I had them put in a tennis court outside my house. When Rania noticed that they had begun to show an interest in our children, Hussein and Iman (who was born in September 1996), then five and two, she put her foot down and insisted that the lions must go. I "regifted" them to a close friend who liked to collect exotic animals.

Back in Amman, I learned that one of my fellow delegates from Davos, John Chambers, had announced that he was so impressed by the potential opportunities in Jordan that Cisco would invest $1 million here in a venture capital fund for high-tech companies. Cisco, a manufacturer of the infrastructure that powers the Internet, subsequently became a key partner, helping us to increase Internet access throughout the country. Chambers has been an outstanding friend to Jordan, donating computer equipment and opening an office in Amman, and has been very vocal in promoting our country, telling other business leaders about the opportunities in Jordan.

But we could not rely only on outsiders to develop our information technology industry. Soon local entrepreneurs started to spring up. In 1994, Randa Ayoubi founded Rubicon, an education software company. Using venture capital investment, she expanded into animation, creating a multimillion-dollar company with offices in Amman, Los Angeles, Dubai, and Manila. Rubicon produced a children's cartoon series, Ben & Izzy, about two boys — one American, one

Jordanian — who go on adventures together through history. She signed a deal with MGM to promote the Pink Panther cartoon in the Middle East and received a further multimillion-dollar investment from a Gulf buyout firm.

In 1997, two young Jordanians, Samih Toukan and Hussam Khoury, started an Arabic-language Web-based e-mail service. Named Maktoob ("it is written" in Arabic), the company became one of the region's largest online Web portals, with over sixteen million users, and attracted millions of dollars in venture capital investment. In August 2009, Maktoob was acquired by the American Internet company Yahoo!. For a high-tech start-up to be bought by a technology giant may be nothing new in Silicon Valley, but this was a first for Jordan, and for the Arab world, and I was immensely proud of the founders for showing that we could compete on a global stage.

One of the benefits of information technology is the impact it can have at all levels of society. From my time as an army officer, I knew how quickly my soldiers could learn to operate a Challenger I tank with its computer-aided firing system. I was tremendously proud of their intelligence and adaptability and knew that they would be successful in any environment, given the right opportunities. A lot of these people had entered the army as enlisted men because that was the only route of advancement open to them. Many had the potential to go to university, but they could not afford the cost.

Many of these talented men left the army when they were young, in their late thirties and early forties, and still had much to contribute. So through the Royal Court we provided scholarships for all retired servicemen who wanted to learn computer skills. These men were extremely dedicated students, and almost all graduated. Many went on to work as technical experts in schools, training teachers in the latest computer technologies.

We also instituted sweeping educational reforms, making it mandatory for computer skills and English to be taught in all schools across the country from the first grade onward and increasing standards in math and science. Our efforts have paid off. Every four years, the International Association for the Evaluation of Educational Achievement, a nonprofit group dedicated to improving education, conducts an international assessment of science and math teaching. In 2007, Jordan's eighth graders ranked the highest in the Arab world — in science they came out ahead of Malaysia, Thailand, and Israel.

Our first public university, the University of Jordan, was founded in 1962, and our first private university, Al-Ahliyya Amman University, in 1990. There are now twenty private universities and ten more public universities attended by 243,000 students across the country. A large number of students from both the public and private institutions graduate with technical and engineering degrees, providing a skilled pool of employees for foreign companies investing in Jordan, local start-ups, and high-tech businesses across the region. We also began to set up IT skills clinics in remote areas across the country where local people could learn about computers free of charge.

Information technology and education are both key to improving a nation's economy, but to develop further we would have to continue opening up to the world. Joining the WTO was only the first step.

In June 2000, I returned to the United States and met with President Clinton, who congratulated me on our membership in the WTO. Again, he asked what he could do to help Jordan. And again I think he half expected me to ask for an increase in aid. This time I said, "I want a free trade agreement with the United States." Going far beyond the general terms of the WTO, a free trade agreement (FTA) reduces tariffs on trade between two countries to the lowest practical level. FTAs are extremely prized for the access they give to the American market. At that time the United States had FTAs with only three countries: Canada, Mexico, and Israel.

Though somewhat taken aback, President Clinton said he would provide his full support. We began negotiations on June 6, 2000, and the U.S.-Jordan FTA was approved by the U.S. Senate on September 24, 2001. Jordan became the first Arab country to sign an FTA with the United States. Boosted by the reduction in tariffs, total exports from Jordan to the United States rose from $18 million in 1998 to about $1 billion by 2009 — outstripping the level of our total exports worldwide when I took office.

Remembering our conversation from the previous year, President Clinton told me that he had met with President Assad of Syria in Geneva a few months earlier, but the meeting had been disappointing. No progress was made and it did not look likely that Syrian-Israeli negotiations would resume.

Domestically, we continued the effort to make Jordan attractive to foreign investors by creating a special economic zone in the southern port of Aqaba in May 2001. The economic zone had zero customs duty and greatly reduced tax rates, and it aimed to attract $6 billion of investment by 2020, an ambitious target. The incentives were more popular than we ever imagined, and by the end of 2008 we had already attracted over $20 billion in foreign investment, including funds from the UAE, Qatar, Kuwait, and Lebanon.

The Kuwaitis, and in particular Emir Sabah Al-Ahmad Al-Jaber Al-Sabah, have been some of Jordan's strongest supporters, and among the largest investors in our economy. Rania was born in Kuwait, and the emir always refers to her as his daughter. Every time we meet, he treats me like a member of his family. "How is our daughter?" he asks.

Building on the success of Aqaba, we set up additional special economic zones, offering reduced tax and customs duties in Mafraq, Maan, Irbid, the Dead Sea, and Ajloun. These zones have also begun to attract major foreign investment, including from Saudi Arabia, Japan, and Lebanon.

Our companies were now playing on a global stage. A few of our larger businesses, such as Aramex, a courier company, and Hikma, a pharmaceutical manufacturer, were successfully competing internationally. Our membership in the WTO opened new markets for them. But many smaller companies were struggling. We needed to build on our local advantages, and began to devise mechanisms to help. The King Abdullah II Fund for Development provides capital and infrastructure to promising Jordanian entrepreneurs. And we soon found exactly the type of project we were looking for.

In the mountains of Ajloun, in northern Jordan, are some of the oldest olive trees in the world. But many farmers were using fifty-year-old equipment to produce olive oil, and a few were employing methods that had not changed for millennia, using small presses and selling their wares locally in old glass jars. The rest of the crop would be sold for pennies to foreign companies, including Italian and Spanish ones, which, using the most modern equipment, processed our olives into expensive oils and sold them for a large profit. The fund invested in advanced pressing, bottling, and packaging equipment and set up a specialist company to help with branding and marketing. The resulting product is now sold in some of London's most exclusive department stores.

One of my priorities has been to strengthen the Jordanian manufacturing and industrial base, particularly in the area of military technology. The King Abdullah II Design and Development Bureau (KADDB), founded in 1999, has been a key part of this strategy. Through KADDB, Jordanian tanks and armored vehicles have been upgraded and new projects initiated (many of which are classified). We have expanded our collaboration with other nations' armed forces, including those of the United States, Brunei, and Azerbaijan. Deals have been signed with European defense companies to maintain F-16 aircraft, develop military vehicles, and manufacture unmanned aerial vehicles. Working with a Russian partner, KADDB developed a new and extremely powerful shoulder-launched antitank missile, the RPG-32. Our products have been sold to Yemen, Libya, and Oman, among other countries.

One new project with enormous ramifications is the development of Jordan's significant but unexploited uranium deposits. Although we had long known that our country had considerable uranium deposits, we had not moved to explore their commercial potential. In 2008 we set up the Jordanian-French Uranium Mining Company, a joint venture with the French power company AREVA. After initial surveys revealed a large quantity of uranium in the central desert, estimated at some 4 to 6 percent of the world's total uranium reserves, we began working on setting up Jordan's first uranium mine. We have signed additional exploration agreements with the Chinese firm Sino Uranium and the Anglo-Australian company Rio Tinto. Under the guidance of the Jordan Atomic Energy Commission, we are developing a nuclear energy program, which would reduce our dependence on costly imports of oil and gas. A domestic nuclear reactor, provisionally planned to be built in the south, could supply up to a third of our country's energy. But that is only the first step. The large amount of electricity it is expected to generate would allow us to power desalination plants, providing affordable water and thus achieving two goals at once.

Jordan is a signatory to the Nuclear Non-Proliferation Treaty (NPT) and a member of the International Atomic Energy Authority (IAEA). We are more than just a signatory, in fact; we have committed to cooperating fully with these organizations, with complete transparency. We want to be a model of how to develop a nuclear energy program.

In 2009 I gave an interview to the Israeli newspaper *Haaretz,* saying that Jordan intended to develop nuclear power for peaceful purposes, and adding, "I personally believe that any country that has a nuclear program should conform to international regulations and should have international regulatory bodies that check to make sure that any nuclear program moves in the right direction."

The nuclear power issue is particularly sensitive in the Middle East. Israel, the only nuclear power in the region, continues to refuse to join the NPT or to allow inspection of its nuclear facilities. The international community has taken little or no action to pressure Israel to joint the NPT or to open its facilities for inspection. Lately, the controversy over Iran's nuclear program has become a global concern, as the international community is adamant on preventing Iran from developing its uranium enrichment capacity, fearing that its real intentions are to develop a military nuclear program. Israel's "privileged" nuclear position has led public opinion in the region to again point to double standards in applying international law.

Our nuclear program is not seen in that controversial context. Jordan's credibility as a force for peace in the region and the transparent approach to developing nuclear energy in cooperation with international organizations and compliance with international standards have won our program the endorsement and support of the international community.

As important as negotiating trade agreements, reforming our educational system, boosting our domestic industry, and reducing our energy dependence have been in putting Jordan on the path of sustainable economic growth, sometimes our economy has been boosted in less expected ways.

In 1988, Steven Spielberg and George Lucas came to Jordan to film scenes for *Indiana Jones and the Last Crusade*. They were accompanied by the stars of the film, Harrison Ford and Sean Connery. My father asked me to meet them when they arrived in Aqaba and to take them to Petra, eighty miles to the north, where they would begin filming. Built by the Nabateans over two thousand years ago, the ruins at Petra are among the most spectacular ancient monuments in the world. Spielberg thought the massive temples, carved from living rock, would be the perfect location for the Canyon of the Crescent Moon, where the movie's final scene takes place.

I was an army officer at the time, and my father offered to take Spielberg, Lucas, Connery, and Ford to Petra by helicopter so that they could view the dramatic scenery from the air. I got the job of pilot. As we were strapping ourselves in, my copilot leaned over and, pointing to Sean Connery, said in Arabic, "Who's that guy? He looks familiar."

"That's Sean Connery," I told him. "He played James Bond."

"Right," my copilot said with a chuckle as we took off. "We'll show him who's the *real* James Bond!"

We flew low out of the airport, barely clearing a fence at the end of the runway, and headed north up the valley toward Petra, hugging the ground. After about twenty minutes, Spielberg, his knuckles white from holding on to the seat, leaned over and asked if we really had to fly so low.

I decided to play along with my copilot's joke. "Sir," I replied, "we could go higher, but we are flying along the Israeli border, and there's no telling what they might do. . . . Of course, if you are willing to take the risk, no problem." Spielberg nodded, and we increased our altitude a nudge and flew a little higher.

We landed near the ruins, and the cast and crew soon set to work transforming the narrow, winding gorge that opens onto Al Khazneh, a temple carved out of the valley's sandstone wall, into the Temple of the Sun, the film's mythical hiding place for the Holy Grail.

I was not able to attend the movie's premiere the following year, but my brother Feisal was there. He met Harrison Ford and introduced himself, saying, "My brother was the helicopter pilot who flew you up to Petra."

"That guy scared the crap out of us!" Ford said.

Years later, after my father died, I met Steven Spielberg again, and he still remembered that ride. "Why did you do that to us?" he asked.

"Well," I said, "sooner or later I figured you were going to make a film about helicopter pilots. And you would have remembered those two crazy pilots in Jordan!" Many other movies, including *Transformers: Revenge of the Fallen, The Hurt Locker,* and *The Mummy Returns,* have been partially filmed in Jordan since Spielberg's *Last Crusade.*

Spielberg and I remained in touch, and when I became king I approached him for help in developing the Jordanian film industry. Thankfully, he had forgiven my youthful antics, and he introduced us to the dean of the University of Southern California School of Cinematic Arts, the oldest film school in America. With help from USC, we founded the Red Sea Institute of Cinematic Arts in Aqaba, a graduate school devoted to teaching filmmaking. The institute opened in September 2008 with its first class of twenty-five students.

Creative industries such as film, media, and information technology hold the keys to Jordan's future economic development — even if the path toward growth will sometimes be a little unexpected.

We can now look back on eleven years of progress. Opening up our economy to global trade has allowed our exports to rise sixfold between 1998 and 2008, the rate of unemployment to fall from 15.3 percent to 12 percent, and GDP per head to double. A UN survey in 2007 ranked Jordan 6th highest in the world in attracting foreign investment relative to the size of its economy, up from 132nd in 1995. The 2008 annual survey by the World Economic Forum rated Jordan the 48th most competitive economy in the world, ahead of Italy, Russia, Brazil, and India.

Jordan has not been immune from the impact of the global economic crisis. Growth slowed dramatically and the 2009 budget deficit, which stood at about 8.5 percent of GDP, is almost unprecedented in the history of the kingdom. Like countries the world over, Jordan had to take tough measures in 2009 to reduce its spending. But unlike many other countries, we did not have the means to offer financial stimulus packages that could get the economy moving again. We had to review policy, improve our investment environment, and ensure a more efficient management of the economy.

The global economic crisis was a challenge, but it also offered opportunities. Many international companies, especially those based in the rich neighboring Gulf region, were examining means to reduce their costs and improve their competitiveness. I was determined to put Jordan on their radar screens. Our highly educated professionals, strong infrastructure, strategic position in the heart of the region, and access to some of the biggest global markets and an open business environment give us a valuable competitive edge. So we began identifying specific opportunities that could attract investors and modernizing our economic legislation. In the past when I met investors, I would tell them that Jordan was a great place to invest. Now I can refer to specific projects and point to clear advantages to encourage companies to do business in Jordan.

We have embarked on a number of "megaprojects" to secure our food and water needs and develop our infrastructure and our position as a regional energy and transport hub. The government has been directed to better manage these vital resources. But political events have sometimes hijacked our economic growth. The only thing that can bring lasting prosperity to our region, replacing bombs and bullets with tourists and entrepreneurs, is a lasting solution to the conflict between Israel and the Palestinians, the root cause of much of the violence and instability in our region.

My dream is that we will link the economies of Israel, Palestine, and Jordan in a common market — patterned on Benelux in western Europe. We could combine the technical know-how and entrepreneurial drive of Jordan, Israel, and Palestine to create an economic and business hub in the Levant. The potential for joint tourism is massive, as is that for foreign investment. The possibility for cooperation is immense. The Israelis are world leaders in agriculture but lack land and workers. We could work together to make the desert bloom.

But such visions of economic cooperation are a mirage in the absence of political leaders with the courage to make peace. For the sake of all of us in the region, we must pray that we can overcome the hatreds and suspicions that have kept us so long divided.

We have done a great deal in the last eleven years, but I will be the first to admit that there is still a long way to go. Political reform could have progressed faster, and we could have done a better job of explaining some of the reasons for what we were doing. Economic reform has been a priority for me because of the direct impact sound economic policies have on the quality of life of Jordanians, but I have always believed that it will not reach its full potential unless it is part of a broader agenda of political, social, and administrative reforms. Unfortunately, political development has sometimes been two steps forward and one step back. Resistance to change has come from different camps for different reasons. Some have resisted change out of fear of losing privileges they have long enjoyed, while others simply lacked imagination, preferring a status quo that they knew and accepted. On many occasions, I found some officials did not have the courage to push forward with difficult changes or were more concerned with promoting their own interests than with the well-being of the people they were appointed to serve. Another factor that has slowed the modernization process has been the terrible regional situation, which often poses challenges that make security and stability the priorities. But we are determined to address these shortcomings. I know that Jordan's future dictates that we move forward with democratization, to ensure that all Jordanians feel they have a a larger say in their government and a stake in their country's future.

In November 2009, I called for new parliamentary elections, and a few days later I designated a new prime minister to form a new government. Many Jordanians were expressing a growing dissatisfaction with the performance of the lower house of Parliament. Many members of the house were impeding essential economic and social legislative reforms. Political bickering and pressure to win personal perks created a dysfunctional relationship between the two branches of government, hindering efforts to address broader economic and social issues. Approval rates of the house were so low that, according to polls, over 80 percent of the population welcomed its dissolution. It was time for change, not just in persons but also in approach. In my letter of designation to the new prime minister, Samir Rifai, the Harvard graduate who had worked with me on economic reform when I first assumed office, I laid down a set of economic, social, administrative, and political reform objectives that government must work toward achieving in accordance with clear timelines. I made it clear that a new Parliament must be elected as soon as possible and that the holding of free, fair, and transparent elections must top the government's agenda. I instructed the new government to amend the election law, and to reform all election procedures in a way that would make it easier for people to vote and for civil society organizations to monitor the election process.

I also asked the government to implement a decentralization program, which would allow people to elect their own local councils and to play a major role in running affairs in their governorates, especially in setting out development priorities.

Sixty days after it was sworn in, the new government presented me with a detailed working plan, with each ministry outlining clear objectives and projects that it would be implementing within specific timelines. The performance of the government will be measured by its progress toward meeting these objectives, which have to be posted on all ministries' Web sites. The government also committed to a new code of conduct inspired by international best practices and identified major reforms, including measures to fight corruption, increase transparency, protect the rights of women and children, and remove all obstacles to the development of a free and professional media industry.

The government's plans are geared to achieving progress in seven key areas, in the form of well-identified initiatives. These are: strengthening government performance and accountability; encouraging political and civic participation; enhancing the business and investment environment; empowering Jordanian citizens with the skills to succeed and enter the labor market; feeding and fueling growth and security through mega-infrastructure projects; expanding the middle class and empowering the underprivileged; and improving citizen services. I have long believed that the presence of a robust and stable middle class is a key driver for social development. By focusing on economic programs that will expand our middle class, we will strengthen the bases for the emergence of civil society organizations that can challenge the government, hold it more accountable, and pressure it to be more transparent.

As this book went to press, Jordanians were preparing to go to the polls to elect their new representatives in Parliament under a new election law. Major changes that better protect the rights of women and children were introduced to the penal code, and a few people are now facing trial on corruption charges. The budget deficit has been reduced and newspapers are reporting some good news about the economy. I believe we are on track in what will be a lengthy reform process that will take much more hard work to finish, and will have its good and bad days. From the beginning I knew that we would have to invest more in the skills of Jordan's main national asset: our people. That means providing the best education possible to our young people. I have given much thought to the subject, and having been educated in Jordan, England, and America, I've brought some unconventional views.

# CHAPTER 16
## DESERT DEERFIELD

In May 2000, twenty years after graduating from Deerfield, I went back to give the commencement address. I was met by the headmaster, Eric Widmer, a tall, distinguished-looking Deerfield alumnus who had taught Chinese history at Brown University before coming back to lead the school. Memories flooded back as we walked past the Ephraim Williams House, with its white wood walls and slate roof, which had been my dorm. I reflected on the quality of the education I had received. Deerfield had taught me to be curious, to question what I was told, and to come up with my own solutions to problems. It taught me how to think, not what to think. It encouraged critical thinking, problem-solving, and creativity. I began to think that a school modeled on Deerfield would be a great benefit to Jordan and the region. I had seen how my classmates had grown up to become leaders in business, science, and politics. Why was there nothing like this in Jordan? A young boy or girl in Jordan, Palestine, Egypt, or the Gulf states should not have to travel to America to get a first-class education.

The next day the Deerfield community gathered for the commencement ceremony. Friends, family, and staff applauded as two bagpipers led the class of 2000 down Albany Road, through the center of the village, and toward a large green-and-white-striped pavilion.

In my commencement address I reflected on the values taught by a Deerfield education — honesty, independence of mind, integrity, and friendship — and said that these values would be needed now more than ever by young people as they faced the hectic pace of change in the modern world. I remembered all that Deerfield had taught me: the wisdom and patience of the teachers; the egalitarian spirit, taking turns to clear the tables after our fellow students; the chance to meet and befriend people from different backgrounds, many of them on scholarship; and the lifelong curiosity and excitement for learning. As I looked out over the young faces, their eyes shining, I became determined to bring the Deerfield experience to the Middle East.

After the ceremony, I told Dr. Widmer that I wanted to set up a school in Jordan on the model of Deerfield and that it would be the first New England–style boarding school in the Middle East. He said that sounded like a great idea and offered to lend a hand and give advice insofar as he could. The seed of what would later become King's Academy had been planted.

Throughout the Middle East there are many private schools for the children of the elite, who show up in their chauffeur-driven Mercedes, cell phones clamped to their ears. But there are no schools in the Deerfield tradition, open to all talented young people and offering scholarships for those unable to afford the fees. I wanted to create a new tribe in a region often riven by ethnic and sectarian conflict: the tribe of the talented meritocracy.

Back in Jordan, I immediately began to work on turning this vision into reality. Safwan Masri, a Jordanian expatriate teaching at Columbia University in New York, was invited to lead the project, and I convinced my good friend Gig, who at the time was a senior banker at Citigroup, to help with fund-raising. Over the next few years, Safwan, Gig, and a small team worked hard to raise money, locate a site, and choose an architect to bring the project to life.

We found a perfect spot just outside Madaba, fifteen miles south of Amman. This is the location, at the Greek Orthodox Basilica of St. George, of the sixth-century Madaba Mosaic Map, one of the earliest maps of the Holy Land. The site we selected for the school was on the historic King's Highway, an ancient trade route that ran from Heliopolis in Egypt across the Sinai to Aqaba, turned north through Jordan, and continued on to Damascus, ending at Resafa on the banks of the Euphrates.

We began construction on July 22, 2004. But I was well aware that if I really wanted to re-create the spirit of Deerfield, I would need more than buildings. Eric Widmer, the school's fourth headmaster since 1902, was due to retire from Deerfield in 2006. This was my chance. I managed to persuade him to be the founding headmaster of King's Academy.

When I returned to Deerfield for my twenty-fifth reunion in 2005, my classmates were excited to hear the news of King's Academy, and I invited them all to visit Jordan. That August nearly one hundred classmates and their family members traveled to Madaba to see the new school for themselves and to tour the country. For many it was their first trip to the Middle East, and all commented on the warm and generous reception of the Jordanian people. Proving that the spirit of the class of 1980 remained strong, they raised over $1 million for King's Academy. To this day they continue to provide strong support for the school, dedicating time and money to its growth and success.

The next year I was again invited to be the commencement speaker at Deerfield, and gladly accepted. On May 28, 2006, I stood in the green-and-white-striped tent, once more looking out at a crowd of jubilant young men and women. Eric Widmer, presiding over his last convocation as headmaster, turned to me during his introduction and said, "I am tempted to introduce you as my new boss, then I'm tempted to say you have to be nice to me even so, because of the likelihood I will be overseeing the education of your children." Indeed, it was my dream that my children, joined by young boys and girls from Jordan and the region, would soon draw the same kind of inspiration from King's Academy that I had received from Deerfield.

In my remarks I stressed the importance of building unbreakable links between America and the Middle East and spoke of my dreams for King's Academy. "We want to bring the Deerfield model to the Middle East," I explained, "a coed boarding school where faculty and students are close, academic studies greatly encouraged, and life enriched with competitive sports, lively arts, and real community service." To give our students the best chance of competing in the modern global economy, we decided that we would follow the American Advanced Placement curriculum, and all teaching would be in English. We would also offer classes in classical Arabic, grammar, and literature, as well as courses in Middle Eastern politics, religion, and society. I also wanted King's to be coeducational. Although Deerfield was single-sex when I was there, it began admitting girls a few years later, in 1989. I knew that some in the region would object to the idea of educating young girls and boys together, but I was determined that our daughters should have the same opportunities as our sons.

In July 2006, I inducted Dr. Widmer as headmaster in a small ceremony, after which we all ate dinner together in the King's Academy dining hall, seated at round tables to facilitate discussion and interaction, following the Deerfield tradition. The construction team had done a fantastic job, and the 150-acre site contained over twenty buildings and extensive sports fields. There was a theater, a dining hall, a gymnasium, a library, boys' and girls' dorms, and a spiritual center. The adobe-walled, red-tiled buildings were sturdy and elegant. Now all we needed was people to fill them.

For the next year, Eric Widmer and his team worked tirelessly to hire faculty, many from the United States with boarding school backgrounds, supervise the construction, set up the admissions process, and receive applications for the first entering class. They traveled across the Middle East, describing and explaining the idea of a coed boarding school, with instruction in English, to worried mothers and skeptical fathers. Because the idea of a boarding school — and a co-educational one at that — was so new to the region, some parents were wary. But many others saw the potential for their children's futures.

Setting up a new institution from scratch is never easy, but Eric and his team pulled off miracles. They scoured the globe and put together a team of some of the finest teachers imaginable. They also managed to develop the curriculum and instill something less tangible: the ethos of the institution. Deerfield has had more than two centuries to develop the "Deerfield Way." But at King's, Eric was creating new traditions as he went.

King's Academy opened on August 29, 2007. As bagpipers played, faculty and trustees gathered in a courtyard on the campus and said a few words to mark the beginning of the first term. There were 106 students in the entering class, from Jordan, Egypt, Palestine, and several Arabian Gulf countries. There were also students from the United States and from as far afield as Taiwan. The sixty-six boys and forty girls were divided between the ninth and tenth grades, with both full-time boarders and day students, most of whom were commuting from Amman. The following year, over 150 new students arrived in August for the start of the new school year, bringing the total to over 250, still split 60 to 40 percent between boys and girls. Among the group were representatives of twenty-one nationalities, including new arrivals from Iraq and Afghanistan. And in August 2009, King's opened with 400 students from twenty-four countries.

Among the entering students was my eldest son, Hussein. Like all parents, we want the best education for our children, and I considered sending him overseas to be educated, as I had been. But as a parent, it was too hard to send my son away, and thankfully, there was now a local school where he could have an education rivaling the one I received in America.

Although it is never entirely possible in Jordan for members of the royal family to lead a normal life, Hussein has had to learn to make his bed and share a bathroom, and to wait on tables for other students. The first weekend he came back home, Rania, the other children, and I were all waiting eagerly to see him; we had missed not having him around the house. As soon as he got through the door, he said, "Hi, I have homework to do, so I'll see you all later." Hussein going to do his homework? That was a shocker.

One of my aims for the school was to have a diverse student body, representing not just different countries but also varied economic backgrounds. Some of my closest friends at Deerfield were there on scholarship, and I saw the value to the school and society of helping able young men and women rise as high as their talents would take them. We were able to offer almost half the students need-based financial aid. This enabled the school to accept the brightest students, regardless of their backgrounds. We decided that the top student in each of the twelve governorates of Jordan, plus the top student from the refugee camps, would be given a scholarship. I personally provided scholarships at King's for some thirty students, known as King's Scholars, who were given a spending stipend, and took a particular interest in their development. Proving that poverty is no indicator of intelligence, in 2008 as much as 70 percent of the honor roll comprised children on scholarship. These are young men and women who are reaching the potential their extraordinary talents deserve.

Inside the school, the students are treated equally: in the honored Deerfield tradition they take turns waiting tables in the dining hall and are required to wear the same uniform of blazer, tie, and slacks. But outside the school walls, many enjoyed opportunities that those there on scholarships did not. With this in mind, I organized a camping trip for the thirty scholarship students whom I had personally sponsored. I took them to Wadi Rum, a series of massive dry river valleys that run for some eighty miles through the desert near Aqaba.

One of Jordan's best-known natural features, Wadi Rum was described by T. E. Lawrence as "vast and echoing and godlike." The tallest rock walls rise some thousand feet above the desert, and above them is Jabal Rum, at over five thousand feet the second highest mountain in Jordan. We flew low over the rock formations and headed for the campsite deep in the heart of a massive valley.

We had set up a camp with tents and brought in all-terrain vehicles, various games, and a shooting range. As the sun set, the students gathered around fires and we cooked lamb in the traditional manner, burying it in the desert sand, lighting a wood fire above the buried meat, and roasting it slowly. After dinner I sat cross-legged in the sand and all thirty students gathered around the fire. Among them was a Kurdish girl from Iraq, an orphaned girl from Afghanistan, a Pakistani girl, and Jordanian students from all over the country. We sat by the fire and talked for three hours, in Arabic and in English. The students asked me questions on every topic imaginable, from what it is like to be a king to Middle Eastern politics. I told each of them that I would help them with college and, for those students not from Jordan, said that I hoped afterward that they would use their new knowledge to help their countries. They promised enthusiastically that they would. I barely had a chance to take a bite of the dinner. The conversation and the sophistication and focus of these kids were electrifying. I turned to Gig, who had accompanied me on the trip, and said, "I don't care what it takes, just find me more of these kids. The investment in them will come back to Jordan and the region a hundredfold."

Finally, everyone went to bed. The next morning we were up at dawn, and again I spent many hours talking and debating with the students. The enthusiasm, dedication, and passion for learning these young people showed were remarkable. In the course of my duties as king, I meet many inspirational people, but that camping trip with King's Academy students was the highlight of my year.

In June 2010, I was full of pride as I handed out graduation certificates to the eighty-four students of King's first class of seniors. All of them were going on to university. Fourteen would be pursuing their education at some of the best schools in the Middle East, ten would be attending universities in the UK, and nine would be studying in Canada. A full forty-four graduates had enrolled in American universities, including Harvard, Stanford, Yale, Brown, Columbia, Cornell, Princeton, Johns Hopkins, and Georgetown.

I know that every one of them will be well equipped to go out into the world and do remarkable things. I can only hope that they built the same strong bonds of friendship as I did at Deerfield, and that the seeds planted there in the desert will blossom into a new generation of leaders who will spread the message of hard work, intellectual curiosity, and tolerance throughout the region.

Sadly, one of my scholars was not among the graduating class. Ahmad Tarawneh was a young man from Kerak, who had never studied in English before. He was one of the best students in his class and was planning to apply to a top university in the West to study engineering, until he died in a tragic car accident only two months before his graduation. I felt as if I had lost one of my own sons.

We remembered Ahmad at the graduation ceremony. My fellow Deerfield classmates had offered King's a trophy to be presented as the King Abdullah II Award to the student who most embodies King's guiding principles of respect, love of learning, responsibility, an integrated life, and global citizenship. The award was given posthumously to Ahmad.

The school remains one of my proudest

achievements. The copyright for the English-language edition of this book has been transferred to King's Academy and the proceeds from the sale of the book will support its scholarship fund for needy students.

■■■■

# PART IV

■■■■

# CHAPTER 17
# JERUSALEM AT THE HEART
# OF CONFLICT

On May 17, 1999, as I was about to embark on my first visit to the United States as king, Israelis went to the polls. Under Prime Minister Benjamin Netanyahu, the peace process had stalled badly, and we all hoped that a new Israeli leader would bring new momentum. The previous year in Washington, Netanyahu and Arafat had signed what was intended to be a framework to advance the peace process, the Wye River Memorandum. Supported by my ailing father in the last months of his life, the Wye Accords, which provided for further Israeli withdrawals, in stages, from the West Bank, seemed to represent a breakthrough. But seven months later, after completing only one of the three stages of withdrawal, Netanyahu was stalling, twisting, and turning, and any further progress based on Wye was essentially halted. In Jordan and across the Arab world, we hoped that a change of prime minister might revive the peace efforts.

A former chief of staff of the Israeli army and Israel's most decorated officer, Ehud Barak was riding high in the polls. He had been in the Special Forces, and when he left the army and went into politics, he took on the challenge of peacemaking. Barak won a landslide electoral victory. The results were announced as I was meeting with President Clinton in the White House. We were both optimistic that he would succeed where Netanyahu had failed and take bold action to bring peace between Israel and the Palestinians.

In April 2000, I went to Israel for my first official visit. I had been scheduled to go two months earlier but postponed the trip when Israel arbitrarily struck targets in southern Lebanon. My delegation went by boat from Aqaba to Eilat, where we were met by Barak, who led us on a tour of a fishery and then took us for a working lunch at a local hotel. We discussed the final status talks that, under the Sharm El Sheikh Accord of September 1999, were to lead to a comprehensive agreement. I told Barak that if he wanted relations to improve between Israel and Jordan, he would have to make substantial progress with the Palestinians.

As the Clinton administration neared the

end of its term, the Israeli prime minister was seriously engaged in efforts to create an atmosphere that would enable Israelis and Palestinians to develop a lasting peace. The summer of 2000 was a period of intense diplomatic activity surrounding the peace process. In May, Ehud Barak withdrew Israel's forces from southern Lebanon, which they had occupied for almost two decades. But the withdrawal was not complete; Israel maintained its hold on the area of Shebaa Farms and a few other small Lebanese territories. Had Israeli troops withdrawn completely from Lebanon, we might not have seen further conflict later on. The decision to stop just one step short of total withdrawal was an unfortunate and costly hedge.

In a nod to the famous negotiations between Anwar Sadat and Menachem Begin at Camp David in 1978, President Clinton invited Barak and Arafat to a summit at Camp David in July. The aim was to accelerate progress on the peace talks, which were faltering, and to strive to reach a final agreement. Shortly before they left for America, I met separately with each leader.

I reminded both men of how hard my father had worked with President Clinton and how much he had sacrificed to move the peace process forward. Clinton had decided to go for the great prize. He wanted to cut out the remaining intermediary steps in Israel's phased withdrawal from the West Bank and to hammer out terms that both Israelis and Palestinians could accept for the creation of a Palestinian state. I told them that we should not miss this historic opportunity.

As Arafat and Barak headed to Camp David on July 11, they carried with them the hopes of all the peoples of the region for a peaceful settlement to a conflict that has defined our part of the world for more than sixty years. Unfortunately, those hopes were not realized. Over fourteen days of negotiations at Camp David, the two sides came closer than they ever have, before or since, to a lasting peace. But they could not take the final step. Of the four final status issues that they addressed, Jerusalem and the status of Palestinian refugees were the most difficult and contentious.

Barak presented a package that represented an advance on any previous Israeli proposal, but for the Palestinian negotiators it fell short. Under his proposals, Israel would permanently retain over 10 percent of the West Bank and would control a further 10 percent for a period of twenty years. The return of refugees was treated in the context

346

of a family reunification program and excluded the issue of the Palestinian right of return (the right of Palestinians who were evicted or fled in 1948 and 1967 to return to their homes). On the critical issue of Jerusalem, the Palestinians were offered only administrative authority over the holy sites in the Old City, far less than the full sovereignty that they sought over East Jerusalem.

The Palestinians wanted a breakthrough, but Arafat felt he could not sign an agreement that would sacrifice the rights of over five million Palestinian refugees and give Israel control over East Jerusalem.

Although Barak and Arafat showed great courage, the finger-pointing started almost immediately after that. In the end their negotiations broke down and the summit ended in failure on July 25. In subsequent months Palestinian frustrations would grow, as the Israelis' interest in coming to terms with the Palestinians waned. Ehud Barak would soon be up for election again, and his willingness to give back territories in the West Bank was not well received by the Israeli public. Then Ariel Sharon lit a match that would set the region ablaze. In a sense it was to be expected that Jerusalem would be the flashpoint for the incident that triggered a second Palestinian uprising and finally dashed the hopes of peace.

Jerusalem has always had a special place in the Arab heart. It is a city holy to the three great monotheistic religions, Judaism, Christianity, and Islam, and in part because of this it has often been the cause of conflict. It has been conquered many times in its history. Some of its occupiers brought great bloodshed. But Islam came to the city with great dignity.

In the seventh century, the forces of the Muslim Caliph, who was then based in Mecca, laid siege to Jerusalem, which was under the control of the Byzantine Empire. When the city finally surrendered, Caliph Omar bin al-Khattab entered on foot, accompanied by his servant and a single camel, in recognition of Jerusalem's status as a city of peace. He was invited by the Orthodox Patriarch of Jerusalem, Sophronius, to pray in the Church of the Holy Sepulcher, but he refused, fearing that if he did Muslims would turn the church into a mosque. Instead, he went to visit Al Aqsa, then in ruins, from which the Prophet Mohammad had alighted into the heavens on the night of Ascension. Omar ordered a mosque to be built over this site, and signed a treaty that guaranteed Christians protection and the right of worship. The Pact of Omar, as quoted by Abdul

Latif Tibawi in his book *Jerusalem: Its Place in Islam and Arab History,* reads:

In the Name of God, the Compassionate, the Merciful, this is what the slave of God, Umar, bin al-Khattab, the Amir of the believers, has offered the people of Aelia (Jerusalem), of security granting them protection of their selves, their money, their churches, their children, their lowly and their innocent, and the remainder of their people. Their churches are not to be taken, nor are they to be destroyed, nor are they to be degraded or belittled, neither are their crosses or their money, and they are not to be forced to change their religion, nor is any one of them to be harmed.

Not all rulers of Jerusalem have been quite so compassionate. In the late eleventh century, Pope Urban II called for the recapture of Jerusalem. Knights and their followers gathered from all over Europe and marched toward the Holy Land, in what came to be known as the First Crusade. In 1099, when Jerusalem finally fell, the Crusaders entered the city and slaughtered thousands of its Jewish, Muslim, and Orthodox Christian defenders, including many Muslims who had taken shelter in the Al Aqsa Mosque.

The Crusaders didn't last long and were kicked out of Jerusalem less than a hundred years later. After that, the city remained in Muslim hands for more than seven hundred years. When the Ottoman Turks were pushed out, after World War I, responsibility for the city fell upon my family, the Hashemites, and the people of Jerusalem pronounced their allegiance to my great-great-grandfather, Al Hussein bin Ali. In 1948 Jordanian forces under my great-grandfather, King Abdullah I, managed to protect the West Bank, including East Jerusalem, from the new state of Israel. Later, in 1950, the West Bank became part of the Hashemite Kingdom of Jordan under the Act of Union in accordance with the declaration of the Jericho Conference. One year later, my great-grandfather was assassinated on a visit to Jerusalem, with my father standing next to him. When my father became king, he inherited both the Hashemite family's responsibility as guardians of the holy city of Jerusalem and his great-grandfather's legacy of a unified West Bank. My father was emotionally attached to Jerusalem for religious and family reasons. He did his utmost to fulfill his responsibility as guardian and protector of the city and its holy shrines. Even after the Israelis seized East Jerusalem in 1967, Moshe Dayan, the Israeli defense minister, agreed that the holy sites should continue to be administered by the Jordanian government, through a religious trust called the waqf.

It is difficult to overstate Jerusalem's significance to Muslims. Chapter Seventeen of the Holy Quran describes the miracle of Isra and Miraj, when the angel Gabriel took the Prophet Mohammad from Mecca to Jerusalem. The Foundation Stone, housed under the Dome of the Rock, marks the place from which the Prophet ascended to the heavens on that night to be shown the signs of God. There he met the prophets who had come before him, led them in prayer, and was returned to Mecca.

In the early days of Islam, all Muslims faced Jerusalem when they prayed. In time, the Prophet Mohammad was instructed by God to shift the direction to Mecca. The Prophet Mohammad proclaimed that religious pilgrimages should be restricted to the mosques in Mecca, Medina, and Jerusalem, and that a prayer in Jerusalem was worth hundreds elsewhere. The area around Al Aqsa Mosque that includes the Dome of the Rock came to be known as Al Haram Al Sharif, or Noble Sanctuary.

In Arabic, we call Jerusalem Al Quds,

"The Holy One." The city's loss to Israel in 1967 shocked Arabs and Muslims around the world. The anger and sadness over the occupation of Jerusalem by Israel was expressed in angry demonstrations as well as poetic and artistic expressions. The famous Lebanese singer Fairouz captured the hearts of millions of Arabs when she mourned the loss of the "flower of cities" in a song that continues to mesmerize audiences today. For Arabs, Jerusalem is also a symbol of the Arab nationalist uprising led by my great-great-grandfather Sharif Hussein.

My father always retained a special place in his heart for Jerusalem. He sold his house in London in the early 1990s so that he could repair the gold covering on the Dome of the Rock. I am proud, too, of the work done by Jordanian engineers and craftsmen in constructing and installing in Al Aqsa Mosque in 2007 a replica of the Salaheddin Minbar, a decorated pulpit from which imams have delivered their sermons for centuries. The minbar was burned down in 1969 when a radical Zionist planted a firebomb in the mosque.

I take very seriously my responsibility to preserve the Arab identity of Jerusalem and protect its holy sites. But Jerusalem's identity is being threatened by Israeli unilateral measures, which aim to drive Muslims and Christians out of the city. Jerusalem is a tinderbox that could ignite the whole region and inflame passions around the globe. We have repeatedly warned Israelis that terrible consequences will come from their actions in Jerusalem, which include excavation works that threaten Muslim and Christian holy sites, the building of settlements, and the demolition of Palestinians' houses, in addition to trying to push Muslim and Christian Jerusalemites out of the city. In every meeting with Israeli officials I warn that Jerusalem is a critically sensitive issue. Unilateral and illegal actions can only deepen the conflict and inflict more suffering on the Palestinians and the Israelis alike. But nothing seems to stop Israeli governments from taking these actions that risk derailing Israel's relations with Jordan and destroying all of our efforts to seek a lasting regional peace.

Sharon, the leader of Likud, did just that when, in September 2000, he announced his plans to visit Al Haram Al Sharif. Jews call this area the Temple Mount. They believe that the First and Second Temples were built on that site, and some hold that the Temple Mount will be the site of the Third Temple, whose construction will herald the coming of the Messiah. But some Israeli zealots do not want to wait any longer for the coming of the Messiah. A radical group that calls itself the Temple Mount Faithful, led by an Israeli officer, Gershon Salomon, has called for the demolition of the Al Aqsa Mosque and the Dome of the Rock and their removal to Mecca, so that the Third Temple can be erected in their place.

Many Muslims saw Sharon's planned visit as evidence that the ideas of the Temple Mount Faithful had entered mainstream Israeli politics. Arafat argued that he should not be allowed to enter the holy complex. Sharon ignored the protests, and on September 28, 2000, he entered Al Haram Al Sharif compound with a group of Likud members. Protected by around one thousand Israeli riot police and in disregard of the sensitivities of Muslims worldwide, he walked across the site as an angry group of Palestinians protested this incursion into one of Islam's holiest sites.

The next day the Palestinians' reaction to Sharon's provocation escalated. In violent clashes at least four Palestinians were killed and over two hundred wounded by the Israeli forces. After that, the situation quickly spiraled out of control. The violent demonstrations spread from East Jerusalem across the West Bank and Gaza. On September

30, at the Netzarim Junction in Gaza, an incident occurred that horrified the world. A carpenter, Jamal Dura, and his twelve-year-old son Mohammed were caught up in a violent clash between Palestinian demonstrators and the Israeli army. Trying in vain to take shelter behind a wall, they were showered with bullets. This gruesome scene was filmed and millions watched in shock as Jamal vainly tried to protect his son, who was killed in his arms. Across the Muslim world this image came to symbolize the brutality of the Israeli occupation of Palestine. In five further days of violence, around fifty Palestinians were killed and hundreds more wounded. Three Israelis died in the clashes.

The violence sparked by Sharon's visit triggered what came to be known as the Al Aqsa intifada. I condemned Sharon's provocation and argued that the only way to stop the violence was to get back to the negotiating table and to reach an agreement that fulfilled the legitimate right of the Palestinian people to statehood on their national soil, with East Jerusalem as their capital. But Sharon had his own approach.

Some lower-level Israeli-Palestinian talks continued during the fall, but no one put much stock in them. In a final push before leaving office in December 2000, Clinton offered some proposals, which became known as the Clinton Parameters, to address the outstanding issues of settlements, Jerusalem, and refugees.

Clinton proposed an end to the conflict on the basis of a solution that would give 94 to 96 percent of the West Bank to the Palestinians, with a land swap of 1 to 3 percent. Four-fifths of Israeli settlers would be in the land kept by Israel. He also proposed that territorial arrangements such as permanent safe passage between the West Bank and Gaza be part of the deal. The parameters further stated that Israeli withdrawal from the West Bank would take place over three years, during which international forces would be gradually introduced.

Clinton proposed that the Palestinian state would be the focal point for Palestinians who chose to return to Palestine, without ruling out that Israel would accept some of those refugees. The guiding principle for solving the issue of Jerusalem would be that Arab areas are Palestinian and Jewish areas are Israeli, with Palestinians having sovereignty over Al Haram Al Sharif and Israelis over the Western Wall. An agreement along those parameters would mark the end of the conflict.

From January 21 to January 27 at Taba in

Egypt, Barak and Arafat tried one last time to come to terms. But Barak was slipping daily in the polls, and after a fraught and contested election, a new president had just been inaugurated in the United States and no one knew what approach he would take. Talks soon ended and violence escalated. In Israel, commentators began to pronounce the Oslo peace process well and truly dead.

In the months that followed, controversy raged over the question of who bore responsibility for the collapse of the peace negotiations. In this debate the sticking points in the negotiations and the failure of the sides to agree were conflated with the consequences of Sharon's provocative visit to Al Haram Al Sharif. Some blamed Yasser Arafat for the ensuing violence as well as for the negotiations' collapse, saying that he had orchestrated the violence in order to win more Israeli concessions. Others suggested that the Americans had sided with Barak and had not pressed him for sufficient concessions. Some pointed out that not enough preparation had gone into Camp David and that what was offered to the Palestinians fell short of what they deserved or wanted. But the truth is that in the seven long years since the signing of the Oslo Accords, too many promises had been broken and trust had frayed. Palestinians knew that Ehud Barak would soon be voted out of office and doubted his ability to deliver given the weakening state of his government. It was a tragic and costly failure.

# CHAPTER 18
## SEEKING PEACE, GETTING WAR

During the Clinton administration, Iraq and America exchanged many violent words and a few missiles but stopped short of outright war. But in January 2001, as the administration of George W. Bush came into office, that dynamic began to change. Neoconservatives such as Paul Wolfowitz, Doug Feith, Elliott Abrams, and Richard Perle had long harbored ambitions to take down Saddam Hussein and finish the job that Bush's father, in their eyes, had begun. Many of these neocons began to take up strategic positions in the Pentagon, the National Security Council, and the State Department. They had the access; now all they lacked was the opportunity. All too soon, one would present itself.

The Bush administration showed little or no interest in building on the work of the Clinton administration. The day after Bush came into office, on January 21, 2001, the Israelis and Palestinians met at Taba in Egypt to try to follow on from the previous year's negotiation at Camp David and, with the assistance of Clinton's last-minute proposals (the Clinton Parameters), to bridge their final differences. But the talks soon broke down. After Taba, the revolving door in Israel began to spin again.

Ehud Barak was defeated in March by the Likud Party, led by Ariel Sharon. By electing Sharon, the Israeli public was sending a clear message. As his actions would soon demonstrate, Sharon had little interest in peace.

As dusk fell on the evening of May 18, 2001, Israeli F-16 fighters took off from their bases, heading for the West Bank and Gaza. Some of their bombs struck at the Palestinian security headquarters in Nablus, flattening the complex and killing eight people. Others hit targets in Ramallah and the Gaza Strip, killing eleven people and wounding many more. It was the first time since the 1967 war that Israel had attacked the Palestinians with fighter jets, and the strikes brought international condemnation. An unrepentant Ariel Sharon said in an interview with an Israeli newspaper, "We will do everything necessary and use everything we have to protect Israeli citizens."

360

The Israeli attack was the culmination of a week of escalating violence. On May 14, five Palestinian police officers were killed by Israeli soldiers. Four days later, on the morning of May 18, Hamas sent a suicide bomber to attack a shopping mall in the coastal resort town of Netanya, killing five shoppers and wounding around a hundred more. Later that evening the Israelis deployed their warplanes and bombs. Each side seemed to be trying to outdo the other in atrocities. Every human life is sacred, and I believe it is simply wrong to target innocent civilians, whether using suicide bombers or F-16 jets.

U.S. vice president Dick Cheney appealed for calm in a television interview a few days later, saying, "I think they should stop, both sides should stop and think about where they are headed here, and recognize that down this road lies disaster." But neither side was listening.

Later that year, on September 8, 2001, I sent a letter to President Bush urging him to speak out on the Palestinian problem, and I was quickly invited to travel to the United States and discuss my plan with him. On September 11, 2001, I was flying across the Atlantic on a private plane, on my way to the Baker Institute in Texas to give a speech before going on to meet President Bush in

Washington. I had taken a sleeping pill, so I was knocked out when my brother Ali came and shook me awake, saying, "We have a major problem. Something has happened in the States." We had received reports from the BBC that an airplane had crashed into the twin towers in New York, but as we had no access to television, we could not fully comprehend the horror and destruction of the attack.

Back in Jordan, Rania was glued to CNN, watching the devastating events unfold minute by minute. She managed to get a call through to the onboard telephone and urged me to turn the plane around and go back to Britain. But I had been raised to support close allies in times of crisis and told her I would stick to my plan. "We're going to continue to the United States," I said. "I want to show solidarity with my friends."

"Abdullah, you don't understand what's happened," she said. "They're not going to be interested in looking after you."

While we were talking, the pilot had contacted U.S. air traffic control and obtained clearance for our plane to land in America. But as we approached Labrador, Canada, I made the decision to turn back. In the cockpit we managed to catch a BBC broadcast that was reporting on the attack and I started to realize the magnitude of what had happened. Several hours later we landed back in the UK, at Brize Norton Air Base in Oxfordshire, about sixty-five miles west of London. While the crew was refueling, I walked across the tarmac in the dark and headed for the passenger lounge. As I went through the main doors, I saw the awful images of the two airplanes crashing into the twin towers. I was shocked by such naked aggression against civilians. Then I thought, "Oh my God. All hell will break loose if this has been done by an Islamist group."

My next thought was, "How can Jordan help?" I found a secure telephone and began to place calls to the United States. President Bush was very busy at that point, but I managed to get through to George Tenet, the director of the Central Intelligence Agency. "George," I said, "whatever we can do, Jordan is behind the United States." He confirmed my fear that Al Qaeda was behind the attack and mentioned that there might be forthcoming operations in Afghanistan.

Then I called General Tommy Franks, who was commander of U.S. Central Command (CENTCOM) and would be in charge of any military operations covering the Middle East. Tommy was someone I had known for many years, going back to my Special Operations days. I said, "We're committed to helping you."

When I got back to Jordan, I gathered my senior military officers and told them that I was determined to help in the fight against these madmen. My officers were ready for Jordan to join in the fight; they had been battling militant extremists in Jordan for years, so they well knew the harm they could do.

When the United States and its allies went to war in Afghanistan in October 2001, we sent a field hospital and Special Forces detachment to Mazar-e-Sharif in the north. After 9/11, the first priority of the United States was to go after its enemies.

From that point on, the Israelis would do their best to link their fight against Arafat and the Palestinians to what the Americans were now calling the "global war on terror." I noticed this disturbing development early on and feared what might happen if they succeeded.

Early in the morning of January 3, 2002, a battered blue ship moved through the calm waters of the Red Sea, rounded the Horn of Africa, and headed north along the coast of Saudi Arabia. The 4,000-ton freighter *Karine A* had stopped in Dubai to pick up a cargo of mattresses, sunglasses, and sandals. The captain of the ship, a former senior officer in the Palestinian naval police, had made an earlier stop at an island off the Iranian coast. At dawn, the quiet of the ocean was broken by the sound of Israeli army helicopters heading toward the ship, accompanied by Israeli naval vessels. Israeli commandos seized control of the vessel, subdued her crew, and diverted the *Karine A* to the southern Israeli port of Eilat. Beneath the flip-flops and bedding, the Israelis found boxes of Kalashnikov rifles, Katyusha rockets, and plastic explosives.

The seizure of the *Karine A* further damaged the already reeling peace process. Yasser Arafat had been under siege at his Ramallah headquarters for nearly a month, his authority severely undermined by Israel's high-handed actions. Sharon's government had ordered the killing of several leaders of Hamas in targeted assassinations and the intifada was growing more violent daily as Palestinians began to despair. Eight years after the signing of the Oslo agreement, little had changed for the Palestinians, as subsequent Israeli prime ministers had reneged on its promises and prescriptions. Sharon periodically closed off access to Israel and sealed off Gaza and parts of the West Bank, making it impossible for Palestinians with jobs in Israel to go to work.

On January 7, Sharon held a press conference in Eilat next to the captured ship. He displayed the seized weapons and called Arafat a "bitter enemy," claiming that he had bought deadly weapons from Iran with the intention of smuggling them into the West Bank and Gaza Strip and launching further attacks against Israel. President Bush could have used his influence to calm the situation, but his attention was focused elsewhere, and he seemed to have no desire to rein in Sharon. His administration appeared to have decided to stand aside and watch as the peace process sputtered and died.

On January 31, after the State of the Union address in which Bush described Iran, Iraq, and North Korea as an "axis of evil," I headed to the State Department for a meeting with Secretary of State Colin Powell. I wanted to stress the importance to the entire region of setting the peace process back on track, and to get a better understanding of the administration's new focus on Iraq. In February of the previous year, Powell had visited Jordan as part of a wider trip to the Middle East, and I had met him at the airport. Typically, this is a practice reserved for visiting heads of state, but I had known him for many years and considered him a good friend. We spoke about Iraq and the stalemated peace process in a long meeting at Raghadan Palace. I was preparing to take him back to the airport when, having taken a liking to my new Mercedes S500 sedan, he asked if he could drive instead. He drove us both to the airport, surprisingly sticking to the speed limit the whole way. Powell was heading to the West Bank for a meeting with Chairman Arafat, and as we got out he pointed to his security detail and said, "I wanted to drive it to Ramallah, but they said no."

When I saw Powell in January, he raised the *Karine A* incident and said that it was unfortunate, because up until then things had been improving a bit. Even Sharon had said as much. But the capture of the ship and its cargo of weapons had undercut U.S. efforts — Powell's envoy, General Anthony Zinni, had been shuttling between the Israelis and Palestinians to negotiate a cease-fire — and made it difficult to move forward. He insisted that there would have to be relative quiet, and that Arafat would need to say something about the ship for the U.S. domestic audience.

I told Powell that the United States needed to send a message of hope to the Palestinians.

It had to reinforce their belief that peaceful negotiations would lead to statehood, and to reach out and help those who had been hurt by the intifada and had lost their jobs because of the closures. I also said that the United States needed to be more transparent about what exactly Arafat would have to do to relieve the situation. I suggested that a plan detailing the obligations of both Palestinians and Israelis would help achieve this. Then we started to discuss the only subject anybody in Washington wanted to talk about: Iraq. Ever the diplomat, Powell sought to soften the impact of the president's State of the Union address, saying that if Iraq abandoned its support for terrorism and its weapons of mass destruction program, then the United States would change its attitude.

The next day I met with President Bush in the Oval Office. I raised the one topic that was then and is now to my mind the most important issue for America in the region — the peace process. I told him that all too often it was relegated to a sideshow, but it was in fact the central issue. Solving the Israeli-Palestinian conflict, I said, would remove a rallying cry for the likes of Al Qaeda and make other Arab leaders more supportive of America's goals in the region.

But Bush was in no mood to talk about the peace process. He quickly revealed his frustration with recent developments. He said that Arafat had "led us down a path and then reneged." He insisted that Arafat had to do a better job in controlling extremists; otherwise, the United States would not spend political capital trying to resolve the conflict. "We can't be hypocrites on terror," he said, and then he made it clear that he felt Arafat was siding with terrorist organizations. As I had feared, he began to elide his own struggle to tackle Al Qaeda with the Palestinian-Israeli conflict.

I defended Arafat, saying that he was a national symbol for the Palestinians, and warned Bush that he would slip away if he felt cornered. I described the situation in the region as two old warriors fighting each other while their peoples suffered, and said that the United States should formulate its demands of Arafat in a way that would be understood by Palestinian people. We kept getting bogged down by problems relating to the leaders on both sides, I said, while the majority of Israelis and Palestinians wanted to improve the situation.

The president said he would look into the idea and discuss it with Sharon. He emphasized that the United States would tell

Sharon on his upcoming visit to Washington that if he went overboard it would undermine America's ability to fight terror. Bush also mentioned that he had told Sharon he would have a real problem if the Israelis killed Arafat.

I asked Bush for his help in convincing the Israelis to let Arafat leave his compound in Ramallah, where he had been kept under "house arrest" by the Israeli military since December 2001, so that he could attend the Arab League Summit in Beirut in March, noting that preventing Arafat from attending would only energize the radicals. Bush promised to raise the issue with Sharon, and then we moved on to a discussion of Arafat's role in the larger peace process. Again Bush said, "We can't be hypocrites on terror." He repeated his claim that Arafat was siding with terrorist organizations, and then he said, "Maybe there is someone better?" He said he was not suggesting overthrow but pointing out that there was a need to think over time about who could best replace Arafat and lead the Palestinians to a better future.

I was alarmed by this turn in the conversation. I said that there was no alternative to Arafat. He had become a symbol of the Palestinian people, and the more pressure Israel put on him the more support his people would give him. Israel had also "cantonized" the Palestinians, leading to a fragmentation of political authority in the West Bank and Gaza. I added that Sharon had a very short-term view, and that while it did not mean we could not eventually be partners in peace, we definitely disagreed with his methods.

At this point Bush steered our discussion to Iraq. Taking a harsher line than Powell had done, the president criticized the Iraqi regime, saying, "Saddam needs to be taken to task."

"You are going to create a major problem in the Middle East," I said, slowly and deliberately. "The problem is not with the United States removing Saddam — but what happens next?" But Bush remained adamant in his position.

I returned to Jordan the next day. In subsequent conversations with fellow Arab leaders, including President Hosni Mubarak of Egypt and Crown Prince Abdullah of Saudi Arabia, I learned that they had had very similar discussions with members of the Bush administration. "What happens the day after you remove Saddam?" they had asked. The inability of the administration to give a concrete answer left us all very uncomfortable.

It had become clear that America would no longer take the lead in pressing for a resolution to the Israeli-Palestinian crisis. But American disengagement from the peace process would almost certainly kill any hope of progress. So we continued to pressure for the resumption of negotiations, and this time around with a collective Arab peace initiative that we believed would encourage a more active U.S. role in the peace process.

In the last years of his reign, my father developed a new approach to the Israeli-Palestinian problem — one that would include all Arab states and commit them to collective peace with Israel in return for Israel's total withdrawal from all occupied Arab land. Under such an approach — wider than the Madrid process and designed to win international support — all twenty-two members of the Arab League would offer a collective peace to Israel, backed by security guarantees, provided that Israel agree to meet specific requirements. These included the establishment of a Palestinian state, agreement on the status of Jerusalem and the rights of Palestinian refugees, returning the Golan Heights to Syria, and ending the occupation of Lebanese territories. My father wanted to set out what the generic concept of "land for peace" would mean in practical terms, and to eliminate some of the political maneuvering that had taken place between different Arab countries. Unfortunately, his proposal did not gain momentum and stalled with his death. On becoming king, I took the opportunity to revive my father's plan and asked our government, in concert with the Egyptians, to discuss it with Saudi Arabia. Eventually the Saudis developed the idea into what first came to be known as Crown Prince Abdullah's initiative and later became the Arab Peace Initiative, after Saudi Arabia presented it to the Arab League, which adopted it at its summit in Beirut in 2002.

As I was preparing to leave Jordan for the Arab League Summit in Lebanon in March 2002, our intelligence service learned of a plot to assassinate me and the Egyptian president, Hosni Mubarak, when we arrived in Beirut. I called Mubarak and passed on the intelligence. He agreed that the security concerns were real, and we both decided that it would be best if we did not travel to Beirut. Not wanting to offend our hosts, I let it be known that I had been struck by a severe cold and would be unable to travel.

Also missing was Yasser Arafat. True to his word, President Bush had sent Vice President Cheney to Israel to try to persuade

Prime Minister Ariel Sharon to let Arafat attend the summit. This was the summit that would launch the Arab Peace Initiative, and it was, therefore, extremely important for Arafat to attend it. But Sharon was unmoved. He said that if Arafat went to Lebanon he would not be allowed to return to his headquarters in Ramallah. Arafat stayed in his compound and tried to join in via videoconference. Showing its petty side, Sharon's government jammed the signal, and Arafat was reduced to sending a taped message.

On March 28, 2002, the twenty-two members of the Arab League formally endorsed the Arab Peace Initiative. This proposed that, in return for a full Israeli withdrawal from all Arab territories to the June 1967 boundaries, a just and "agreed upon" solution to the refugee problem, and the establishment of a sovereign independent Palestinian state in the West Bank and Gaza with East Jerusalem as its capital, Arab states would consider the Arab-Israeli conflict ended, enter into a peace agreement with Israel, provide security for all the states of the region, and establish normal relations with Israel.

For the first time since the start of the Arab-Israeli conflict, Arab states had formally and unanimously made an offer to Israel for normal relations as a basis for ending the conflict. The Israeli response was swift and unambiguous.

On March 29, 2002, Sharon ordered Israeli troops into West Bank cities in an operation called "Defensive Shield," the largest Israeli military operation since the invasion of Lebanon in 1982. Israeli forces reoccupied almost all of the Palestinian self-rule areas it had redeployed from under the Oslo process. Ramallah, Bethlehem, Jenin, and Nablus were once again under Israeli occupation. A refugee camp in Jenin suffered the worst attack during a two-week siege that was supported by blanket bombardment of its neighborhoods.

The next day Israeli tanks and soldiers assaulted Yasser Arafat's compound in Ramallah, smashing through the walls, cutting the electricity, and leaving the Palestinian leader isolated in his second-floor office, working by candlelight. The crudeness of Israel's handling of Arafat made even his staunchest detractors soften toward him. Because he was imprisoned for so long, up to a few weeks before his death in November 2004, and treated so badly, many became sympathetic to his plight. He essentially became a hero.

The violence continued to escalate when a

Palestinian suicide bomber blew herself up in a Jerusalem supermarket, killing two people. In April 2002, some Palestinian fighters, fleeing from Israeli soldiers who were hunting them, took refuge in the Church of the Nativity in Bethlehem. The Israeli army quickly surrounded the church and blockaded the Palestinians inside, along with some 250 priests, nuns, and other civilians. People across the world watched appalled as a sacred place of worship was surrounded by Israeli armored vehicles and snipers huddled on nearby rooftops, with their guns trained on the church.

On April 21, Israel halted its military operations and pulled out its troops from Palestinian areas but kept the siege on the Church of the Nativity and Arafat's compound in Ramallah. The UN General Assembly convened in an emergency session on May 7 and issued a resolution that expressed grave concern at the deteriorating situation in the Palestinian territories. It demanded that Israel, as an occupying power, abide by its responsibilities under the fourth Geneva Convention. It also condemned Israel's attacks on religious sites and its refusal to cooperate with a UN fact-finding team that was ordered by the Security Council in a resolution adopted on April 19 to investigate its attack on the Jenin refugee camp.

The siege on the Church of the Nativity lasted for over a month. What was shocking was that the Israeli government had no compunction about allowing its soldiers to open fire on this most sacred site. At one point, two Japanese tourists wandered into the middle of the armed standoff, and were saved by nearby journalists, who motioned for them to get out of the way. Eventually a peaceful solution to the standoff was negotiated, but there was little progress in the larger conflict. It was clear that Sharon had no intention of making peace. The decades-old struggle would have to wait for new leaders to emerge.

In June 2002, the Council of Foreign Ministers of the Organization of the Islamic Conference (OIC), meeting in Sudan, endorsed the Arab Peace Initiative. They decided to make every effort to win international support for its implementation. The OIC, established in 1969 at a historic summit in Rabat, with fifty-seven members, is the world's second-largest intergovernmental organization after the United Nations. By endorsing the Arab Peace Initiative, the OIC had given the proposal the explicit backing of the entire Muslim world. Holding out the promise of normal relations with Israel with all of its members, the OIC put a fifty-seven-state solution on the table.

The OIC again reaffirmed its support for the Arab Peace Initiative the following year, at the foreign ministers' meeting in Tehran in June 2003 and at the full OIC summit meeting of heads of state in Malaysia in October. But the Israelis showed no interest in this unprecedented opportunity.

In April 2002, in one of its most controversial decisions, Israel announced that Sharon had authorized the construction of a twenty-six-foot-high wall between Israel and the West Bank. Although the stated purpose was to prevent "terrorists" from crossing into and attacking Israel, parts of the wall were built on West Bank territory occupied by Israel in 1967, not along the 1949 armistice line. Reaching into the West Bank, in some cases up to twelve miles, the wall was constructed so that some 80 percent of the settlers in the West Bank would be on the Israeli side. Its path in some cases cut through the middle of Palestinian villages and in others trapped Palestinian towns on the Israeli side.

We, along with the whole Arab world, suspected that Israel's real intention was to create a de facto border and, contrary to international law, to annex land occupied in

war and thereby preempt final status negotiations. In December 2003, the UN General Assembly requested a ruling from the
International Court of Justice (ICJ) on the
legality of the wall.

The Palestinians began to prepare their
case, and in light of our historical and legal
responsibility for Jerusalem, Jordan offered
to assist them. Civilized nations settle dis-
putes through the law, and we were determined to present the best case possible. We
recommended to the Palestinians that they
engage Professor James Crawford of Cambridge University, a recognized expert in
international law, and the Jordanian team
engaged the services of Sir Arthur Watts, a
distinguished British lawyer who formerly
had been the legal adviser to the Foreign
Office.

In February 2004, assisted by our permanent representative to the United Nations,
Prince Zeid bin Ra'ad, the Palestinian and
Jordanian teams presented their case to
the ICJ, arguing that Israel had no right
to build a wall, or anything else, on territory occupied illegally in the 1967 war. On
July 9, 2004, the court ruled by a majority
of fourteen to one, with the dissenting vote
cast by the American judge, Thomas Buer-
genthal, that the wall violated international

law, saying, "The construction of the wall being built by Israel, the occupying Power, in the Occupied Palestinian Territory, including in and around East Jerusalem, and its associated régime, are contrary to international law." The ruling further stated that Israel should stop violating international law and that it should pull down the existing wall and compensate Palestinians for damage caused by its construction. The Israeli government ignored the ruling, and Prime Minister Sharon ordered construction of the wall to continue.

Throughout history, from the Warsaw Ghetto to cold war Berlin, walls built to divide or imprison people have never proved strong enough to stand against the tide of human hope. In the end, Israel cannot gain the security it seeks by imprisoning the Palestinians in a ghetto of their own construction, or by re-creating the Berlin Wall in East Jerusalem. The security that all Israelis and Palestinians crave most, that of a normal life, can be achieved only by tearing down the barriers that separate them and learning to live in peace.

The war drums continued to beat throughout the spring and summer of 2002. I returned to the United States in the spring, and on May 8 again saw President Bush at the White House, where I continued to stress the importance of restarting the peace process. The month before, I had pointed out in a letter that we had been "instrumental in building consensus for the Saudi initiative, which had been translated into a collective Arab commitment to end the conflict with Israel, guarantee its security and establish normal relations between all Arab states and Israel." This effort to line up the Arab world behind a plan for peace was threatened by Israeli actions. I urged Bush to work for the withdrawal of Israeli troops from Palestinian cities, which they had taken almost complete control of by then, and to press for the restarting of negotiations.

But the president seemed to view Arafat as a failed leader, and kept stressing his inability to deliver on his promises. He also bemoaned the fact that Sharon, by attacking Arafat's headquarters in Ramallah and keeping him a virtual prisoner, had increased Arafat's domestic support. "I don't know who else can emerge," he said. Bush said Sharon made a hero out of Arafat, who would remain on the stage. But he pointed to the need for ideas that would allow younger people to come out and lead.

I warned the president that there was a

false impression of quiet in the region and that a great deal of anger was simmering under the surface. The temporary period of quiet, I said, was due to the hope generated by Powell's visit the previous month and America's subsequent efforts to restart the peace process, but more violence could easily erupt if there was no movement in the next few months. I restated the position that political change would depend on a political settlement with a timeline and a Palestinian state as an outcome.

The president listened but stressed his desire to avoid what he saw as the mistakes of the Clinton administration in focusing too much on the details of finding a solution to Jerusalem and forgetting about Israel's security concerns. "I can imagine how Sharon feels when he starts his meeting with me with the news of a suicide bombing," he said. The tragic events of 9/11 had understandably given the president greater empathy with other leaders whose people were targeted by suicide attacks. But it also obscured the administration's grasp of Palestinian suffering. Then the president told me that he still had his eyes on Iraq.

President Bush continued to criticize Arafat, notably in a speech he gave on June 24, 2002, when he set out his policy toward Israel and the Palestinians. He began by stating his commitment to a two-state solution. "My vision is two states," he said, "living side by side in peace and security. There is simply no way to achieve that peace until all parties fight terror. Yet at this critical moment, if all parties will break with the past and set out on a new path, we can overcome the darkness with the light of hope." "But," he continued, "peace requires a new and different Palestinian leadership, so that a Palestinian state can be born. I call on the Palestinian people to elect new leaders, leaders not compromised by terror." In return, Bush said, the United States would support a provisional state of Palestine pending negotiations between the Israelis and Palestinians on borders and other issues, with a settlement envisaged in three years.

The idea of "leaders not compromised by terror," sadly, was one that would be hard to implement — on both sides. In American eyes, the Palestinian leader, Yasser Arafat, was compromised by terror. But in Palestinian eyes, the Israeli prime minister, Ariel Sharon, was equally compromised by his role in the massacres at the Sabra and Shatila refugee camps in Lebanon in 1982. In the Middle East, everyone was stunned by Bush's comments. Arafat had represented the Palestinian people, for better or worse, since the 1970s. He had won the Nobel Peace Prize in 1994 for his bold partnership with Rabin and Peres. How could the U.S. administration imagine that it could sweep him under the table? Sharon harbored an old animus against Arafat and had decided to lock him into his compound in Ramallah. But what I did not want was for the U.S. administration to take the same line.

In April, to try to revive the stalled peace process, we floated the idea of a "road map," a set of specific actions accompanied by a timeline that could be used to measure progress by both sides. On a visit to Jordan in early June, William Burns, the assistant secretary of state for Near Eastern Affairs, said he thought the idea of a detailed action plan with benchmarks was a good one and promised to promote it inside the U.S. government.

Many in the Bush administration, however, continued to be obsessed with Iraq. The desperate situation in Israel would be relegated to the back burner, with disastrous consequences.

Israel supported the approaching war. By constantly conjuring an imminent threat in the public's imagination, Israeli politicians have managed to keep their citizens in a state of perpetual alarm. This approach has its risks, because it can easily be exploited by those seeking short-term political gain. That is not to say that Israel does not face real threats. But the most effective way to neutralize these threats would be to do the one right thing: negotiate a lasting peace with the Palestinians. If Israel were to do so, it would be recognized by the entire international community, and accepted by the Muslim world. Sadly, many decision-makers inside Israel are ideologically opposed to this. Others are unable to quantify, and therefore to understand, the long-term gains that peace would bring.

Since the 1960s Israel has tried to play the United States against the countries in the Middle East that it has perceived as its biggest threat. In 1967 the Israelis made the argument to the United States that they would have to strike first against Egypt because it was preparing to attack them. In the run-up to the 2003 war they encouraged the United States to launch war on Iraq. Israeli politicians tried to portray Saddam Hussein as a strategic threat to Israel's existence. At the same time in the United States a group of neocons with administration ties played up the threat to America, fanning the flames of war. Iraqi expatriates, with personal interests in mind, joined in, feeding the government of the United States with inaccurate and exaggerated information.

On July 29, 2002, concerned that the march to war in Iraq was gaining momentum, I gave an interview to the *Times* of London. "Ask our friends in China, in Moscow, in England, in Paris," I said. "Everybody will tell you that we have concerns about military actions against Iraq. The international community is united on this. . . . Military action against Iraq would really open a Pandora's box." I criticized the neoconservative members of the Bush administration, saying they were "fixated on Iraq. . . . You can talk till you're blue in the face and they're not going to get it." The United States was now irrevocably heading down the path to war.

Many leaders in the Middle East stayed away from Washington to express their displeasure with the Bush administration's policies. But I thought it was important for me to go to Washington regularly to attempt to influence the debate and remind the Bush administration of the importance of moving forward on the establishment of a Palestinian state. I went back again at the end of July, traveling to Washington via Europe, where we discussed the rising tensions between the United States and Iraq with

President Jacques Chirac of France in Paris and Prime Minister Tony Blair in London. I knew that my plain speaking would not be welcomed by some in Washington. But Jordan is an old friend of America, and we would be doing the United States no favors by hiding our concerns at such an important moment.

In preparation for my visit, I asked my foreign minister, Marwan Muasher, to prepare a draft of a proposed road map for peace that we could discuss with the president. He reported back that he and Bill Burns had made great progress but that Condoleezza Rice, who was then the U.S. national security adviser, was dead set against the idea, believing it was a "nonstarter." Rice never gave a rationale for her objections.

I told Marwan that no matter what she thought, we would present our proposal to the president. When I landed in the United States I discovered that my candor with the European press had provoked an angry reaction inside the administration. I was welcomed on arrival by a call from Condoleezza Rice, who said, "The president is very upset with your statement."

"I'm just saying in public what I heard from Chirac and Blair," I said. "So don't shoot the messenger."

The morning of August 1, 2002, I met President Bush at the White House. Our main agenda item was the peace process, particularly the concept of the road map to move the process forward and reach a two-state solution. Normally the president greeted me warmly, but this morning he was quite stiff and formal. As we walked into the Oval Office, he was drinking a Coke with plenty of ice. Crushing the ice cubes between his teeth as he spoke, he said that he was upset about my recent newspaper interview outlining the risks of war. But President Bush and I had developed a good personal relationship and he warmed up as the meeting progressed.

Giving his views on Iraq, he said that there was a huge amount of hyperventilating about Saddam. He said we were facing a historic moment and that he did not want people thirty years from now to say that President Bush and King Abdullah had the opportunity to forge a lasting peace but did not do it. "We should not be threatened by thugs," he said.

I reiterated my opposition to war and then said, "Mr. President, if you've decided to go to war in Iraq just be straightforward and tell your friends."

His reply was firm. "I haven't made that

decision yet," he said. "When I do, you will know." Then he said he had to deal with the Europeans, who did not understand that what was happening in Iraq was a crime against humanity. He said he would not allow it to go on any longer.

Then we moved on to a discussion of the peace process, and I asked Marwan to present the concept we had come up with in Amman. "We need to assure people of our seriousness," Marwan said. "We need a road map that starts with security and institutions, and addresses the humanitarian situation in the Palestinian territories, but that also outlines the remaining steps to be taken going forward until mid-2005, so that Palestinians know exactly what they are getting, and so the international community can gain more support for their work on security."

"I thought I made that clear in my speech," the president said, referring to his controversial remarks on June 24. "If it wasn't clear, we are willing to work with you on outlining these steps," the president added. He said he had no problem with what we suggested and that after improving security and building institutions, issues such as occupation, settlements, and Jerusalem would be dealt with.

"We can take the speech and translate it into steps," interjected Bill Burns, who was also in the meeting. The president agreed and called the meeting to an end. Condoleezza Rice later approached Marwan and reversed her earlier opposition to the road map, saying that the United States could work something out with Jordan. By December the road map draft was completed. The new initiative was eventually launched in mid-2003.

The larger meeting gave way to a smaller tête-à-tête in a side room off the Oval Office. But before that, the subject returned to Iraq. At one point President Bush said, "You and I have two great fathers, and we both believe in God, and we have an opportunity to do the right thing." The president spoke as if going to war against Iraq was a religious duty.

My brother Ali was with me and we were both surprised to hear the president invoke religion as a factor in his decision. Bush's statement gave us a clear impression that, despite earlier assurances, he had already made up his mind to go to war. Back in Jordan, when I met with senior officials to brief them on the visit, I said, "We've got to prepare. This war is going to happen."

# CHAPTER 19
# WAR IN THE DESERT

January 12, 2003, was a sunny winter's day in Portsmouth. A crowd of ten thousand people packed the docks and streets of this historic British naval city, waving good-bye to the *Ark Royal,* the Royal Navy's 20,000-ton flagship aircraft carrier. As the ship moved slowly out of the harbor, the sailors on deck stood at attention, listening to the shouts and cheers of the crowd. *Ark Royal* was heading up a naval task force of sixteen vessels, carrying three thousand Royal Marines. Although the fleet was officially headed for "exercises" in Asia, its course would take it through the Arabian Gulf and, it was widely believed, to Iraq. As soon as I heard that the Royal Navy had set sail, I knew war in Iraq was imminent. From my time at the Staff College in the UK and in the British army, I knew that Her Majesty's Treasury would never spend that much money unless war was inevitable.

I was against the war, though deeply sympathetic to the continuing suffering of the Iraqi people. I thought then, and still think now, that the Iraq war was a big mistake for the United States. I was alarmed by the prospect of another conflict on our borders, but there was little I could do to stop the war. Part of my responsibility as head of state was to anticipate the likely turn of events, and I was convinced that there could only be one outcome: the United States would win. I did not want Jordan to be damaged afterward by appearing to have sided with Saddam. From my father's experience in the first Gulf War, I had seen the adverse impact on Jordan when we were perceived to be taking Iraq's side against the West. We had been frozen out by the Americans and British, as well as by a number of Gulf countries. I was determined to keep Jordan out of this fight while ensuring that we not be punished for our position.

This was probably the most difficult time I have faced in the last eleven years. Some people wanted me to side with Saddam Hussein, but I did not think that was the right thing to do. I was determined to do the right thing for Jordan no matter how unpopular our position would be. I felt that was what my father had expected me to do when he had given me this responsibility.

I was determined to fulfill my responsibility toward Jordan to the best of my ability. And, as ironic as it may sound, to be able to do this job well you have to come to terms with the fact that, more often than not, the right decision is not necessarily the popular one. Often the job of a leader is to resist the temptation to give in to widespread and strongly held popular sentiment. A leader has to make decisions based on reason and judgment, and on the long-term interests of his country.

The train was coming down the tracks and I was not going to be able to stop it. The best I could do was get Jordan out of the way.

I tried to walk the tightrope of opposing the war and staying out of it. But I was certain of one thing: the longer the war lasted, the more terrible the consequences would be and the more intense the pressures on Jordan would become. Adding to the complexity, at this time I came under sustained pressure from the American administration to allow U.S. troops to be based in Jordan. In the months before the Iraq war, Jordan began to be dragged into the debate about the staging of ground forces. Our long land border with Iraq was attractive to American planners, who saw it as an ideal strategic location from which to launch an attack into western Iraq.

The looming conflict was an emotionally charged topic, both in Jordan and in the wider Middle East. Throughout January, tens of thousands of people demonstrated from Ankara to Beirut, expressing enormous hostility to what they believed was an unnecessary war. On February 1, around five thousand protesters, organized by opposition parties, marched in Amman against war in Iraq, waving pictures of Saddam and chanting, "Terrorist Bush, get out of our lands."

We were determined to keep our borders sovereign and not to allow any of the potential combatants to cross over into Jordanian territory. During this period, one night an unidentified aircraft flew over Jordan without permission. It flew fast and low to avoid being spotted, but we picked it up on our radar and sent two Mirage fighter jets to intercept it. The plane was heading toward Iraq and our fighters intercepted the aircraft as it was approaching the Jordanian-Saudi border. They flew up next to it and identified it as a C-130 military transport plane, flying in the dark with no lights. It refused to answer repeated requests for identification.

As part of the coalition's military buildup, there were many C-130s and other transport planes in the air near our borders, and we wanted to know what this plane was and why it had entered Jordanian airspace covertly. We called coalition headquarters, as well as the Israeli military, but no one would admit to ownership of the mystery plane. The Jordanian pilots radioed my brother Feisal, who was the commander of the air force, and asked whether they should shoot it down. If we made the mistake of shooting down a coalition transport craft, it would create a major international incident. As the plane approached the Saudi border, Feisal told his men to hold their fire.

The next day Feisal followed up with the American military, who assured him that it was not a coalition plane. The United States agreed to try to track where the plane had gone after leaving Jordan. We subsequently learned that after entering Saudi airspace, it had landed in Israel.

The chief of staff of the Israeli air force at the time, Dan Halutz, called Feisal to assure him that it was not an Israeli plane. He said that it was most likely a cloud of chaff. A couple of days later a senior Israeli officer was visiting Jordan. I asked Feisal to go speak to him and to set out Jordanian policy clearly and directly. Feisal did not mince his words. "We know it was a C-130, and we know it was yours," he said. "I want to make it very, very clear that the next time this happens we will pursue it very aggressively. We will not allow anybody to fly through our airspace. Anything that crosses the border will be shot at."

During this period, General Tommy Franks was in charge of war planning. I had gotten to know General Franks when he took over at CENTCOM in 2000. One of the finest soldiers I have ever met, he was hard-bitten, no-nonsense, and profane. We hit it off right away. When I was commander of Special Operations, we went out in the field on military exercises together, and I learned that he, like me, was an enthusiastic biker. On my last visit to Tampa, where CENTCOM has its headquarters, he served me an amazing beef brisket. Although I had gone to school in New England, I understood enough about Texas to know that it is almost impossible to get a Texan to share a barbecue recipe. After lots of wrangling, he finally relented, and I now serve his beef brisket to official guests in Jordan.

General Franks was famous for his ability to chew out people using colorful and imaginative phrases. In fact, there should be a book written about his use of expletives. Provided the cursing is not being directed at you, it is pretty hilarious to watch.

He visited Amman to brief me on the war preparations, hoping to get my permission to deploy U.S. troops. Pulling out a huge board, he said, "I want to bring twenty-five thousand troops into Jordan." Then he proceeded to outline a detailed plan for the operation. He had a list of military units he wanted to deploy inside our country. He wanted to bring a Joint Special Operations Command, logistics units, Patriot batteries, and many other units.

I have the highest regard for General Franks, but in this case I could not give him what he wanted. We went down the list one by one. I pointed to the logistics unit and asked, "What's this group?" He said, "We need them to take trucks and equipment from Aqaba into Iraq after the war is over. The idea is to send supplies in once we move toward Baghdad. We have the transportation corps coming with a large number of drivers and trucks."

"Well," I interrupted, "it seems to me the Jordanian army could do that. I mean, if we are going to be working together, you will have to trust us, so you don't need to bring those men. We will ship the stuff to the border."

He continued, describing how he wanted to put a Special Operations headquarters and helicopter transport hubs inside Jordan.

"Look," I said, "headquarters can be put anywhere, don't put them in Jordan. And I really don't want helicopters flying from our border. I don't want an attack launched from Jordan into Iraq."

He agreed to move the headquarters and to shift the Chinook helicopters and other air transport elsewhere, to places like Qatar. After a lengthy debate, soldier to soldier, we agreed that only a few Patriot air defense batteries would be placed in Jordan to defend against Iraqi Scud missiles that could be fired over our territory.

With this agreement, General Franks left, and I continued to prepare for the coming conflict. But no military plan can remain intact for long in the shifting politics of the Middle East. The United States wanted to move an infantry division through Turkey, in preparation for a strike into northern Iraq. But on March 1, the Turkish parliament voted no. The Turkish vote disrupted the U.S. war plans, and shortly afterward I received a call from Vice President Dick Cheney, who asked me to respond positively to requests that Tommy Franks would make during a meeting that had been scheduled between us the next day.

"Mr. Vice President," I said, "Tommy Franks and I have a very good relationship and a lot of trust. Let us two military men work something out between ourselves." Cheney agreed, and we ended the conversation. I made sure to try to have breakfast with the vice president whenever I went to Washington. Sometimes we would meet alone, while at other times he would be joined by a member of his staff or his daughter Liz, who was then a State Department official. Cheney was a tough character, dead set in his views but always very supportive of Jordan and sympathetic to our financial problems. Because he was so influential within the administration, I would often make the points I wanted to drive home on subjects such as the peace process and Iraq to him a day or so before my meeting with the president. His reaction would give me an early warning of the arguments I was likely to hear in the Oval Office.

The next day General Franks was back in Amman. "We're not looking at moving troops into Jordan at this stage," he said. "But we would like to base some of our assets out of the Mediterranean. That would mean firing Tomahawk missiles and launching air strikes from our carriers across Jordanian airspace into Iraq."

"Tommy," I said, "why do you want to mess with a friend? If you want to launch over somebody, launch over a different country. Why put us in the line of fire? And can you even guarantee that Israel would not slip in and attack Iraq through our airspace?"

Eventually General Franks understood my concerns and agreed to shift everything elsewhere. To this day I owe General Franks a tremendous debt of thanks — in part because of our personal friendship forged over the years. During his visit he willingly listened to my objections and concerns and agreed to change his plans. If the United States had pushed to fly over Jordan, I would have continued to say no and that would have put Jordan in a tremendously difficult position.

Shortly after the debates over basing ended, the fighting began. On March 20, 2003, the war started with cruise missile strikes. As dawn broke over Baghdad, U.S. Tomahawk missiles slammed into a bunker where Saddam Hussein was thought to be staying. Later that day, around 8 p.m., the ground invasion began. American and British tanks poured across the border from Kuwait, heading for Baghdad and Basra.

The invasion was covered live on satellite television. Like many Arabs, I watched these images with a mixture of sadness and alarm. I was no friend of Saddam, who was the leader of a brutal regime, but I was saddened to see so many innocent Iraqis paying the price for his ambition. The Iraqis are a great people and Baghdad is one of the historic seats of Arab culture, famous for its House of Wisdom, which preserved and translated the works of many Greek philosophers. Iraq produced many famous Arab scientists, musicians, writers, and poets, including Al Mutanabbi, known as the "Arab Shakespeare." It was heartbreaking to see this ancient city pulverized by American missiles. Many Arabs were alarmed at American forces invading a brethren Arab country. Across the Middle East, we felt plenty of shock, but little awe.

Knowing the concerns that were uppermost in many Jordanians' minds, I spoke about the efforts I had made to stop the war, saying in an interview with the Jordanian press:

We have used all our relations with influential countries in order to avert the day in which we see Iraq exposed to this invasion with all that it entails of suffering of innocents and suffering of the entire region. . . .

The Jordanian people, and I am one of them, strongly condemn the killing of women and children. . . . As a father I feel the pain of every Iraqi family, of every Iraqi child and father.

I spoke my heart, yet the war had begun and my hands were tied. There was nothing I could do to reverse it. The best I could do was rely on my instinct that I was doing the right thing for Jordan.

Although the conflict was hundreds of miles away, it did not take long before its tremors were felt inside Jordan. I was sitting at home watching the news on television when the telephone rang. It was Saad Khair, the head of my intelligence services (who very sadly passed away in late 2009). "We have discovered an Iraqi plot to poison the water supply in Zarqa and other locations," he said. "The leader is the military attaché at the Iraqi embassy, and he is planning to strike soon. What should we do?"

The poisoning of our main water supply would have killed hundreds if not thousands of innocent Jordanians. Dealing with the plot would not be easy — as "diplomats,"

Saddam's men had immunity, and arresting them could cause an international incident. I went through the evidence and decided it was too conclusive not to act.

I said, "If this is going to risk the life of Jordanians, forget diplomatic immunity. Go arrest them, right now." The intelligence services burst into Iraqi embassy housing and grabbed the military attaché and two of his accomplices. This created an uproar. The public did not know the evidence that we had seen of what the Iraqi regime was planning, and many were critical, saying, "How could you break into embassy property and arrest Iraqi diplomats?" I told them to trust me, that I was acting on the basis of good information and that Jordanian lives were in danger.

The next day the Iraqi ambassador came to see me. He was furious. "I've got a message from Saddam," he said. "He's really upset that you've done this."

"I am quite willing to come out publicly and say that I've arrested these three people because they were plotting to kill hundreds, if not thousands, of Jordanians," I said. "I am looking beyond the war, Your Excellency. I don't want to have to say anything now that would destroy the long-term relationship between Iraq and the Jordanian people. So please send this message back to Saddam: if this is how you want to do it, I will publicly reveal how your regime is trying to kill Jordanian civilians." The ambassador — to his credit — came back to me and assured me that he had sent my message back to Baghdad. "Problem solved," he said. The ambassador had told his Foreign Ministry that they had made a mess and that we would go public and cause an international incident if they continued to pursue it. So the issue died. We expelled the three men to Baghdad, and accusations from the Iraqi government stopped. At this point, they had more pressing concerns.

On March 28, after Friday prayers, thousands of demonstrators took to the streets across Jordan to protest the Iraq War. In Amman, a crowd of eight hundred people gathered near the Israeli embassy, chanting, "Our beloved Saddam, use your chemical weapons on the invaders!" They then tried to march on the embassy a few streets away, but the crowd was dispersed by Jordanian riot police, who fired live rounds over their heads.

Many of the demonstrators viewed the war as the West attacking the Arab and Muslim world, continuing a long history of violent Western interaction with our region. This perception had been strengthened when, shortly after the 9/11 attacks, President Bush referred to a "crusade" against terrorism. This unfortunate choice of words awakened in many Arabs memories of the violent invasions of the Middle Ages, and the Crusaders' bloody seizure of Jerusalem. Now, hundreds of years later, a Western army had again entered an Arab land. Some also believed that the United States was acting under the influence of Israel to destroy a strong Arab country, while the more cynical suspected that it wanted to replace Iraq's leader with somebody more friendly toward American oil companies.

Three days later a group of ninety-nine prominent Jordanians, including four former prime ministers, tried to ride this wave of public opinion and demanded that Jordan support Saddam in the war and do things I knew, and they knew, would not be in our national interests. However popular such rhetoric might be domestically, I did not have the luxury of making my decisions based on emotions. I had to look to the future and to Jordan's national interests once the fighting stopped. From my knowledge of Iraqi and Western forces, I thought it would be a pretty one-sided fight and would be over quickly. But others in Jordan were less certain.

The U.S. and British forces had some quick military successes, taking the southern town of Basra a few days into the conflict. But then the media, especially Arab satellite TV channels, began to report that they were facing difficulties. Their analysis was so convincing, bringing in retired generals to analyze the war's progress, that a lot of people, including many politicians, began to think the war would last a very long time, and even that Iraq had the upper hand. A week into the war, the U.S. advance on Baghdad was hampered by terrible dust storms. My wife had been watching television, which was reporting that the war was going badly for the Americans. But I knew that you did not get a good sense of a war from watching satellite television. I had traveled to Baghdad with my father before the first Gulf War and knew how the Iraqi regime had a tendency to overestimate its own military capabilities. I knew that the Iraqi army was no match for the United States and its allies, given their superior resources and military capabilities.

On April 9, U.S. forces captured Baghdad, and the world watched live as jubilant Iraqis toppled a statue of Saddam Hussein in Firdos Square. I felt a mixture of both sadness at the needless death and suffering the war had caused and hope as I looked at the many Iraqis celebrating the promise of a better future. When the statue fell, it was like a switch had been thrown across the Arab world. The images flashed on TV from the Arabian Gulf to Morocco and around the world. Even before it hit the ground, my phone began ringing. On the other end were many of the ninety-nine prominent Jordanians who had questioned our position. They were calling to congratulate me on "my wisdom and judgment" in keeping Jordan out of the conflict. "We knew Saddam would not last," they said. "We were with you all along." I was amazed how easily some of the elite would change their colors to win favor.

I was sure that the United States and its allies would win the war, but I had no idea how badly they would handle its aftermath.

# CHAPTER 20
## "WE WILL BE GREETED AS LIBERATORS"

Conventional wisdom in Washington held that removing Saddam Hussein and imposing a new Iraqi government would be as simple as replacing a lightbulb. In an interview shortly before the war, Vice President Dick Cheney said:

> I think things have gotten so bad inside Iraq, from the standpoint of the Iraqi people, my belief is we will, in fact, be greeted as liberators. . . . The read we get on the people of Iraq is there is no question but what they want to get rid of Saddam Hussein and they will welcome as liberators the United States when we come to do that.

Once the war ended, this rosy view began to look more and more misguided. "It's going to be a bloodbath," I had told my friends in America. In my conversations with friends in the region, we almost universally shared a sense of foreboding about the aftermath of the war in Iraq. I remember several conversations with Egyptian president Mubarak in which we both expressed concerns that the invasion would lead to unforeseen negative consequences that we would be dealing with for decades.

In June 2003, two months after the fall of Baghdad, Jordan hosted a meeting of the World Economic Forum at the Dead Sea, and during the conference I met L. Paul Bremer, the newly appointed head of the Coalition Provisional Authority (CPA), the interim Iraqi government established by the United States. The previous month, on arriving in Baghdad, Bremer had issued two now infamous orders: to pursue an aggressive de-Baathification policy, and to dissolve the Iraqi army.

I pleaded with Bremer not to dissolve the army, and warned him that it would blow up in all of our faces. I told him that I understood the rationale behind the process of de-Baathification, but that it needed to apply only to those at the top with blood on their hands. To be a taxi driver or a teacher in Saddam's Iraq, you had to be a member of the Baath Party. I said I hoped he understood that if he was going to de-Baathify across the board, he would be setting himself up for major resistance and would create a power vacuum that someone would have to fill.

The army was one of the only functioning institutions inside Iraq. Together with other security networks, it guaranteed Saddam's survival. But it was also in large part responsible for social stability. Disbanding it was crazy — like deciding to fire all the cops, firefighters, and ambulance drivers in New York City all at once because you do not like the mayor. You would have hundreds of thousands of people with military training and access to small arms and explosives, sitting at home with no jobs in a desperately poor and brutalized country that had just come through a war. Baathists, feeling vulnerable, would organize and strike back. How would these people feed their families? It was a recipe for anarchy and chaos.

"I know what I'm doing," Bremer said brusquely. "There's going to be some sort of compensation. I've got it all in hand, thank you very much."

But despite Bremer's supreme confidence, things started to fall apart quickly. The Sunnis felt isolated and threatened, because they believed they were being shut out of the new Iraqi government. They started organizing military operations against coalition forces.

At the same time, ideologically motivated Iraqi Islamists opened the door for foreign Arab jihadists. If anybody rejoiced at the chaos in Iraq after the American invasion, it was Al Qaeda, as they quickly realized that they could shift their operations from Afghanistan into the heart of the Arab world.

Although it is hard to determine the origin of these two policies — Bremer denied responsibility in his memoir and said they came from the White House — I believe the ideas originated from the Iraqi émigré politician Ahmad Chalabi and his supporters. When he lived in Jordan in the 1970s and 1980s, Chalabi was an active businessman and a close friend of Crown Prince Hassan. One of his most notorious ventures was the Petra Bank, founded in Jordan in 1977. In the late 1980s, the Petra Bank ran into financial trouble, and the government began to investigate, suspecting financial fraud. Investigators believed that Chalabi had been illegally taking funds from the bank. When they began closing in on him in 1989, he smuggled himself out of the country to Syria. He was tried in absentia and in 1992 was convicted of embezzling $70 million and sentenced to twenty-two years in prison. There is still an active warrant for his arrest in Jordan. After he left, his name was connected with the controversy surrounding the collapse of a Lebanese bank and a financial institution in Switzerland.

After an unsuccessful career as a business-man, Chalabi tried his hand at politics. During the 1990s he was one of the leaders of the Iraqi National Congress, the main opposition group dedicated to toppling Saddam Hussein. He was supported by the Clinton administration, and also became close to neoconservatives Richard Perle and Paul Wolfowitz. When Bush came to office in 2001, Chalabi increased his efforts to push his ideas for influence and cash. He is said to have secured substantial amounts of both from the U.S. State and Defense departments.

I warned President Bush about Chalabi when I saw him in 2002, telling him that he was the worst person possible to be giving advice to the United States. Bush said that he would "deal with Chalabi." But Chalabi's star continued to rise.

Chalabi's grandiose schemes may have been popular in Washington, but on the ground in Baghdad, a grim reality began to take hold. As one of the first Arab countries to reopen our embassy in Iraq, Jordan was soon drawn into the chaos. On August 7, 2003, a truck pulled up outside our embassy. As the driver walked away, the truck exploded, killing at least seventeen Iraqi civilians. None of our embassy staff were killed. Later investigation showed this to be a strike by the terrorist Abu Musab al-Zarqawi, who would later become the leader of a new group called Al Qaeda in Iraq. In pursuit of a wider goal, Zarqawi and his followers wanted to ride on a tide of violence and brutality, and struck at Jordan to discourage others from helping the nascent Iraqi government.

The looming chaos in post-invasion Iraq called for a coordinated approach by all of its neighbors. And one neighbor in particular was positioning itself to play a dominant role in Iraq's future. In early September 2003, I traveled to Tehran to meet with the Iranian leadership. This was the first trip to Iran by a Jordanian head of state since the Iranian Revolution in 1979. My father had been close to Shah Mohammad Reza Pahlavi, and I remember visiting Tehran as a young teenager. We went to a holiday camp on the Caspian and explored the resort island of Kish, in the Arabian Gulf.

I remembered Tehran from my childhood as a grand imperial city, edged by mountains like Amman, but as I drove into the city in 2003 I found it looking a bit run-down.

413

Little seemed to have changed since the revolution. I met Iran's president, Mohammad Khatami, at the Sadabad Palace northeast of the capital, and after inspecting the honor guard and the requisite formalities, we began to discuss business. Khatami was quite relaxed and jovial. He pointed to his defense minister, who was an Arab Iranian, and said jokingly, "This fellow is an Arab; we have to keep a close eye on him." We discussed possible areas of economic and cultural cooperation between Iran and Jordan. After the meeting was over, he took me on a tour of the Iranian defense industry.

The Iranians did have some serious business to conduct. Some Iranian officials wanted to reach out to the Americans and knew I would shortly be going on a scheduled visit to Washington. So they asked me to act as an intermediary. They said they wanted to discuss cooperation over the future of Iraq. They also said they were holding under house arrest or some kind of detention around sixty to seventy Al Qaeda members who had escaped from Afghanistan into Iran. They asked me to tell the Americans that they were ready to talk about handing over these individuals to U.S. forces in Afghanistan. They were also prepared to discuss their nuclear program, Afghanistan, and Iraq. I agreed to relay the message to President Bush.

The morning after my meeting with Khatami, I met with the supreme leader, Ayatollah Khamenei, the most powerful man in Iran. We pulled up to a walled compound and were handed over by our escort to the supreme leader's personal guard. Unsmiling, serious, and barefoot inside the compound, they led us to the room where we would meet Khamenei. In contrast to the grandeur of Sadabad Palace, the supreme leader's residence was austere, with a simple table and chairs and a few carpets.

While President Khatami had been open and friendly, Khamenei was reserved. "Welcome to Iran," he said as we shook hands. "As a Hashemite, you are very important in our branch of Islam."

We discussed common challenges facing Muslims and the need to coordinate our efforts. We each play a leadership role in our branch of Islam, and we spoke about the problem of the takfiris, extremists who denounce as infidels those who don't follow their rigid interpretation of Islam. Although our two countries had not been close, we had a common interest in combating the takfiris, who have been inciting sectarian strife throughout the Muslim world.

After the meeting with Khamenei ended, I returned to Amman, hoping that this visit would mark the start of improved relations between Jordan and Iran, not least around a common approach to the growing problems in Iraq. Relations did not improve, however. Differences in our positions on regional politics and the peace process, as well as Iran's interference in the affairs of the Arab countries, would prevent that from happening.

Since the election of Mahmoud Ahmadinejad in August 2005, Iran has been at the top of the agenda in many Western capitals. But it is too easy to blame a people for the actions of their government when in fact the two are quite separate. Iran is a great nation with a tremendous historical heritage and a remarkably educated and sophisticated population. Most Iranians feel no hatred toward America and the West and would like to see a peaceful resolution of the conflict between Israel and the Palestinians.

It is common in the West to portray the Iranian government as a single structure, with all elements following the same rationale and motivation for action. But the truth is that the Iranian political structure is complex and opaque, even to those of us in the region. The only certain truth about the Iranian government is that anybody who tries to give a simple explanation is certain to be wrong.

Rather than a monolith, Iran is a mosaic, formed of numerous interlocking political elements. There are those who are deeply religious, and whose motivation toward iconic Islamic causes, such as the liberation of Jerusalem from Israeli occupation, is sincere and deeply felt. But there are others who, acting out of political motives, adopt the banner of Jerusalem merely as a rallying cry for their own illegitimate purposes, exploiting the legitimate frustrations of young Arabs over continued occupation. Many people in Iran and the rest of the region are tired of this manipulation.

A few days after my visit to Tehran, I met with President Bush at Camp David. We drove out to the president's famous weekend retreat high in the mountains of northern Maryland on September 18, 2003. Outside the windows of the wooden lodge, the heavens darkened as Hurricane Isabel thundered inland from the Atlantic Ocean. I asked the president why, despite repeated promises that the money would stop, Chalabi was still being paid $350,000 a month by the U.S. Defense Department.

Bush, dressed casually in a gray jacket

417

and light blue shirt without a tie, was furious. He leaned across the wooden table and said, "You can piss on Chalabi." Members of my delegation were not exactly sure what the president meant, but they dutifully wrote down his comment in their notes of the meeting. There was an uncomfortable silence from the president's advisers, as his mood matched the skies outside.

We then began to discuss Israel and Palestine. Although this was the same spot where Barak and Arafat had come so close to an agreement only three years earlier, peace seemed farther away than ever. The road map, a concept that Jordan had put forward the previous year to provide a set of specific steps toward peace, now seemed to be in disarray.

But Bush continued to blame Arafat for the deadlock in the peace process. "The road map is darn specific!" he said, raising his voice. "Palestinians failed the first test. Arafat does not want peace."

Demonstrating that Sharon's campaign to link Israel's conflict with the Palestinians to the wider American "war on terror" had in large part succeeded, the president said he was still in a war frame of mind and that part of this war on terror is in the Palestinian territories. Stressing his view that Arafat was unable or unwilling to make peace, the president made it clear he believed that Arafat was a failed leader and said he would no longer deal with him. He would spend political capital on winners, not losers, he said. Then, angry at Arafat's inability to control Palestinian violence, he added, "What we asked of him is doable, and he did not do it!"

The U.S. administration seemed to have a very one-sided view of the situation. Bush was sincere, but appeared not to have been receiving the best, or most impartial, advice. I tried to give him a more comprehensive view of the situation. I defended Arafat and told him that Arafat was the leader of the Palestinian people. You may or may not like him, I said, but he is viewed by the Palestinian people as their legitimate representative.

Shifting gears, Bush asked about my recent trip to Iran. I told him that it had been positive, and relayed the Iranian offer to hand over the Al Qaeda prisoners they were holding and to embark on a wider, more comprehensive discussion on their nuclear program and on cooperation in Afghanistan and Iraq. He told me his staff would follow up. I never heard any more about the matter, but I know that custody of the Al Qaeda members, including a number of senior leaders, was never transferred.

Although we made good progress on several issues, I emerged from Camp David convinced that the peace process would not be moved forward this time around.

A few months later the Iranians would receive some welcome news from Baghdad regarding their old enemy, Saddam Hussein. On December 13, 2003, Saddam was captured by U.S. forces at a farmhouse near Tikrit, around one hundred miles north of Baghdad. The next day satellite news stations showed pictures of a bearded, disheveled Saddam and his underground hiding place. It was a surreal moment. Many Arabs felt let down, almost humiliated, by the way Saddam had capitulated so meekly. Even those who really hated him had expected him to face his enemies with courage and determination and to go out fighting, like his sons Uday and Qusay, who had been killed in July 2003 in a shootout with U.S. troops in Mosul, in northern Iraq. But when he was captured without a fight, his mythical, fearsome image was damaged.

I remember talking to the king of Saudi Arabia that day, and we were both shocked to see this man, who had been one of the most powerful leaders in the Middle East, hiding underground in a hole. It was humbling. Saddam Hussein had been a powerful Sunni Arab leader who had stood up to both the United States and Israel, and by doing so he had gained popularity throughout the region. I had met him in Baghdad with my father when he was at the height of his power. To see him diminished, with gray unkempt hair, blinking on television, was sobering. Those across the region who had looked to him as a modern-day Salaheddin felt badly let down.

But Saddam's capture did not bring an end to Iraq's troubles. For the most part, things continued to deteriorate. Some of the strife was caused by historic tensions and hatreds that had been brutally suppressed by Saddam's regime. But some of the problems that drove the insurgency were entirely of America's own making.

In late April 2004, the American television news program *60 Minutes* revealed that American troops had abused Iraqi prisoners at the Abu Ghraib military prison. The graphic images of hooded and shackled prisoners caused an uproar inside Iraq and across the region. On May 5, President Bush gave an interview to the Middle Eastern television station Al Arabiya in an effort to control the damage. "I want to tell the people of the Middle East that the practices that took place in that prison are abhorrent, and they don't represent America," he said.

The next day, May 6, I arrived in the United States for a previously scheduled visit to the White House, and the controversy was raging. Although the president had decried the actions at Abu Ghraib, the Arab world noted that he did not apologize for them. Bush took the meeting, accompanied by Condoleezza Rice and Donald Rumsfeld, his secretary of defense. After some pleasantries, he turned to me and said, "I'm really upset about Abu Ghraib. What do you think?"

Although we had our differences over policy, President Bush and I had by that point formed a strong personal rapport, which allowed me to speak candidly when needed. Some in the Middle East may be surprised to hear this, but in person he is quite different from the caricature painted by the media. He is a very sincere person who strongly believed that what he was doing was right. I think he was badly misled by some of his advisers, however. I knew he would want to hear the truth from me, even if it would upset some of his staff.

"Mr. President," I said, "you're the leader of the strongest and most powerful nation in the world. I think it is very easy from a position of strength to apologize, and I think an apology from you, because you are the president of the United States, would go a long way."

The president looked at me and scowled for a second, and then he said, "You're right." He turned to Condi and Rumsfeld and said, "I'm going to listen to my friend here." I guessed that some of his senior staff had been telling him not to make a public apology out of fear that it would make him seem weak. But there is also strength in humility.

After the meeting, we went outside the White House to the Rose Garden for a press conference. We stood side by side at podiums in the early afternoon sun as the president said:

> We also talked about what has been on the TV screens recently, not only in our own country, but overseas — the images of cruelty and humiliation. I told His Majesty as plainly as I could that the wrongdoers will be brought to justice, and that the actions of those folks in Iraq do not represent the values of the United States of America.
>
> I told him I was sorry for the humiliation suffered by the Iraqi prisoners, and the humiliation suffered by their families. I told

him I was equally sorry that people who have been seeing those pictures didn't understand the true nature and heart of America. I assured him Americans, like me, didn't appreciate what we saw, that it made us sick to our stomachs.

After the press conference I went to the State Department to meet with Secretary of State Colin Powell. We discussed Abu Ghraib again, and Powell said the pictures hurt the image of the United States all over the world, and even at home. He said these images created a major problem that the president knew he needed to deal with and do more about than just appear on Arab networks. This implicit criticism was only the most visible sign of the infighting that had begun to break out in the Bush administration.

On one side were the neocons — Paul Wolfowitz, Douglas Feith, and Elliott Abrams — and on the other the moderates, led by Powell and his deputy, Richard Armitage. Although I typically would not meet with Wolfowitz and the others in person, my senior staff in Washington, who did, told me that they were dogmatic and inflexible. Like many politicians who are ideologically driven, they had little time for compromises.

If you are dealing with a pragmatic decision-maker, there is scope for give-and-take. But if you are dealing with an ideologue, it can be very hard to find common ground.

My staff said Feith and Abrams were impossible to deal with. The minute they walked into the room there was a feeling that this would be yet another awful meeting. They acted as if they were superior to everyone else. They had a plan, and they would see it implemented — no matter what.

The next month, after a year in existence, the much-hated Coalition Provisional Authority (CPA) was finally dissolved, and Bremer handed over power to an Iraqi government headed by Ayad Allawi, a prominent Iraqi Shia politician, in anticipation of national elections scheduled for January 2005. Allawi was a strong leader who had a chance to succeed in Iraq. Educated, worldly, and well rounded, he believed in a unified Iraq, but because some people in Washington were still backing Ahmad Chalabi, he did not get the undivided support of the American government.

The know-it-all attitude among some in Washington was perfectly illustrated during a visit I made to the United States in September of the following year. While in

New York to attend the annual United Nations General Assembly meeting, I was invited to a dinner given by Lally Weymouth, a senior editor at *Newsweek* magazine and the daughter of the late Katharine Graham, publisher of the *Washington Post*. One of the other guests, as I recall it, a female American news anchor, asked whether I thought women's rights were better or worse in Iraq since the war. "They're ten times worse," I said. "When you had a secular regime under Saddam, men and women were pretty much equal." Liz Cheney, the vice president's daughter, who was also present, leaned over to Bassem Awadallah, my chief of the Royal Court, and told him that I should not say those kinds of things in public. She had a smile on her face, so he was not sure how serious she was.

The next day Bassem received an unexpected follow-up call from Liz Cheney, saying that she had discussed my comment with Paul Wolfowitz, who had recently become president of the World Bank, and they had both agreed that I should not be expressing such opinions. When Bassem told me about the conversation, I suggested that he tell Wolfowitz to get stuffed. What I had said over dinner was true. I was shocked that some members of the administration and their supporters seemed to feel that there could be no dissent on Iraq — and that in America, a country that prides itself on opinionated self-expression, they would try to muzzle inconvenient news.

I had been warned by others in Washington, including a prominent journalist who had covered the Middle East for years, to tread with caution. "You've got to be really careful with some in this administration, because they're vindictive," he told me.

Thankfully, there were still some people in D.C. who were more interested in results than ideology and petty politics. One was William Burns, the assistant secretary of state responsible for the Middle East. A fluent Arabic speaker, Bill had once been the U.S. ambassador to Jordan. At that time I was still in the army, and Rania and I had invited him and his wife to our home for dinner. A kind, soft-spoken, and gentle man, Bill is everything that you would want from a diplomat: worldly, nuanced, knowledgeable, and extremely intelligent. We have remained good friends ever since. Another person I came to know well was George Tenet, the CIA director. George had worked closely on the peace process, and subsequently developed a plan for a cease-fire and security arrangements between the Israelis and Palestinians. He was later used as a scapegoat for some American policy failings, but I always found him considerate of our views and as dedicated to finding an equitable resolution to the Palestinian-Israeli issue as anyone in Washington.

George and Bill both helped me to navigate the rough waters of Washington politics, giving me an inside sense of when to try to push policy in a better direction and when to hold my breath.

*With Hussein, my first child, in the Azraq area in eastern Badia observing a presentation by the Desert (Badia) Police in 2001.* (YOUSEF ALLAN / ROYAL HASHEMITE COURT)

*With my daughter Salma during an army-themed garden party at our house in Amman to celebrate Hussein's seventh birthday on June 28, 2001.* (NASSER AYOUB / ROYAL HASHEMITE COURT)

*On a pilgrimage to the Holy City of Mecca in 2001.* (YOUSEF ALLAN / ROYAL HASHEMITE COURT)

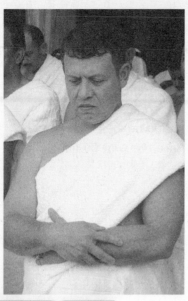

*Taking Rania, Hussein, Iman, and Salma for a motorcycle ride in Aqaba in April 2001. We often retreat to Aqaba, a resort town on the Red Sea, to relax and escape from the pressures of Amman.* (MAHER ATTAR / TRAVEL CHANNEL, LLC)

*At the beach in Aqaba on another visit in 2001 with Hussein, Iman, and Salma.* (TROY WORD / ROYAL HASHEMITE COURT)

*Teaching Hussein to ride a motorbike in 2003. My father and I shared a love of motorcycles and fast cars, and I proposed to Rania on the Tal Al Rumman hill, where I used to take part in hill climbs in my racing days.* (YOUSEF ALLAN / ROYAL HASHEMITE COURT)

*Admiring the view with Rania on the beach in Aqaba in 2004. Neither one of us imagined, when we were married, how much our lives would change. We've done our best to give our children a normal experience of childhood, and Rania has become a powerful advocate for women in the region and the world.* (YOUSEF ALLAN / ROYAL HASHEMITE COURT)

Meeting with President George W. Bush at the White House on August 1, 2002. My brother Ali is seated on the left between Field Marshal Sa'ad Khair and then chief of the Royal Court Fayez Tarawneh. To the right are National Security Adviser Condoleezza Rice and White House Chief of Staff Andy Card. After this meeting, I knew war was inevitable. (YOUSEF ALLAN / ROYAL HASHEMITE COURT)

The Middle East Peace Summit at Aqaba, with Palestinian president Mahmoud Abbas, U.S. president George W. Bush, and Israeli prime minister Ariel Sharon, June 4, 2003. (YOUSEF ALLAN / ROYAL HASHEMITE COURT)

*In Tehran with Iranian president Mohammad Khatami in early September 2003. Everyone in the region recognized, after the Iraq war, that Iran would play an important role going forward. This was the first visit to Iran by a Jordanian head of state since the Iranian Revolution in 1979.* (YOUSEF ALLAN / ROYAL HASHEMITE COURT)

*At Camp David with Rania and President and Mrs. Bush, September 18, 2003. I brought a message to President Bush from President Khatami, but the discussions that the Bush administration had established with the Iranians in 2000 broke down soon after that.* (YOUSEF ALLAN / ROYAL HASHEMITE COURT)

*Surveying the destruction caused by a terrorist attack on the Radisson SAS Hotel in Amman on November 10, 2005. I was visiting Kazakhstan when suicide bombers blew themselves up simultaneously at three different hotels, and I flew back as soon as I heard the news. The attacks had been planned in Iraq and I pledged to hunt down the mastermind, Abu Musab al-Zarqawi. He was killed in a joint U.S.-Jordanian operation on June 7, 2006.* (YOUSEF ALLAN / ROYAL HASHEMITE COURT)

*Greeting a Jordanian woman during a visit to a Bedouin tribe in the south in 2005.* (YOUSEF ALLAN / ROYAL HASHEMITE COURT)

*At the airport in Riyadh, where I was received by King Abdullah of Saudi Arabia, in 2007. As a boy I visited Prince Abdullah with my father at his home in Jeddah. Now, years later, we work together closely in the interest of both our countries.* (YOUSEF ALLAN / ROYAL HASHEMITE COURT)

*Students hurrying to class at King's Academy in Madaba, Jordan. Modeled on Deerfield Academy, which I attended as a boy, King's opened its doors in 2007. It is the first coeducational boarding school in the Middle East. All proceeds from this book will go to providing scholarships for needy students from Jordan and across the Middle East.* (KING'S ACADEMY)

*Driving Senator Barack Obama to the airport after his visit to Amman on July 22, 2008.* (NASSER AYOUB / ROYAL HASHEMITE COURT)

*In Baghdad in August 2008. Security was tight; I postponed an earlier visit on learning shortly before I was scheduled to go that an Al Qaeda assassination team had been sent to Baghdad to welcome me. Jordan was the first Arab country to reestablish its embassy in Baghdad after the war, and the embassy was attacked by different sides.* (YOUSEF ALLAN / ROYAL HASHEMITE COURT)

*With my daughter Iman, after she won a medal at the King Abdullah II Award for Physical Fitness in 2008. Tens of thousands of students compete for this award, which I sponsor to encourage sports among students.* (YOUSEF ALLAN / ROYAL HASHEMITE COURT)

*Sharing a joke with Hashem and Rania in 2009.* (SVEN ARNSTEIN / ROYAL HASHEMITE COURT)

*Preparing to receive Pope Benedict XVI during his visit to Jordan in 2009.* (YOUSEF ALLAN / ROYAL HASHEMITE COURT)

# PART V

# CHAPTER 21
## MY ISLAM

I remember the first time I saw Mecca as if it were yesterday. I was almost fifteen when I accompanied my father on Umra (the lesser pilgrimage, which, unlike Hajj, can be made at any time of the year). Years later I performed the Hajj, one of the five Pillars of Islam. There were well over a million pilgrims that year, each clothed only in a white sheet tied around the waist with a piece of rope. I felt an amazing sense of community and brotherhood as I stood with these pilgrims gathered from all over the globe, all dressed alike, signifying our equality before God.

We performed the tawaf, walking counterclockwise round the ancient Kaaba, the most sacred site in all Islam, and the place toward which all Muslims turn when they pray. My father had taught me about our ancestry, and the historical role the Hashemites had performed as guardians of Mecca, but to actually be there and to touch the Kaaba left me speechless. I sat down, humbled and overwhelmed, waiting to begin the afternoon prayer. I could hear a faint hum, and felt that I was present before God.

Islam is a religion that requires believers to perform daily rituals that act as a framework for the exercise of faith. But its deeper meaning lies in the spiritual values it awakens within its faithful, and the way believers come to manifest these values in daily life. The five Pillars of Islam consist of the Shahadatayn, or the acknowledgment of God and of Mohammad as God's messenger; prayer, which Muslims are instructed to perform five times a day, symbolizing their attachment to God; Al Zakat, giving alms to the destitute and the poor, a sign of detachment from the world; fasting in the holy month of Ramadan, to reveal detachment from the ego; and performing the Hajj, a pilgrimage to Mecca.

I am troubled by the way in which many today view Islam, as a strict system of rules, instead of reflecting on the deeper meanings of our faith. We should think about how we can help a neighbor who is in trouble, a colleague at work who needs our advice, or a family member who needs our love and support. I feel at peace when I say my prayers, but I am also comforted when I can help others and show compassion and kindness. Islam stands for justice, equality, fairness, and the opportunity to live a meaningful and good life. These virtues have unfortunately been corroded by empty adherence to reactionary interpretations of our sacred texts.

When I pray, I often ask for protection for my loved ones and family, my government, my soldiers, and my country. As the head of a country, I pray for my people, for improvement in their standard of living and health. Sometimes I pray for specific things, like creating more jobs for young people. And sometimes I even pray for rain.

One of the things in the last two decades that has saddened me the most is the misinterpretation of a great faith as a result of the misguided actions of a very few. An example is the meaning of the term "jihad." Many associate this term with violence and war, yet jihad literally means "struggle" and refers primarily to the internal struggle to better oneself. It is a struggle for self-improvement but also a wider struggle to improve the lives of others around you. Victory does not come as the result of a single battle, but as the result of many small triumphs throughout the day, some of which may be so small as to be almost invisible to others.

I am pained by the twisting of my religion by a small band of misguided fanatics. Such people embrace a deviant form of Islam. While claiming to act in its name, they are in reality just murderers and thugs. They constitute an unrepresentative minority of the 1.57 billion Muslims in the world, but they have had a disproportionate impact on how the faith is perceived. These people are called takfiris, which in Arabic means "those who accuse others of being heretics." They rely on ignorance, resentment, and a distorted promise of achieving martyrdom to spread their ideology, turning their backs on over a thousand years of Quranic scholarship and commentary in the name of what they presume to be the authentic ways of seventh-century Arabia.

Takfiris are a small part of a larger fundamentalist movement, the Salafi movement. Salafi ideology (Salafi in Arabic means "going back to the past") proposes to go back to the "fundamentals" of the early faith, but the majority of Salafis do not condone terrorism or the killing of innocent civilians. They declare total war on their enemies and believe that people who kill themselves in suicide attacks go straight to heaven. For them there are no limits on how war can be waged against their enemies, and they disregard traditional Islam's moral codes, enshrined in the Quran and in the Hadiths. Almost all Muslims are aware of the tradition set in the early days of Islam in the seventh century by the first Muslim Caliph, Abu Baker Al Sediq, whose instructions to his armies were to not kill women or children or elderly people and to not cut any tree that bears fruit. In what can be considered the Muslim "Geneva Conventions," Abu Baker's first act as Caliph said:

Do not betray; do not carry grudges; do not deceive; do not mutilate; do not kill children; do not kill the elderly; do not kill women. Do not destroy beehives or burn them; do not cut down fruit-bearing trees; do not slaughter sheep, cattle, or camels, except for food. You will come upon people who spend their lives in monasteries, leave them to what they have dedicated their lives.

The actions of the takfiris have nothing to do with Islam and its message. Islam celebrates life; they seek to destroy it.

Takfiris have turned their back on this

tradition of clemency and compassion. They aim to overthrow governments across the Arab world by violent means in order to declare a worldwide "Islamic" republic. For the sake of what they imagine to be Islam, they are killing Muslims and corrupting Islamic ethics, and they also seek to destroy the world embraced by 99.99 percent of all Muslims.

The takfiri movement, which can be traced back to the revival of a doctrinaire jihadi tendency in Egypt in the 1970s and had connections to the 1979 uprising in Mecca, would spawn many violent terrorist groups, including Al Qaeda. Takfiris are drawn to wars where Muslims are under attack, and they swarmed into Afghanistan. Many, including Osama bin Laden, learned about war, strategy, death, and terror while fighting the Soviet occupation forces in the 1980s. After that conflict ended in the early 1990s, large groups of these fighters returned to their native lands, bringing their new "skills" with them.

In Jordan we have been following the activities of these takfiris for many years. A large number of them flocked to Afghanistan in the 1980s and to Bosnia and Chechnya in the 1990s. After France and the UK, Jordan was the largest contributor of troops to the UN forces in the former Yugoslavia, sending three battalions, or over three thousand troops, from 1993 to 1996. A Jordanian general even commanded UN forces in Croatia. We saw takfiri fighters coming to take part in the conflict, and we knew we were facing a new and lethal combination of nationalism, religious extremism, and violence.

Along with veterans of Afghanistan who returned to Jordan and were linked to the so-called Prophet Mohammad's Army, we also had to cope with a group of fighters returning from Chechnya. Jordan is home to a sizable community of Chechens, and some of these, in addition to other Jordanians, went to support their kin in what they saw as a jihad against the Russians. So in the 1990s we faced a new problem in the form of highly trained mujahideen fighters who had come home from Afghanistan and Chechnya. Unfortunately, some groups knew all too well how to use their skills, and they began carrying out terrorist attacks throughout the region.

When these takfiris began to unleash a more wide-ranging campaign of terror at the beginning of the twenty-first century, we knew exactly who we were dealing with. Their brutality came as a shock to many in the West and prompted some people to lump all Muslims in with them, using terms such as "Islamo-fascism" or "Islamic extremists." But these labels insult the faith and intelligence of 23 percent of the world's population. I repeatedly tell my friends in the West, "Do not be taken in by their pretense of religion. These people are murderers, pure and simple. Be careful not to paint their deeds with such a broad brush that you would seem to include the entire Muslim world."

The first time I was personally threatened by Al Qaeda was in the summer of 2000. I had decided to take a short vacation with my family, and we had chosen the Greek islands. On June 22, 2000, I flew from Amman to Rhodes with my son Hussein, who was then five, and my daughter Iman, then three. Rania, who was pregnant with Salma, was scheduled to join us in Greece the next day. Also with me were my brother Ali, who was responsible for my personal security, and two of my sisters.

As we flew into Diagoras airport on Rhodes, I looked down at the rocky mountains and ancient buildings below. Famous as the site of one of the original Seven Wonders of the World, the Colossus of Rhodes, a gigantic statue that once stood near the harbor, this historic island had not been immune to the conflicts of the Middle East. Part of the Byzantine Empire, it was conquered by the Muslim warrior Muawiyah I in the seventh century and recaptured for the Byzantines in the First Crusade four centuries later. It was ruled after that by a fierce band of warrior knights, who were driven out in the sixteenth century by the Ottoman emperor Suleiman the Magnificent. In the twentieth century the island had been the scene of peace negotiations between my great-grandfather, Abdullah I, and the leaders of Israel, Egypt, Lebanon, and Syria. The talks resulted in the armistice agreements of 1949 that produced a cease-fire between the newly formed state of Israel and its Arab neighbors.

We drove from the airport to the harbor, where I had arranged to borrow a yacht from a Saudi friend, a beautiful 177-foot craft with a dark blue hull and a white superstructure. We set sail that afternoon, gliding across the clear blue water of the Mediterranean, followed at a discreet distance by a Greek coast guard vessel. Since we would have to pick up Rania from the same spot the next day, we decided not to go far and sailed around the coast to the town of Lindos.

As we approached the harbor I saw a cluster of white houses huddled around the base of a massive rock, with an ancient acropolis perched at the top. A few people gathered as our yacht pulled up to the dock. We spent a peaceful evening in this small island town. In the morning we went back to pick up Rania.

We had a few hours to wait, so Ali and I left the children with their aunts, rented Harley-Davidson motorbikes, and set off to explore the island. We drove around the dusty roads and small villages and got back just as Rania arrived. We set sail again not long after that, heading for Halki, a small island with just three hundred inhabitants. We had planned to sail for two days through the Greek islands, stopping at Symi, Tilos, and Nisyros before arriving at Santorini, famous for its black volcanic beaches and dazzling white houses.

Around five o'clock in the afternoon I was relaxing with my wife and young children on deck, enjoying the beautiful scenery, when a call came from Amman. I went belowdecks to the communications center and picked up the telephone. On the other end was the head of intelligence. "We have received reports that a group of Al Qaeda assassins are planning to attack your boat when you arrive in Santorini," he said. "You have to turn around immediately."

He told me that the terrorists intended to strike our yacht with rocket-propelled grenades, and said they might be planning a suicide attack, which would involve drawing up alongside the yacht and blowing up their boat to destroy the one carrying me and my family. (This technique was used some four months later, on October 12, when suicide bombers attacked the destroyer USS *Cole* in the port of Aden, in Yemen, killing seventeen sailors.)

As a husband and father, I was furious that these terrorists had threatened my family. Although my first instinct was to fight back, I agreed with my brother Ali that it would be wisest to turn the boat around and get out of there as quickly as possible.

We did not want to cause a panic onboard, so we had to come up with a good reason for the sudden change of plan. As Rania was pregnant, we told the crew that she was having complications and that we would have to cancel the cruise and return to Rhodes. We alerted the airport, and our plane was waiting on the tarmac when we reached the harbor. Once we were airborne, I called the head of intelligence and told him to inform the Greek security services of what he knew. We never found out how Al Qaeda discovered I was in Greece; our best guess was that a local informant had passed on intelligence. Because of Jordan's moderation and its active role in pursuing regional peace and promoting a culture of tolerance among members of different civilizations and faiths, I was viewed by Al Qaeda as a threat.

By this time we had been fighting Al Qaeda for several years, working with our allies to stop their plots across the region, and this may have led to their plot to kill me. It was not personal; they were trying to strike at a larger target. The Hashemite lineage has always commanded respect across the Arab and Muslim world, but our traditional moderation, coupled with our openness to the West, has often made us a target of extremists. By killing me they hoped to kill ninety years of Hashemite rule in Jordan, and more than a thousand years of leadership in Arabia. Part of Al Qaeda's agenda is to overthrow all Arab regimes and replace them with its fanatic and unorthodox vision of government.

The seeds of Al Qaeda's violent radicalism were planted in the region in the turbulent year of 1979, when three events took place that would echo through the decades. In January the shah of Iran fled the developing revolution and was replaced by Ayatollah Khomeini, who gave birth to the Islamic Republic of Iran. Iran's Islamic Revolution inspired and energized radicals throughout the region. Then, on November 20, several hundred radicals seized control of the Grand Mosque in Mecca. The capture of Islam's most holy site by a group of armed extremists stunned the Muslim world. Their leader, a Saudi named Juhayman al-Otaibi, claimed that the Saudi government was corrupt and un-Islamic, and that the Mahdi, a foretold and awaited Islamic leader and descendant of the Prophet Mohammad, had returned to take over the country. The rebels were eventually driven from the mosque and Juhayman and many of his coconspirators were publicly beheaded. The rebellion was over. But its implications lingered on.

One radical Islamist inspired by Juhayman's actions was the Palestinian Isam Muhammad Taher Barqawi, better known as Abu Muhammad al-Maqdisi, who would later repeat many of Juhayman's criticisms of the Saudi and other Arab governments. Born in the West Bank, Maqdisi spent time in Afghanistan in the late 1980s, and as a leading theorist he later would become a key figure in the jihadi Salafi movement in Jordan and would mentor Abu Musab al-Zarqawi, leading him on the path toward using brutal violence in the name of religion.

As the siege of Mecca ended, in December 1979, the third momentous event of the year occurred: Soviet tanks rolled into Afghanistan. This attack on a Muslim country energized fighters across the entire Muslim world. Some wanted Jordan to get involved. An American friend who recently had retired from the armed forces came to see me, saying he had just returned from Afghanistan and wanted Jordan to train a group of mujahideen fighters. I told him it was not my decision to make; I was just a junior officer. But I would pass the request on to my father.

My father said, "Absolutely not." He felt mixing religious zeal with cold war politics was a very dangerous thing to do. He also felt that getting involved in this conflict would set us up against Russia, something he did not believe would serve the interests of Jordan.

One Muslim group at the forefront of the war in Afghanistan was the Salafi movement. Mainstream Sunni and Shia believers base their interpretation of Islam on a deep historical tradition of scholarship and learning and a corpus of grammatical, linguistic, and etymological analysis. In this tradition, Muslim religious leaders, known as imams, spend years, even decades, studying over a thousand years of Muslim scholarship. When they issue religious edicts or judicial opinions, known as fatwas, they generally offer a nuanced interpretation of Islamic thought, based on the wisdom of those who have gone before. But Salafi leaders disregard this tradition of learning and do not accept a plurality of scholarship in Islamic thought. Instead, they insist that they have a privileged understanding of Islam based on their own interpretation of the Quran. One of the problems with this approach is that it does not contain the internal judicial checks and balances of the mainstream faith, and it is not accepting of other learned opinions. In the wrong hands, this can be very dangerous.

The takfiris take this exclusivism further and use it to justify their distorted version of Islam. They believe they have the right to kill heretics, and to denounce as such those who disagree with their doctrines. They would kill whenever and wherever they can.

Early in the morning of October 28, 2002, Laurence Foley, a senior official for the U.S. Agency for International Development

(USAID), stepped out of his white limestone house in an Amman suburb, heading for work. As he walked toward his car a gunman jumped out from behind the car and shot him eight times with a 7mm pistol. The assassin fled to a waiting getaway car, leaving Foley's wife to discover his body lying in a pool of blood.

The head of the intelligence service called me and said, "There's just been an assassination of an American diplomat." I was furious that such a terrible thing could happen to a guest in our country and ordered immediate action to find the culprits.

The next day I went to the U.S. embassy to pay my condolences to Foley's widow, Virginia. I told her we would find her husband's killer. Two months later, in December 2002, Jordanian security forces arrested the gunman, a Libyan, and the driver of the getaway car, a Jordanian.

As our security forces investigated further, we found that the plot had been directed from outside Jordan and that the mastermind was Abu Musab al-Zarqawi. Following a lengthy investigation and trial, in the spring of 2004 a Jordanian court sentenced eight men to death for the killing of Laurence Foley, six in absentia, including Zarqawi. The two men who were in Jordanian custody, the gunman and the driver, were subsequently executed.

Terrible as this act was, it was simply the prelude to a much larger wave of violence that was soon to crash over the Middle East. In early April 2004 in Irbid, a town close to the Syrian border, Jordanian security forces intercepted three trucks filled with explosives. The intelligence services scrambled to uncover who was behind the shipment and what their intentions were. We were fortunate to discover that one of the plotters, a Jordanian named Azmi Jayousi, was still in the country, hiding out in a flat in the Marka neighborhood of downtown Amman with an unknown number of coconspirators. I ordered a Special Forces team to get Jayousi and, if possible, take him alive. We had to know if his cell was acting alone or if there were others waiting to strike.

Jayousi was holed up in a residential area next to a school. The team decided to operate at night to reduce the risk of civilians getting caught up in the fight. At two in the morning on April 20, 2004, a team from Battalion 71 assembled in the street below the flat. Highly trained counterterrorist soldiers, they were accompanied by regular police.

One of the policemen knocked on the

door and was greeted with a volley of machine-gun fire. Six commandos stormed into the apartment, returning fire and killing the terrorist who was shooting at them. A second team rushed into the flat after that and captured the heavily armed Jayousi alive, along with his wife and three children. They found explosives, thousands of dollars and Jordanian dinars, and several fake passports.

Under questioning, Jayousi revealed that the ringleader was Abu Musab al-Zarqawi, whom he first met when they were fighting in Afghanistan. He revealed that there were two more cells still in Amman, planning more attacks. Jayousi did not know where the second cell was, but a quick-thinking Special Operations commander asked him to call its leader and set up a meeting. The Special Forces team set off to intercept the leader of the second cell. They grabbed him in broad daylight, and he led them to his safe house, where they captured the leader of the last cell.

A few days later, Jordanians watched in disbelief and horror as the terrorists revealed the details of their plot in a televised confession. They had planned to mix conventional explosives with deadly chemicals and attack the U.S. embassy, the prime minister's office, and the headquarters of the General Intelligence Department (GID), the internal intelligence service. Trained in explosives in one of bin Laden's camps in Afghanistan, Jayousi had developed a technique for mixing concentrated oxygen with ground-up black cumin seeds to create a substance with greater explosive power than TNT. He hoped to kill many thousands of people.

A few days later, on April 29, around one hundred thousand Jordanians, including my wife, Rania, marched on the streets of Amman to protest. Chanting, "No to terrorists in Jordan," and beating drums, the demonstrators marched to the gates of Parliament, where they burned pictures of bin Laden, Zarqawi, and Jayousi and his accomplices.

The subsequent trial was chaotic, with the terrorists disrupting the proceedings and refusing to recognize the authority of the court. At one point Jayousi took off his slippers and threw them at the judge, yelling that Abu Musab al-Zarqawi would chop off his head and calling those assembled "God's enemies."

When the trial concluded, Jayousi and his fellow plotters were sentenced to death, and Zarqawi was once again sentenced to death in absentia. When the verdict was read aloud, one of the terrorists shouted out, "Bin Laden's organization is rising, and we will be back!"

# CHAPTER 22
## JORDAN'S 9/11

November 9, 2005, was supposed to be the happiest day of Nadia Alami's life. That evening she was to marry her longtime sweetheart, Ashraf Da'as, at the Radisson SAS Hotel in Amman. The young couple had met three years before while working at a local hospital, and had quickly fallen in love. Their families and friends had come from around the globe and gathered at the hotel for the wedding. At around nine o'clock, the bride and groom walked through the lobby, past the cheering and clapping guests. Nadia wore a beautiful white dress with a flowing veil, and Ashraf a dark suit and red tie.

They had been married less than an hour and were about to celebrate the beginning of their life together. But Abu Musab al-Zarqawi had other plans.

Two Iraqi suicide bombers, a husband-and-wife team wearing explosive vests packed with ball bearings under their clothing, had infiltrated the wedding party and were mingling with the guests, each in a different corner of the room. As Nadia and Ashraf approached the door, the band struck up a tune.

Then the male bomber detonated his vest. The ball bearings shot across the ballroom with deadly force, killing the father of the bride outright and mortally wounding the father of the groom. The female bomber tried to detonate her vest, but it failed to go off, and she fled.

Twenty-seven guests were killed, including sixteen of Ashraf's relatives. Both the bride and groom lost their fathers.

At exactly the same time, suicide bombers struck at two other nearby hotels, the Grand Hyatt and the Days Inn, killing thirty-three more people. In all, sixty people lost their lives that night, thirty-six of them Jordanian. Among those killed was Moustapha Akkad, a prominent Syrian-American film-maker who produced the movie *Mohammad: Messenger of God,* depicting the early days of Islam, though he is probably better known to U.S. audiences for producing some of the *Halloween* horror movies.

When the attack took place I was in Kazakhstan on an official visit. We had just finished dinner when a call came in for me from Amman. As soon as I heard the news, I got a cold feeling in the pit of my stomach. In our battle against the takfiris I had always feared that, sooner or later, we would be attacked. But nothing could have prepared me for this.

I excused myself and immediately called for my plane. It was an agonizing trip home. We arrived in Jordan around five o'clock the next morning, and I went directly to the sites of the attacks. When I saw the chaos and devastation, my sadness turned to anger. "How could they do this to us?" I thought. I was furious. These murderers had killed innocent people at a wedding, and as the head of state it was my duty to protect them. I was determined to find those responsible. I paid my condolences to grieving family members and went to several hospitals to visit the wounded. One of the victims was the son of a close friend of mine.

To a large country like the United States, sixty people may not sound like very many, but to Jordan it was a devastating blow, the equivalent of losing three thousand people in a single attack on America. The psychological impact on average Jordanians was dramatic. It turned the population decisively against Al Qaeda and their like. In Jordan, and across much of the rest of the world, when we write a date, we write the day before the month. So the date of the attack, November 9, was 9/11. And in many ways it was as much of a watershed for Jordan as 9/11 was for the United States.

The leader of Al Qaeda in Iraq, Abu Musab al-Zarqawi, issued a statement taking responsibility for the bombings. "After studying and observing the targets," he said, "the places of execution were chosen to be hotels which the tyrant of Jordan has turned into a backyard for the enemies of Islam, such as the Jews and Crusaders." But far from targeting the enemies of Islam, as the terrorists claimed, they had indiscriminately murdered dozens of innocent Jordanians and other innocent people of different nationalities.

The people of Jordan did not accept Zarqawi's hateful attack. That afternoon, a group of angry protesters gathered outside the Radisson Hotel waving Jordanian flags and chanting, "Death to Zarqawi!" For nights on end young Jordanians held vigils and said prayers.

I was extremely angry and said in an address to the nation on November 10, "Let it be clear to everyone that we will pursue these terrorists and those who aid them. We will reach them wherever they are, pull them

from their lairs, and submit them to justice."
We had a policy in Jordan of not interfering
in the internal affairs of other countries, but
that was about to change. I resolved that
from now on, if we learned about a terrorist
group that was planning to target us hiding in another country, we would hit them
before they hit us. I gathered together our
intelligence service, the military, and the
political leadership and said, "We're going
on the offensive. What Zarqawi did was rep-
rehensible. The gloves are off, and I want
you to get him." We reached out to the Iraqi
tribes to see if we could get more information. If the Iraqi government was willing to
help us, fine. But if not, we were prepared to
act alone.

Iraq was a closed country under Saddam
Hussein, and our intelligence services had
not been able to operate easily there. After
the U.S.-led invasion, when things started
to fall apart, it took us a little while to get
our people inside. We knew Zarqawi was in
Iraq. But initially we did not have the capability to move against him. Now we began
aggressively to move into Iraq. We began to
attach teams of Jordanian officers to American Special Forces units. Jordanians had a
better understanding of the mannerisms of
takfiris and were thus able to identify sus-

pects more efficiently. Many takfiris have a distinctive manner of dress and behavior, and we helped the Americans understand what to look for.

Zarqawi had said that this was an attack against the Jordanian regime. But it was not, and people in Jordan clearly saw that killing guests at a wedding was an act of savage barbarity, not a political gesture. What Zarqawi had done was to declare war on Jordan. Now we were coming for him.

Zarqawi was born Ahmed Fadil Nazzal Khalaylah and grew up in the town of Zarqa, seventeen miles northeast of Amman. He was a thug and petty criminal and drifted until his early twenties, when he headed to Afghanistan to join the war against the occupying Soviet troops. Arriving just as the Russians were leaving in 1989, he adopted the nom de guerre of "al-Zarqawi," literally meaning "the one from Zarqa," and met Osama bin Laden and other radicals. On returning to Jordan in the early 1990s he set up a local terrorist group called Bay'at al-Emam, but before he could carry out any attacks he was arrested and sentenced to life imprisonment.

In prison, Zarqawi met the leading thinker of the radical takfiri movement, Abu Muhammad al-Maqdisi, who encouraged his violent desires. But Maqdisi later started to criticize Zarqawi and the two men fell out. In what would prove to be a costly mistake, Zarqawi was released from prison in 1999, as part of a general amnesty declared shortly after I became king. It was not long before he headed back to Afghanistan, where he received further funding and encouragement from bin Laden. Following the U.S. invasion of Afghanistan in October 2001, he returned to the Middle East to continue his plotting.

Zarqawi settled into the Kurdish areas in northern Iraq, where he linked up with a local terrorist group, Ansar al-Islam, with strong ties to Al Qaeda. Working with this local group and with a gang of Al Qaeda fighters who had come with him from Afghanistan, he and his men began experimenting with poisons, including cyanide and ricin, testing them on animals to make sure they worked. He began sending terrorists from his camp on missions to attack targets throughout Europe, including Italy, Germany, and the United Kingdom. Many were subsequently arrested and confessed to Zarqawi's involvement. Zarqawi wanted to expand his reach and influence. Little did he know that a much larger opportunity was about to present itself.

When the Americans invaded Iraq in 2003, Al Qaeda was dancing in the streets. Osama bin Laden was delighted, because he knew that with the instability that would inevitably follow, his supporters would be able to parachute into the heartland of the Arab world and set up a base. But bin Laden was not the only one to spot the opportunities for mayhem. Seeking to step into the vacuum created by the invasion, Zarqawi expanded his own activities. He became increasingly vicious in the methods he used and began to break all boundaries, seeking political influence through extreme violence.

On May 11, 2003, a video titled "Sheikh Abu Musab Zarqawi Slaughters an American Infidel with His Hands and Promises Bush More" was posted on a militant Web site. The video showed a young American civilian contractor, Nicholas Berg, wearing an orange jumpsuit and kneeling in front of five men dressed in black, their faces covered by ski masks and head scarves. The men read a statement, and then one of them beheaded Berg with a knife, yelling, "God is great!"

That was the moment when Zarqawi and his men moved from being barbarians to animals. It was outrageously disgusting, and I could not see how they could pose as defenders of anything, let alone Islam. Zarqawi continued his atrocities, bombing Shia holy places in an attempt to stoke the flames of civil war and beheading several more unfortunate civilians.

In October 2004, in a statement posted on an extremist Web site, Zarqawi proclaimed that he was merging his terror group with Al Qaeda, saying, "We announce that the One God and Jihad group, its prince and its soldiers, has pledged allegiance to the sheikh of the holy warriors, Osama bin Laden." After that he increasingly targeted Jordan. In 2004 and 2005 our security services foiled over 150 attempted attacks by Zarqawi's Al Qaeda group and other takfiri extremists. But we could not stop them all. In August 2005, members of Al Qaeda in Iraq crept into Jordan and from the southern port of Aqaba launched a rocket attack against an American warship. And in November Zarqawi's suicide bombers struck the three hotels in Amman. In addition to being an atrocity, this was a major tactical blunder.

In many other capital cities in the Middle East, luxury hotels are used mainly by foreigners, Western businessmen, and visiting government officials. And so by bombing a hotel, Zarqawi probably aimed to kill Americans or Israelis. But in Jordan, five-star hotels are frequented by our own people much more than by foreigners. Even the waiters are likely to be Jordanians rather than foreign workers. So the attacks provided a wake-up call. Stung by the outpouring of rage, Zarqawi decided to change tack. In an audiotape released the following week, he threatened me personally, saying, "Your star is fading. You will not escape your fate, you descendant of traitors. We will be able to reach your head and chop it off."

That winter and the following spring of 2006, Jordanian intelligence operatives and agents flooded into Iraq, searching for information that might lead us to Zarqawi's hideout. They soon developed a network of sources and informants. While looking for clues, we exchanged information with a Sunni tribe with links to the insurgents. In April 2006, Zarqawi released an online propaganda video, and our analysts were able roughly to identify his location inside Iraq by analyzing the background scenery. We also recruited an informant in Zarqawi's inner circle, who would in time reveal a crucial detail. He was in contact with three of Zarqawi's most trusted couriers, who would meet the terrorist in person to receive and deliver secret messages.

Working closely with the Americans, we

came tantalizingly close several times. On one occasion, Zarqawi was alerted by the sound of approaching Bradley armored vehicles and fled on a moped as American troops arrived. Another time, he jumped out a window and escaped. But we were getting closer.

In May 2006, we learned from the Americans that Zarqawi was planning to meet with his spiritual adviser, Sheikh Abdel-Rahman. We began to monitor the sheikh's movements, hoping he would lead our men to Zarqawi.

On June 7, American forces tracked the sheikh to a house outside Baqubah, thirty miles northeast of Baghdad, and placed a team of Delta Force commandos in the undergrowth nearby, watching. We had asked our informant to be extra vigilant, and he sent a message that Zarqawi and one of his couriers were inside.

Dusk was approaching and, afraid that he would escape yet again, one of the commandos called in an air strike on the house. Shortly afterward, two U.S. F-16 fighter aircraft dropped two 500-pound bombs on the house. American and Iraqi troops pulled Zarqawi from the rubble, still breathing, but he died shortly after.

The families of his victims finally had justice. Zarqawi would never harm anybody again. His wife and family were caught crossing into Jordan from Syria in June 2009, and, demonstrating the difference between violent extremists and the civilized world, we allowed them to go free.

Jordan had long been cooperating with other friendly nations in the global effort to protect innocent people from terrorist organizations. But international cooperation against Al Qaeda has become stronger and more systematic in recent years, in response to the growing terrorist threat. Our intelligence service was the first to penetrate Al Qaeda, long before it was on the radar of the international community, and we had developed in-depth knowledge of its techniques. We have put this knowledge in the service of all our allies in the fight against terrorism. I am proud to say that we have played a major role in saving innocent lives in the region and beyond. We continue to cooperate and share information with other intelligence services in a partnership that is growing more effective in protecting our people and interests from terrorist organizations.

Although we had won an important victory, we cannot prevail in this struggle by just winning tactical battles, using our military and intelligence service to take down cells and disrupt plots. To comprehensively defeat terrorists, we will have to neutralize the appeal of their extremist ideology and combat the ignorance and hopelessness on which they thrive. This is not just a military battle, it is an intellectual one. And it is a battle we started a while ago.

# CHAPTER 23
# THE AMMAN MESSAGE

In late 2004, I brought together a group of leading Islamic scholars in Jordan and asked them how we could combat takfiris and their terrible ideas. I asked my cousin and adviser Prince Ghazi bin Muhammad, a highly respected Islamic scholar with a PhD from Cambridge University, to lead and coordinate their work. The scholars produced a document called the Amman Message, which set out what Islam is, what it is not, and what types of actions are and are not Islamic. Released on November 9, on the eve of the holy month of Ramadan, it states in part:

Today the magnanimous message of Islam faces a vicious attack from those who, through distortion and fabrication, try to portray Islam as their enemy. It is also under attack from some who claim affiliation with Islam and commit irresponsible acts in its name.

We denounce and condemn extremism, radicalism, and fanaticism today, just as our forefathers tirelessly denounced and opposed them throughout Islamic history. . . . On religious and moral grounds, we denounce the contemporary concept of terrorism that is associated with wrongful practices, whatever their source and form may be. Such acts are represented by aggression against human life in an oppressive form that transgresses the rulings of God.

I knew that no statement coming from Jordan alone would be enough to combat the takfiris, who had spread their poison across the entire Muslim world. So Ghazi distilled the Amman Message down to its three most basic points, three questions that would undercut the takfiris' distortions and show them up as fraudulent from the point of view of normative Islam. The three points are:

1. Who is a Muslim?
2. Is it permissible to declare someone an apostate (takfir)?
3. Who has the right to issue fatwas (legal rulings)?

We sent these questions to twenty-four of the leading Muslim religious scholars across the world. Unlike Christianity, Islam does not have an official clergy. But it does have schools with famous religious scholars, known as imams, who command great respect. We included representatives from the four main schools of Sunni Islamic jurisprudence (Hanafi, Maliki, Shafi, and Hanbali), the two main Shia schools (Jafari and Zaidi), the Ibadhi school, and Thahiri scholars.

In July 2005, we invited two hundred of the world's leading Muslim scholars from fifty countries, including Saudi Arabia, Iran, Turkey, and Egypt, to a conference in Amman. These scholars issued a ruling on the three fundamental issues we had raised, and their conclusions became known as the three points of the Amman Message:

1. The scholars specifically recognized the validity of all eight Mathhabs (legal schools) of Sunni, Shia, and Ibadhi Islam; of traditional Islamic theology (Ash'arism); of Islamic mysticism (Sufism); and of true Salafi thought, and came to a precise definition of who is a Muslim.
2. Based upon this definition they forbade takfir (declarations of apostasy) between Muslims.
3. They set forth the subjective and ob-

jective preconditions for the issuing of fatwas, thereby exposing ignorant and illegitimate edicts in the name of Islam.

Over the course of 2005 and 2006, we took these three ideas to every major Islamic conference and institute imaginable and had it ratified by over five hundred of the Islamic world's leading scholars. This created a consensus of Muslim scholars, which is legally binding according to Islamic law. In other words, the whole Muslim world together, for the first time in history, declared the very fundamentals of the takfiri movement to be unacceptable, illegal, and un-Islamic.

To an outsider, this may seem like an arcane debate. But these wise scholars, in putting aside their differences and seeking to define the true meaning of Islam, struck at the roots of the extremists' false ideas. In the end, this is a battle in which ideas are the most potent weapons. I am a military man by training, but I know from experience that no war on terror will neutralize this enemy. We have to convince people of the bankruptcy of the takfiris' ideology and to defeat them in the battlefield of the minds of young Muslim men and women.

Our two greatest weapons against the takfiris are education and opportunity — not only providing better schools and universities, but also improving the quality of our religious education. To make sure our young people hear the true message of Islam, we have to encourage bright and well-educated members of our society to pursue careers in religious affairs.

Of course, this debate about extremism and moderation is not limited to Islam. There are extremists in all religions. The ability of a few extremists to influence perceptions through acts of barbarity places greater responsibility on the moderates, of all religions, to speak up. If the majority remains silent, the extremists will dominate the debate.

After the Amman Message, which aimed to discredit the takfiris within the Muslim world and to bring Muslims together in protecting their faith from their distortions, we started to do what we could to bring Muslims, Christians, and Jews together in peace as religions. We called this initiative the Amman Interfaith Message. On my trips abroad we met with priests, preachers, rabbis, and imams and basically said that our religions do not require us to fight, and that if we do fight for political causes, we should not cloak these fights in religious justifications. Then, on September 12, 2006, in an academic lecture at the University of Regensburg in Germany, Pope Benedict XVI cited the negative comments of a fourteenth-century Byzantine emperor on Islam and sparked a major global controversy. Soon afterward the Vatican expressed regrets, and Pope Benedict himself met with ambassadors of Muslim countries in order to patch things up. But the situation was tense, so I asked my cousin Prince Ghazi to do what he could to defuse tensions globally.

One month later, on October 13, 2006, Prince Ghazi and thirty-seven other major Muslim figures from around the world wrote an "open letter to the Pope," politely pointing out some mistakes in his Regensburg lecture and calling for more interfaith understanding and dialogue. This open letter did not get very far, so exactly one year later, on October 13, 2007, they wrote another open letter, entitled "A Common Word Between Us and You," issued in the name of 138 major Islamic scholars, in order to show that Muslims still wanted dialogue. Proposing that Islam and Christianity, despite many irresolvable differences, nevertheless share in common two golden commandments — love of God and love of neighbor — "A Common Word" became the most successful Muslim-Christian interfaith initiative of our time. Emerging from it, in November 2008, was the first meeting of the Catholic-Muslim Forum, held in the Vatican under the auspices of Pope Benedict XVI. The second will be held in Jordan, God willing, at the Baptism Site, in 2011.

In the meantime we invited the pope to come to Jordan and he accepted our invitation. He came in May 2009. On the afternoon of May 8, 2009, Rania and I flew by helicopter to Queen Alia International Airport to greet the pope. As we flew over Amman, we saw the streets below bedecked with both the yellow-and-white flag of the Vatican and the Jordanian flag. We landed just before the pope's plane taxied up to the waiting red carpet. The honor guard, dressed in tan uniforms and wearing traditional red-and-white-checkered head scarves, stood at attention as the pope descended from the plane. I welcomed His Holiness to Jordan, endorsed his commitment to dispel the misconceptions and divisions that have harmed relations between Christians and Muslims, and expressed the hope that together we could expand the dialogue he had opened. The pope received a very warm welcome in Jordan, with tens of thousands of Jordanian citizens, Christians and Muslims alike, lining the streets in the hope of catching a glimpse of him.

Rania and I flew back home and prepared to receive His Holiness and his delegation that evening. Rania corralled the children and began to get them dressed. The girls, Salma and Iman, were well behaved, but Hussein and our younger son, Hashem, were more of a challenge. We have always brought them up to be "normal," but this was one occasion when a bit more formality would have been welcome. We persuaded Hussein to wear a suit, but Hashem, four years old, would have none of it. Part of being a parent is knowing when to pick your battles, so we dressed Hashem in a blue-and-white shirt and tan pants and headed off to the reception.

In our conversation that evening I explained to the pope that while Jordan had severed its legislative and administrative ties with the West Bank in 1988, we had never renounced our moral and legal responsibility as custodians of the Muslim and Christian holy sites in East Jerusalem, including the Church of the Holy Sepulcher and the Al Aqsa Mosque. In fact, the Jordanian government still pays the salaries of the civil servants who administer those sites.

"Your Holiness," I said, "we all hope and

pray for peace. And nowhere do we hope for peace more than in Jerusalem, that city holy to three great religions."

Two days later, on Sunday, May 10, Rania and I drove to the Baptism Site on Bethany beyond the Jordan, where we met the pope, who had just said mass for some fifty thousand Christians gathered in and around Amman stadium from Jordan and all over the Middle East, including Syria, Lebanon, Iraq, and the West Bank. Sunday is the start of the workweek in Jordan, but in honor of the pontiff's visit, all Christians were given the day off. Although it is not widely known in the West, we have in Jordan a small but thriving Christian community that is perhaps the oldest in the world. Its head — or, rather, the head of its largest denomination — is the Orthodox Patriarch of Jerusalem. His church is an Apostolic church, which means that it dates back to the first Christian community in the years of the Apostles, and he is the direct spiritual descendant of Saint James, the first bishop of Jerusalem, in Jesus Christ's own lifetime. Christians constitute around 3 percent of our population, and they participate in all aspects of life. In fact, by law, around 8 percent of the members of our parliament are Christian.

The Baptism Site is Jordan's most important Christian site. It is here on the East Bank of the River Jordan ("beyond the Jordan," according to John 3:26) that John the Baptist baptized Jesus and where Jesus's mission started and Christianity began. The "Bethany beyond the Jordan, where John was baptizing" (John 1:28), is one of the most important holy Christian sites in the world, together with the Church of the Holy Sepulcher in Jerusalem and the Church of the Nativity in Bethlehem. We have preserved the site in its natural state as best we can, and at the same time have given land there for Christians to build churches. The site attracts hundreds of thousands of pilgrims every year and was visited by both Pope John Paul II in 2000 and Pope Benedict XVI in 2009. It is the most significant among many places in Jordan that are of relevance to Old and New Testament events, as well as events in subsequent Christian history. In Rihab, in northern Jordan, archaeologists have found the remains of a church that they believe may be one of the oldest in the world, dating back to the first century after Christ. There is the church in Madaba, with its important sixth-century Byzantine mosaic map of the Holy Land. And going back over three thousand years is Mount Nebo, a mountain north of Madaba that is the place where Moses saw the Promised Land and where his body was buried.

At around 5:30 p.m., Rania, Pope Benedict, some of our advisers, and I got into a large motorized buggy and rode down to the Baptism Site, where the pontiff blessed the foundation stones of two churches, one Latin, the other Greek Melkite.

Jordan's religious tolerance and diversity come as a surprise to many in the West. I remember when in July 2005, Tom DeLay, a member of a movement called the Christian Zionists, who are strong supporters of the state of Israel and oppose the creation of a Palestinian state, visited Jordan as part of a trip to the Middle East. We met in my father's old house in Amman, and DeLay, Republican majority leader in the U.S. Congress at that time, wasted no time in telling me what was on his mind. "I am very concerned about the treatment of Christians in Jordan," he said. As it happened, a few of the Jordanians who were with me in the room were Christian, and they began to smile. Oblivious to this, DeLay grabbed my hand and said, "Do you believe in Jesus?" looking earnestly into my eyes. "I believe in Jesus Christ as the Messiah," I replied, freeing my hand from his grasp. In fact, all Muslims believe in Jesus as the Messiah and revere him as a Spirit of God and as the Word of God as well as a great prophet and messenger of God. "Listen," I said, "if you're worried about Christians in Jordan, you can ask around here — some of the people by my side in this room are Christian." Then I told him how Jordan takes very seriously its responsibility of protecting Christian rights within Jordan, and also in Jerusalem. I am not certain that DeLay understood or accepted my assurances. I do know that his delegation included no Muslims. Just a few months after his visit to Jordan, DeLay, a vocal evangelical, was indicted by a grand jury in Texas on charges of money laundering and violating campaign finance laws. He subsequently resigned as House majority leader and later gave up his seat in Congress.

But the pope was well aware of Jordan's diversity. His visit was a joyous time, and a celebration of Jordan's religious tolerance. It came at a very good time, and the pope's message of peace and spiritual reconciliation between Christians, Muslims, and Jews complemented our efforts in the political sphere to bring about a political reconciliation between Israelis and Palestinians. It was hard to miss the significance of the pope's religious pilgrimage, which started in Jordan and ended in Jerusalem, by way of the West

Bank. His visit helped inspire all of us who were searching for peace. And we needed that inspiration, for the path to peace had been riddled with potholes and perilous detours.

# PART VI

# CHAPTER 24
## THE END OF AN ERA

Israeli prime minister Ariel Sharon had been in office for three years by the time we first met. His policies in the West Bank and Gaza had created so much tension in the region that it had been politically almost impossible for us to meet earlier. But in early 2004 I invited Sharon to Jordan in an effort to break the stalemate in the peace process. He flew into Amman by helicopter, landing at the headquarters of the General Intelligence Department.

A man with a fearsome reputation, Sharon had served in the Haganah, the Jewish underground resistance that fought Palestinians and later became part of the Hebrew Resistance Movement against the British. He led Israeli Special Forces Unit 101, conducting clandestine raids against Arab targets, and was involved in the attack on Qibya in 1953, when scores of Palestinian civilians were killed. Sharon was infamous across the region for allowing the massacre of some eight hundred Palestinians in the Sabra and Shatila refugee camps during the 1982 Israeli invasion of Lebanon. No Arab will ever be able to forget the searing images of the slaughtered mothers and children of Sabra and Shatila.

Extremists will always criticize me for meeting with Israeli leaders, especially those with a history of violence like Sharon, who to most Arabs is a mass murderer and a war criminal. But leaders do not have the luxury of choosing their counterparts. I do not get to choose the Israeli prime minister. Only the Israeli people can do that. But I can choose how Jordan behaves toward its neighbors and decide how to build upon my father's legacy of peace. Although there might be some emotional satisfaction in refusing to meet Sharon, it would be short-lived and self-defeating.

We had invited Sharon to Jordan because we felt it was essential to somehow reboot the peace process. I had strongly objected to many of his actions and policies, and I hoped to persuade him that the only way to ensure lasting security for Israel was to forge a peace between Israel and its Arab neighbors. My father had interacted with Sharon when he was a minister in the Netanyahu government in the late 1990s and had passed along an insight into his character. He had told me that if Sharon committed himself to something, he would stick to it. He was a man who kept his word.

Although I did not know Sharon personally, I had benefited from the respect he held for my father, and for Jordan. As I sat opposite him in a meeting room at GID headquarters, I told him that my father had said he was a man who would keep his word. So that was how I wanted to begin the relationship, I said.

Sharon seemed shy and somewhat reserved and kept looking down as he spoke. "I care about the security of Israel," he said, "but I also care about the safety and security of Jordan."

I knew that the true national interest of Jordan, and of Israel, would be served only by reaching peace between Israel and the Palestinians. I tried to convince him of this, but by the end of the meeting, after a lengthy discussion of Israeli actions in the Occupied Territories and the need to take effective steps to create an environment conducive to the resumption of serious peace negotiations, I was quite certain that Sharon did not share my view.

Our next encounter, on March 19, was

a secret meeting at his ranch in the Negev Desert. By inviting me to his personal farm, where his wife was buried, Sharon was sending me the message that he was a friend to Jordan and hoped to put old hostilities behind us. Times were very tense. The construction by Israel of the wall dividing the West Bank had begun, and the belief in the region was that the Bush administration wanted to bring about "regime change" in the Palestinian Authority and had little interest in getting the parties back to the negotiating table. All the while, Israel was building more illegal settlements in the West Bank and consolidating its hold on the Occupied Territories. The settler population in the West Bank and East Jerusalem stood at around 265,000 at the time the Oslo Accords were signed in 1993. The number had risen to about 365,000 in 2000, and to over 400,000 in 2003. This growth was a reflection of the fact that Israel never stopped building new settlements in the West Bank and East Jerusalem, a politically incendiary move. The building of new settlements was alarming not just because they were eating away at land that should belong to the future Palestinian state, but also because it was a clear indication that Israel was not committed to a two-state solution.

We had gone to Sharon's ranch to discuss his recent proposal to pull Israeli troops out of the Gaza Strip and some parts of the West Bank. I told him that any such move should be coordinated with the Palestinian leadership and the Egyptians, and that it should be the beginning of a comprehensive Israeli withdrawal from all occupied Arab territory. It should not simply be a unilateral withdrawal by Israeli forces so as to transfer Israeli settlers from Gaza to other locations in the West Bank. I felt as though we were making some progress in building a working relationship that could ultimately help push the peace efforts forward. But in my neighborhood, appearances can be deceptive.

One of the problems with the Israeli government is that everything leaks. Although our meeting was supposed to be secret, a confidence-building measure that would allow us to discuss ways of moving toward a settlement with the Palestinians, news of the trip was leaked to the Israeli press. Shortly afterward the Israelis assassinated Sheikh Ahmed Yassin, the head of Hamas, with a Cobra gunship as he was leaving a mosque in Gaza. Nine innocent people were killed along with the blind, wheelchair-bound Yassin. The assassination of a quadriplegic in his seventies seemed heartless even by Israeli standards. I was infuriated by the murder of Yassin and knew it would open up another cycle of violence. But I was also furious because the operation had taken place so soon after my visit. The next month the Israelis assassinated Yassin's successor, Abdel Aziz Rantisi, sparking renewed violence in the West Bank and Gaza. The Americans did not condemn either assassination and vetoed a UN resolution doing so.

Israelis often, whether on purpose or not, seem to schedule important diplomatic meetings a few days before conducting controversial operations. One recent example was the meeting between Turkey's prime minister Recep Tayyep Erdogan and Israeli prime minister Ehud Olmert in December 2008, a few days before the Gaza war started. Erdogan was furious. He felt the Israeli government was trying to create the impression that he had given his tacit consent to the Gaza attack.

The assassination of Sheikh Yassin was emblematic of the morass of Middle East conflict: one side acts rashly and the other overreacts in return. The path to peace is littered with roadside bombs. The only law that is followed is one whose logic leads to unintended consequences. After the Israelis assassinated Rantisi, Hamas had to find another leader. Who did they turn to? None other than Jordan's former guest, Khaled Meshaal.

In April 2004, I was again scheduled to meet with President Bush at the White House. I planned to push to restart the peace process and hoped that the president would take a broader view of the challenges facing our region. Before my arrival, Bush welcomed another visitor, Prime Minister Sharon. During that visit, on April 14, an exchange of letters between Bush and Sharon was made public. In the days leading up to the visit, Sharon had pressed the president to reveal America's positions on several issues and to support his unilateral disengagement in Gaza. Bush's secret assurances amounted to a major shift in American policy. In his formal letter to Sharon, Bush promised U.S. support for Israel's retention of some West Bank settlements and ruled out the right of Palestinian refugees to return to their former homes, saying that they should settle in a future Palestinian state. The U.S. administration was prejudging one of the most controversial topics in the whole peace process. Bush said:

The United States is strongly committed to Israel's security and well-being as a Jewish state. It seems clear that an agreed, just, fair and realistic framework for a solution to the Palestinian refugee issue as part of any final status agreement will need to be found through the establishment of a Palestinian state, and the settling of Palestinian refugees there, rather than in Israel.

The whole Arab world exploded in anger. It was clear to me that the Bush administration intended to back Israel right or wrong, so I told the White House that I was canceling my meeting. They were stunned. Few people ever turn down a meeting with the American president, and fewer still cancel meetings that have already been scheduled. But I had to make my point. I could not condone the shift in U.S. policy implied by Bush's letter. The peace process was frozen, and despite the best efforts of the Arab states to make a new push for peace, all we were getting were one-sided pronouncements and more violence.

One month later I went to Washington to try to reverse the change in American policy and was partially successful. In our joint press conference, which reiterated the substance of letters we had exchanged before my visit, Bush reaffirmed that he would not prejudge the final status talks. I restated Jordan's position that any Israeli withdrawal should follow the parameters of the road map and lead to the creation of a Palestinian state on the basis of the 1967 borders.

In October, Yasser Arafat was flown to Paris for medical treatment after his health speedily deteriorated. He slipped into a coma and died the following month. His body was flown to Cairo, where he was given a military funeral. An Egyptian plane then took his body to the Sinai, and Jordanian military helicopters carried it from there to Ramallah for burial. The helicopter landed as a distraught crowd of mourners surged forward, desperately trying to get one last glimpse of their beloved leader. Whatever the world may have thought of Arafat, he was a hero to the Palestinian people and his passing marked the end of an era.

Mahmoud Abbas (known as Abu Mazen) was elected president of the Palestinian National Authority the following January. For decades, Israel had claimed that Arafat was a barrier to peace. Now, with his passing, they would have one less excuse for failing to deliver on their promises. Abbas assumed the leadership of the PNA at one of the lowest points in the peace process. The challenges before him were enormous. He had to fill the vacuum left by Arafat and rebuild Palestinian institutions that had been systematically destroyed by Israel in the past few years. The new Palestinian leader also had to work to put the peace process back on track. From the day he assumed office, Abbas sought a political settlement with the Israelis on the basis of the two-state solution. But he would be sorely disappointed.

In August 2005, the Israelis unilaterally withdrew from Gaza three days earlier than announced — without adequate coordination with the Egyptians, who share a long border with Gaza, or with the Palestinian Authority. The Israeli cabinet had voted overwhelmingly in support of this move the previous February. Sharon, the former champion of the settlers, had given the order to bulldoze their buildings and remove the occupants, by force if necessary. Although the withdrawal was welcome, the manner in which it was conducted was not.

By blockading all of the Gaza Strip's entry and exit points, the Israelis had turned Gaza into a virtual prison. And when they withdrew in an uncoordinated manner, they created a security vacuum. This vacuum was soon filled by Hamas and the Islamic Jihad. It was a desolate scene, with heavily armed men moving through a landscape of barbed wire and ruined buildings. There was no management of the transition and no handing over of security and other responsibilities in a coordinated manner to Palestinian institutions.

A few months later, in November, Sharon split from the Likud Party and founded a new party, which he called Kadima. His decision followed months of political infighting with members of Likud over what was known as the "disengagement plan," which involved the withdrawal from Gaza and the dismantlement of four settlements in the northern West Bank. Sharon was joined by key Likud members, including Tzipi Livni, who would later become foreign minister, and Ehud Olmert, the former mayor of Jerusalem, who was his deputy.

In early January 2006, Sharon suffered a stroke and fell into a coma. His duties were assumed by Olmert. It soon became clear that the old warrior would not recover, and Olmert officially became prime minister of Israel in April.

New leaders were taking over on both sides, and many in the region hoped this would lead to a fresh approach to an old conflict. Nowhere was that hope stronger than among those gearing up for the first Palestinian legislative election in a decade, which was slated for January 25, 2006. One of the parties on the ballot was Hamas, which had chosen not to take part in the 1996 legislative elections. Because of Hamas's participation, the Israeli government considered not allowing Palestinians living in East Jerusalem to vote in the election (it considers East Jerusalem to be part of Israel). But in the end, they were allowed to vote.

Many Palestinians and others in the region argued that the conditions were not right for holding elections and urged that they be delayed. But the Bush administration disagreed with this suggestion. In a question-and-answer session with the State Department Correspondents Association on January 5, Condoleezza Rice said:

I don't really believe that we can favor postponing the elections because we fear an outcome. . . . [O]ur position on Hamas has not changed. It's listed as a terrorist organization. We recognize that there's a transition here going on in Palestinian politics. And so this is an internal matter for the Palestinians. We do believe that there should be the ability of everyone to participate — the Palestinian people to participate in the elections.

But what would the Bush administration do if Hamas won?

Many hoped and expected that Yasser Arafat's Fatah Party would win the elections. Fatah had promised the Palestinian people statehood and freedom through the Oslo process, but the long-ago-promised state was still a distant mirage and charges of corruption against Palestinian National Authority officials were rampant. Many felt that Fatah had not delivered on its promises. So when the day came for Palestinians to go to the polls, they gave Hamas a decisive win. Hamas's victory created a major problem. The U.S. government considered Hamas a terrorist organization and would have nothing to do with it. Many European countries followed suit. This in turn allowed the Israelis to freeze tax payments to the Palestinian Authority and to claim that they did not have a "partner for peace."

Americans rightly extol the benefits of democracy, but democracy manifests itself in different forms in different cultures. If conditions are not right, it can cement divisions and fuel hatred. Part of the problem with the Bush administration was its cookie-cutter approach toward the concept of exporting democracy, which basically came down to holding elections. To my mind, developing an effective democracy is a journey. Voting in the absence of a widespread acceptance of democratic values and the existence of an independent judiciary can be a disaster. Democratic institutions are strengthened by the presence of a strong, effective middle class and reputable governing bodies. It is certainly a process that is more difficult to develop under an occupation that could, and would, destroy these institutions at will.

I do not think the Bush administration fully understood conditions in the region and thus it pushed blindly for early elections wherever it could. It sometimes seemed as if the administration was just seeking a quick win to feed the never-ending twenty-four-hour news cycle. But the problems in the West Bank and Gaza were not going to be resolved through the ballot box before the end of the Israeli occupation. If the foundations for a stable society are not in place, extremist groups will capitalize on popular frustrations to seize power. And once the radicals take control, they do not easily relinquish it.

After winning a majority of seats in the parliamentary elections, Hamas took over the government, while Fatah still retained control of the presidency and the PLO. The new Hamas government was sworn in in March 2006. The United States and EU countries refused to recognize the government and suspended aid to it. The situation deteriorated quickly after that, especially after militants close to Hamas killed two Israeli soldiers and captured another, Gilad Shalit, during a raid into Israel from Gaza. Israel reacted by invading Gaza in June.

Almost three weeks before the invasion of Gaza, I expressed alarm at the deteriorating situation in the West Bank, Gaza, and Iraq, as well as the growing dispute between Iran and the United States. The likelihood of a new conflict appeared high to me. In a graduation speech at Mu'ta University on June 7, I warned of the risk posed by both state actors and nonstate groups seeking to ignite conflict and spoke about the devastating consequences of Iranian expansionist policies in our region. I normally address domestic issues in such speeches, but the enormity of the looming threats prompted me to emphasize these concerns instead.

On July 12, 2006, Hezbollah fighters crossed into Israel, killing eight Israeli soldiers and capturing two others. In response, Israel launched an all-out invasion of Lebanon and Hezbollah fired rockets at Israeli border towns. I watched on television as the Israeli army attacked cities and villages in South Lebanon and bombed power stations across the country as well as Beirut's airport, closing that city's lifeline to the outside world. Hezbollah fighters were in the south. They were not going to escape via the airport, nor were they going to fly in more men and military supplies. Closing the airport hurt the civilian population.

I condemned the war. I had seen enough suffering in our region to know that war brings nothing but destruction. Israel's security will be guaranteed only by coming to terms with its neighbors, not by more wars and military action.

The Israeli planes targeted not only power plants but also waterworks, roads, bridges, and other civilian infrastructure. Over the last few years Lebanese expatriates of all backgrounds had come back to the country and the economy was booming. And now the Israelis were systematically destroying Lebanon's economy and infrastructure. This was a terrible act of collective punishment, inflicting pain on the entire country in retaliation for the actions of one group.

Although throughout history there have been examples of states targeting civilians to break the will of the enemy, that is not a decision to be proud of. It is dangerously easy in wartime to demonize the enemy, which can lead to the killing of civilians, women, and children in large numbers. But any leader, whether a platoon commander, a general, or a head of state, has a moral obligation to distinguish between civilians and combatants. And Olmert chose not to do this.

Satellite stations across the Arab world filled their screens with pictures of civilian suffering in Beirut. Public opinion in Arab countries was strongly against the Israeli attack, and many in Jordan and across the region urged that something be done to help the hundreds of thousands of innocent Lebanese caught in the crossfire.

Our peace treaty with Israel allowed us to fly in humanitarian aid to Lebanon. A Jordanian C-130 transport plane was the first to land at Beirut–Rafic Hariri International Airport after Israel severely damaged its tarmac. Our military engineers helped to reopen the airport to supply planes. We then continued to send planes carrying relief supplies into Beirut airport, evacuating some Lebanese and third-country nationals stranded there.

An emergency Arab League meeting convened in Cairo on July 17 and unanimously condemned the Israeli military offensive in Lebanon. Several Arab states, including Egypt, Saudi Arabia, and Jordan, also criticized Hezbollah for "unexpected, inappropriate, and irresponsible acts." Saudi foreign minister Prince Saud Al-Faisal said, "These acts will pull the whole region back to years ago and we simply cannot accept them." Since we suspected that Hezbollah was acting as an Iranian proxy, we believed that its rocket attacks were a direct intervention by Iran into Arab politics. We knew that no good would come out of this increased Iranian assertiveness, but we were widely criticized in the Arab world for our stance.

The war lasted for thirty-four days. More than 1,100 Lebanese and 160 Israelis were killed, and much of Lebanon was destroyed before the fighting stopped on August 14, two days after the Security Council adopted Resolution 1701 calling for the end of hostilities. Hezbollah, which put up a strong fight against the Israeli army and was able to fire rockets deep into Israel till the last minute of the war, declared victory. The majority of public opinion in the Arab world celebrated Hezbollah and took pride in its ability to stand up to the Israeli army. For a brief period, Hezbollah leader Hassan Nasrallah became the hero of the Middle East. The celebration of Hezbollah's survival in the war against Israel as a victory was indicative of a major shift in the Arab and Muslim world. Victory now means survival, rather than defeating the Israeli army. The implications of this new dynamic are dangerous in the sense that, if the conflict persists, people are willing to support armed confrontations no matter what the cost is as long as they can survive and inflict damage on Israel. This new reality gives more credence to the belief that only peace, and not the military superiority of Israel, will ensure the safety of Israelis and all other peoples of the region.

Meanwhile, the scene in the Palestinian territories was getting more problematic. Tensions between the Fatah-led PNA and the Hamas government were on the rise. The uncomfortable cohabitation between the two groups ended in violence on June 14, 2007, when Hamas took over the Gaza Strip after bloody confrontations with Fatah supporters and security forces.

A few months later, on November 27, the Bush administration made a final major push to reinvigorate the peace process by convening an international conference at the U.S. Naval Academy in Annapolis. The road map of 2003 had brought little progress. Though it clearly identified steps to be taken by the Palestinians and Israelis, the road map was not being implemented and the two sides kept accusing one another of not fulfilling their obligations.

The United States invited forty-nine countries and international organizations to the conference in Annapolis, with the purpose of setting in motion a continuous process that would result in the establishment of a Palestinian state. Among the attendees were Israeli prime minister Ehud Olmert and Palestinian president Mahmoud Abbas, as well as the secretary-general of the United Nations and foreign ministers of the Arab League's Arab Peace Initiative follow-up committee, which included Jordan. Also attending were representatives of the Quartet, a four-member group consisting of the United States, the European Union, Russia, and the United Nations, which had been set up in Madrid in 2002 to help overcome obstacles facing the peace process.

In an address to the conference Bush said, "We meet to lay the foundation for the establishment of a new nation — a democratic Palestinian state that will live side by side with Israel in peace and security. We meet to help bring an end to the violence that has been the true enemy of the aspirations of both the Israelis and Palestinians." He said that both Israelis and the Palestinians would have to make tough choices to achieve peace and that he believed leaders on both sides were ready to tackle the major issues and move toward peace.

The conference ended with the announcement of an agreement that raised hopes for a settlement. Abbas and Olmert agreed to immediately implement their respective obligations under the road map and to form a mechanism, led by the United States, to monitor its implementation. The two sides committed to engage in vigorous, ongoing, and continuous negotiations, and to make every effort to conclude an agreement before the end of 2008.

Direct negotiations between the Palestinians and the Israelis followed. They tackled the final status issues of borders, Jerusalem, refugees, and security, with a view to delivering a final settlement. The talks, which proceeded on the understanding that "nothing is agreed until all is agreed," appeared to be making some headway, especially on the essential issue of borders. The discussions were thorough and detailed, and the two sides exchanged maps and were negotiating the percentage of land to be swapped within the context of a final agreement. But the talks lost momentum in July when Olmert's authority was undermined by charges of corruption that forced him to announce his resignation.

Abbas's authority was also undermined by Hamas's electoral victory, which had opened another front. The 2006 elections had divided the Palestinian leadership, leaving Gaza under the full control of Hamas and the West Bank under Fatah's control. Gaza was in continual confrontation with Israel until Egypt succeeded in brokering a truce in June 2008. Popular pressure was mounting for reconciliation between Hamas and Fatah. But that would prove an extremely difficult task.

In hindsight, a Palestinian election in which Hamas took part created more problems than it solved. And, as with the Iraqi elections the previous year, sometimes the democratic process throws up surprises.

# CHAPTER 25
# THE MASK SLIPS

Iraq's first general elections were held one year before the Palestinian elections, on January 30, 2005. Parties were competing for seats in a Transitional National Assembly, which would draft a new constitution to be submitted to the Iraqi people. The likely victory of Shia political parties backed by Iran had led to talk of a strengthening of Shia power throughout the region. Iran was thought to be providing money and support to one or more of these parties, and many in the region feared that it was plotting to stage a behind-the-scenes takeover of Iraqi politics. The Sunni community in Iraq, unwilling to trust a process that they believed was being rigged to marginalize them, decided to boycott the elections. This proved to be a big mistake.

Just over a month before the election I was interviewed on *Hardball with Chris Matthews* on MSNBC. Matthews asked me my opin-

501

ion of the upcoming Iraqi election, and in particular the implications of a radical Shia victory. I said:

> The worst outcome is, you don't have a secular state. In other words, the new government is strongly represented by those who might have support from Iran. We hope that's not the case. As you are aware, there's an issue of the Sunnis; we want them to go to the elections, we want them to be part of the process. If they're not, then there could be more difficulties.

In those days I often expressed my concerns about the area covering the old Levant and the Fertile Crescent, an area stretching from Syria and Lebanon to Iraq and Iran. During that interview with Chris Matthews, the image of a crescent popped into my head as a good metaphor for the potential spread of Iranian influence. "If it was a Shia-led Iraq that had a special relationship with Iran, and you look at that relationship with Syria and Hezbollah and Lebanon," I said, "then we have this new crescent that appears that will be very destabilizing for the Gulf countries and for the whole region."

After that interview, all hell broke loose. I was criticized by many people for being anti-Shia. The Iraqi politician Abdul Aziz Hakim, the head of the Shia party SCIRI (the Supreme Council for the Islamic Revolution in Iraq), who had spent many years in exile in Iran, called the idea of Iranian influence in Iraqi politics "ridiculous." But by then no one doubted that Iran was actively meddling in, if not guiding, Iraqi politics.

The controversy illustrates some of the difficulties of speaking to the media. I was talking politics, not religion, but my comments were deliberately distorted. My concern was that some Iranians were trying to invoke sectarian sentiments to serve their own agendas, thus creating conditions that could lead to Sunni-Shia confrontations across the Muslim world. I accept and respect the Shia as one of the legitimate branches of Islam and strongly believe that it is not acceptable to judge people according to their faith. Shias have made an enormous contribution to Arab and Muslim culture as well as to the defense of the Arab nationalist cause, and they have been loyal to their countries, whether in Lebanon or Iraq. I never meant to suggest that they would, by virtue of their faith, automatically align with Iran — only that the Iranian government would manipulate the situation to its advantage and foment divisions. In fact, Iraqi Shia fought valiantly in defense of their country in its war with Iran in the 1980s.

Contemporary Shia thought covers a broad spectrum of beliefs. At one end are some of the most conservative thinkers in the Muslim world, and at the other some of its most liberal. Iran is the home of some visionary clerics, who are leading the Middle East in addressing certain social issues. When we in Jordan were looking at different ways of tackling birth control, we turned to Iran to understand how religious authorities there support contraception, a sensitive subject in the Arab world. The late Lebanese Shia cleric Muhammad Hussein Fadlallah believed that women should have equal rights and play a role equal to that of men in society. So clerics can be a force for positive change, but they can also be reactionary.

My fear was that some in the Iranian regime were setting in place the conditions for a devastating sectarian conflict that could speedily spread from Beirut to Bombay. Across the centuries, some of the most violent moments in human history have been preceded by politicians' decisions to use religion to justify a war or political interest. From the Crusades to the Spanish Inquisition, great cruelty and suffering have often been imposed by those with the divine conviction that they are in the right.

Speaking in the name of God can all too easily serve as a justification to suppress debate. Putting yourself on a moral and spiritual pedestal allows you to condemn any challenger as morally bankrupt. And this absolutist view becomes dangerous when it is combined with politics. Suddenly, your political opponents become not merely people with differing values and ideas about how to organize society, but enemies of God.

I wanted to point out the risk of this potential new sectarian conflict. Unfortunately, the controversy over my interview generated more than hostile words.

On Christmas Eve 2004, a tanker truck packed with explosives heading for the Jordanian embassy in Baghdad blew up, destroying a nearby house and killing nine people. Subsequent investigations revealed that the attack had been planned by a certain well-known Shia political group with support from the Iranian Revolutionary Guards. My hopes that my visit to Tehran the previous year would lead to improved relations between Jordan and Iran literally went up in smoke. This was the second attack on our embassy in Baghdad. The first, in August 2003, was a car bombing by Sunni extremists linked to Al Qaeda. Now we had also been attacked by Shia extremists linked to the Iranian government. In the Middle East, moderates have no shortage of enemies.

As the New Year began, people across Iraq were getting ready for the elections. I asked my people to prepare an analysis, based on what we were hearing and seeing, of the Iraqi political situation for President Bush, who had just been reelected to a second term. To keep it simple, I asked them to use a traffic-light system. They put together a large chart with three colored columns, in which they placed pictures of thirty Iraqi politicians, organized by party and affiliation. In the green column were the Interim Government's prime minister, Ayad Allawi, and his supporters, as well as the Kurds — people who were moderate and with whom we shared the same values. The red column was made up of people who were allied with Iran and working to promote Iranian influence inside Iraq as well as Sunni extremists. And the yellow column comprised people who shifted in their allegiances but whom the international community could work with, like Nouri Al Maliki, of the Shia Al-Da'wa party, technocrats and businessmen, and some of the more conservative Sunni tribal sheikhs.

We also gave the American president and his staff a detailed plan for reconstruction in western Iraq to help bring the Sunnis back into the political process. It was crucial that the tribal sheikhs not become hardened in opposition — Iraq could not survive without the Sunnis onboard. We were concerned that the traditional tribal instincts of the region would take over, and that all groups would begin to fight for political power and influence. Our goal was to make sure the Americans understood that if there was to be any hope of stability in Iraq, it would depend on having a government that was inclusive and representative of Iraqi society. To my shock, not all American officials agreed with this logic. A senior American general did not waste any time in brushing aside our argument that the Sunnis' involvement in the political process was essential for the stability of Iraq. He was adamant that the Sunnis were America's enemies in this war and said that if they did not behave themselves, the United States would crush them militarily. Such an alarmingly simplistic view of the situation was very disconcerting.

Our plan outlined how to use social and economic assistance to provide political support to Iraqi tribal leaders in western Iraq. As we shared a common border, this was an area of Iraq we knew well. Some of the larger tribes had members in both eastern Jordan and western Iraq. In one area there was a run-down phosphate plant. We suggested that if the United States could help get that factory up and running again, this would create jobs, thereby providing a pocket of stability, which could in turn serve as a base for local tribesmen to fight back against Al Qaeda in Iraq.

U.S. defense secretary Rumsfeld took bits and pieces of our plan, focusing mainly on security and the creation of tribal militias. But the administration did not pay much attention to the economic and political recommendations, treating the occupation and administration of Iraq primarily as a military undertaking. They liked the idea of using the tribal militias to fight Al Qaeda, but they were far less interested in providing them with economic support so that they would become representatives of the central government in remote regions of Iraq.

By now, the Americans were not the only ones encountering problems in Iraq. In the south, the British were also struggling. The British Foreign Office has a deep knowledge of the Middle East, and its diplomats were known for their insight into the region and experience in dealing with its complicated and interconnected issues. But surprisingly, when the British went into the south, they seem to have been blind to the potential for problems from Iran. With Iranian surrogates fomenting unrest and Revolutionary Guard units being sent across the border, the whole place blew up in their faces. In some places you could hear Farsi spoken more often than Arabic. The British could have used fewer Whitehall bureaucrats and more people with deep cultural and historical knowledge of Iraq, especially as the Iranians began to make a stronger play for political influence in the south.

In the run-up to the elections, Iranian agents were determined to influence the result, supporting those Shia parties affiliated with Iran with money and resources. A large influence in Iraq where U.S. troops are spread across the country could be extremely useful for the Iranians in any future confrontation with the United States.

In the January elections, the United Iraqi Alliance (UIA), a coalition of Shia parties, won a majority of the seats in the Transitional National Assembly, and one of its leaders, Ibrahim Al Jaafari, replaced Ayad Allawi as prime minister. Ahmad Chalabi's party failed to win a single seat. The assembly fulfilled its main mandate of drafting a new Iraqi constitution, and Iraqis, voted again in December to elect a new parliament for a four-year term. The UIA again won the majority of seats and Jaafari was again chosen as prime minister. But he was forced to step down amid criticisms of ineffectual leadership. He was replaced by Nouri Al Maliki in April 2006.

The security situation in Iraq was gravely deteriorating when Maliki took over. Sectarian violence was on the rise. According to UN reports at the time, an average of one hundred civilians were killed a day in Sunni-Shia confrontations that started to escalate after an attack at an important Shia religious site, Al-Askari Mosque in the city of Samara, in February 2006. People began to speak about the possibility of a country-wide civil war.

In an attempt to restore security, Maliki announced a national reconciliation plan in June. The plan included steps to rein in militias and to open dialogue with rebels. But violence continued, raising concerns that the plan was not achieving its objectives. The Iraq Study Group, an American bipartisan panel established by Congress in March 2002 to assess the situation in Iraq, said in a report in December that the situation in Iraq was "grave and deteriorating."

In the beginning, I got a lot of positive reports about Maliki from the Shia and Sunni tribal sheikhs, in part because he took on the Iranian-supported militias. But over time, the reports became more mixed, with some in Iraq and the region arguing that he started to become more sectarian, supporting Shia over Sunni communities and refusing to spend government money in Sunni provinces. He took over at a terrible time, when Iraq was racked by sectarian strife and multifaceted violence. It is to Maliki's credit that the country started to stabilize during his premiership.

As things slowly began to improve in Iraq, with levels of violence subsiding, many Iraqis began to ask why Arabs were not coming to talk to them and why no Arab leaders were visiting Baghdad. And the truth is, it was not all that easy to do. Though some other Arab leaders did want to reach out to Iraq, they did not want to appear in front of their people to be in cahoots with the Americans. Even now, when Iraqis are running the country, the government still bears the stigma of being seen as American-led. People use this to attack Arab leaders who are perceived to be too close to Iraq.

In December 2006, Saddam Hussein was executed. A widely circulated amateur video of the execution showed men crowding around the gallows chanting, "Muqtada! Muqtada! Muqtada!" as the noose was placed around Saddam's neck. They were referring to Muqtada al-Sadr, the firebrand Shia cleric who leads the powerful Al Mahdi Army and who is believed to be an ally of Iran and Hezbollah. Arabs have, in the main, a common language and culture, so one image on satellite television can impact the whole region. In a flash, the mood in the Arab world changed. Saddam's execution was seen not just as an act inspired by the West against an Arab dictator. Many Sunnis around the region saw it as an act of revenge by Iran and Shia groups allied with it. The implications of this perspective were serious. Following Saddam's death, violence in Iraq took a new course, degenerating into Sunni-Shia tit-for-tat assassinations. Militias roamed the streets. It was widely felt that a dangerous divide between Shia and Sunni was threatening to spread across the region. The legitimacy of Hezbollah leader Nasrallah and others like him linked to Iran was diminished as a result. Many now saw them as proxies, working for Iran against the interests of the Arabs. The mask had slipped.

I tried to explain to the Bush administration, and in particular to Secretary of State Condoleezza Rice, that the mood of the region had changed and the moderates were back on top. Moderate Arab leaders could now band together and be more vocal — from the end of the Lebanon war in the summer until Saddam's execution, all of us had just been keeping our mouths shut and our heads down.

I said, now that we have regained momentum, empower us to push the peace process forward. But I do not think the message got through. The Bush administration's new priority was democracy promotion, and it had its hands full trying to stem the wave of violence in Iraq.

The Iranians lost some ground when Maliki took on the Iranian-backed militias in a series of confrontations and arrest campaigns, which eventually forced Muqtada al-Sadr to leave the country in February 2007. The security situation started to improve after that due to a combination of an increase in U.S. troops in Iraq and the efforts of the Awakening Councils, launched by Sunni tribes who took up the fight against Al Qaeda in their areas. Over time, however, Iranian-backed groups rebuilt their strength. I think Iraq's Arab neighbors bear some responsibility for this. The best way to guard against further Iranian interference in Iraq is for Arab countries to step in and support Iraq's new government as it gets onto its feet. If not, a vacuum will result and the Iranians will come back and restore the influence they briefly lost. Iran is offering sizable amounts of money to different sectarian groups inside Iraq, and is inviting children, both Sunni and Shia, in need of medical attention or a better education to Iran. They have opened up all of their borders and are trying to put Iraq under their sphere of influence. The turbulent security situation inside Iraq made it difficult for Arab countries to set up diplomatic missions in Baghdad and strengthen their relations with Iraq. But the fact is that Arab engagement with Iraq is essential for consolidating it against Iranian government expansionism and ambitions for hegemony.

In 2008, I decided that it was important to show that Iraq was moving in the right direction and that the political situation was stabilizing. One practical step I could take was to visit Iraq. A very real problem was security, because neither the Iranians nor Al Qaeda in Iraq wanted me there. I would be the first Arab leader to visit Iraq since the invasion, and my visit would be a symbol that things in Iraq were beginning to return to normal.

News of my trip leaked out, and Al Qaeda in Iraq sent a hit squad to welcome me. We heard that they had smuggled in surface-to-air missiles and were planning to assassinate me. I postponed the trip and took action that showed the terrorists they were playing a dangerous game. Working with the Iraqis, we made sure we would have no more problems from that particular cell. Once the security problems had been resolved, I resumed plans for the visit.

On August 13, 2008, I flew with my brother Ali and a small Jordanian delegation east from Amman in a C-17 military transport aircraft, heading over the Jordanian desert and across the border into Iraq, a journey I had last made with my father. As we neared Baghdad, the crew began to strap on body armor and peered anxiously out of the windows to see if there was any missile signature. They did not offer us any armor, but luckily I was allowed to sit in the cockpit. As we approached the airport, the plane dove sharply to avoid missiles. This was part of the standard operating procedure for landing at Baghdad's airport. Banking like a jet fighter, the bulky aircraft groaned as it hurtled toward the tarmac. As we landed, I thought back to my previous visits to Baghdad. Now I was returning — and Iraq was ruled by a very different government.

Once on the ground, we transferred to a helicopter and took off, flying low over the streets and buildings of Baghdad. I saw a puff of something white, which I then realized came from the helicopter next to us when it activated its flares and chaff systems designed to prevent missile lock-on. We swerved left, then continued on. Below, the sunlight glinted off what looked like lakes and ponds in the middle of the city. I did not remember these from previous trips and thought perhaps they were a new feature. As we flew closer I saw that they were cesspools festering in the streets. Baghdad once had been a jewel of the Middle East. It produced some of the finest scientists, engineers, and educators in our region. A grand nation of proud and capable people had been reduced to utter devastation. It was depressing to see the damage the city had suffered. All over the streets, every sixty yards were duck-and-dive shelters, bomb shelters that pedestrians could jump into to avoid mortar attacks.

When we arrived at the compound where I had been scheduled to meet Iraqi prime minister Nouri Al Maliki, things were quite confused, as we had not been able to publicize my arrival widely in advance, for security reasons. I was received by Maliki and he and I got along well. In a way, the substance of that meeting was less important than the fact that it took place in Baghdad.

As word of my arrival spread, more and more Iraqis began to arrive at the compound. We tried to meet with a number of other Iraqi officials, but the logistics proved problematic. They had not been told in advance that I was coming to Baghdad. They were therefore given late invitations to come to meet with a senior foreign visitor, but they had trouble reaching the location of this mystery guest because of long delays getting through checkpoints. We waited and waited for one senior parliamentarian, but he did not show up. The head of my security detail was uncomfortable with our party staying at one location too long. Finally he said, "Right, that's it," and we headed back to the airport. We were all subdued as we entered the aircraft. Our plane shot straight up, engines screaming, and we were slammed back into our seats. Once we were out of missile range, I glanced back out of the window.

Remembering the Baghdad I had seen twenty years ago, it was a shock to see it such a shattered mess. My brother Ali told me that the visit left him very depressed. "You too?" I said.

Over time, U.S. policy shifted and combat troops began to leave Iraq. A Status of Forces agreement was ratified by the Iraqi parliament in November 2009, providing for U.S. forces to leave Iraq by the end of 2011. This is a good objective, and I would be the first to say that all foreign troops should leave. But you do not want, as a result of too speedy a withdrawal, to create a political vacuum that a few years later somebody would have to come back and fix. If establishing a strong Iraqi government means withdrawing a little more slowly, that may be the best course. When you talk to those Iraqis who are in government, many will admit privately that they do not want a vacuum, so the withdrawal must be well planned to ensure that the security of Iraq does not suffer.

U.S. combat troops completed their withdrawal from Iraq on August 31, 2010, and President Obama announced the end of U.S. combat operations in Iraq. The security situation deteriorated soon after, as the Iraqi security forces moved in to fill the vacuum. About fifty thousand U.S. troops will remain in Iraq until the end of 2011 to train the Iraqi army and help it assume its responsibilities in securing the country. The hope is that Iraq will stabilize by then and the Iraqi army will be fully equipped to maintain security.

# CHAPTER 26
# A NEW VOICE FROM AMERICA

In March 2007, in a rare honor for a foreign head of state, I was invited to address a joint session of the U.S. Congress. After careful thought, I knew that there was only one topic I could speak about: the urgent need for peace in the Middle East.

I said that throughout the region, the people of the Middle East were searching for a new beginning, and hoping for a future of prosperity and peace. We have seen the danger and destruction of violence, hatred, and injustice, but we have also seen what people can achieve when they are empowered, when they break down walls, when they commit to the future. And we know that peace between the Israelis and Palestinians would offer new possibilities for our region and the entire world. No Palestinian father should be helpless to feed his family and build a future for his sons and daughters. No Israeli mother should feel fear when her child boards a bus.

We cannot afford for one more generation to grow up thinking that violence and conflict are the norm.

After my speech, many American friends came and asked me what they could do to help. Others were more skeptical. Some said, "What does this conflict have to do with us? Why should we get involved in a local struggle halfway around the world?"

I would like to say very clearly now what I told them: resolving the Arab-Israeli conflict is in the national interest of the United States, Europe, and the rest of the international community. The Palestinian issue is of paramount importance to more than a billion and a half Muslims across the world; as such, it truly is a global issue. Many men of violence use the Israeli occupation of Arab lands, especially East Jerusalem, as a rallying cry. They portray the West — and America in particular — as a blind supporter of Israel, and therefore hold "Satanic America" and its allies responsible for the injustice of the Israeli occupation. Terrorist organizations exploit the legitimate frustration of Muslims over the failure to end the Israeli occupation of the Palestinian territories to serve their illegitimate agendas and to generate support for their anti-American rhetoric and actions. It is imperative that

521

we resolve the Palestinian-Israeli conflict in order to deprive these extremists of one of their most potent appeals.

Al Qaeda feeds on the continuation of this conflict. The creation of a Palestinian state would significantly diminish its global appeal and would limit its reach, turning Al Qaeda into a localized threat restricted to certain conflict zones. For more than ten years, the United States, Britain, and their allies have been involved in two wars in the Muslim world. We will witness more violent conflicts that Al Qaeda will exploit to further its reach unless the Palestinians and Israelis find peace. The link may not seem obvious to Americans, but any Muslim will tell you that the injustice suffered by the Palestinian people is a festering sore that radicalizes and mobilizes young men throughout the Muslim world. Al Qaeda won't disappear the moment a Palestinian state comes into being. But it will have a harder time finding new recruits and winning support for its criminal actions.

One of the most vital functions that the United States can play is to help its friends set aside their emotions to think in strategic terms. All too often in my region we are consumed with the latest injustice or act of violence and lose sight of the larger view.

We sometimes need help to raise our eyes to the future, to consider where we want to be in ten, twenty, or thirty years, and to act in such a way as to make that vision a reality.

Unfortunately, when it comes to the Israeli-Palestinian conflict, we do not have the luxury of time. All of the stalling and waiting, the deferred promises, have seriously compromised people's confidence that peace is even a possibility. This undermines moderates and plays directly into the hands of extremists. By failing to act now, we are dooming the Middle East to a future of wars that will reverberate way beyond its borders, a future dominated by terrorists and extremists as moderates lose all credibility.

The elements of a peace settlement are clear. A two-state solution has been endorsed by the entire international community. But we need some help getting there. In the past few years the peace process has stalled, producing little but empty rhetoric, disappointment, and violence.

On November 5, 2008, when Barack Obama won the U.S. presidency by a big margin, many throughout Jordan and the Middle East breathed a sigh of relief. People hoped his administration would bring a new approach to the region and that he would rise to the historic challenge of the peace process — as mediator, middleman, and honest broker. Although it may seem that the complex negotiations should be solely between Israel and the Palestinians, America plays a crucial role. The United States has in the past too often appeared as an uncritical supporter of Israel, but everyone in the region knows that America is the only country Israel will listen to — even if Israel sometimes chooses to disregard what it is told.

In July 2008, Senator Obama paused from campaigning to make an overseas tour around Europe and the Middle East. Accompanied by Senators Jack Reed and Chuck Hagel, he arrived in Jordan on July 22, 2008, after visiting Iraq and Afghanistan. Amman, our capital, was originally built at the intersection of seven hills, and Obama chose the Citadel, a historic site atop one of these hills, to hold a press conference. One of the oldest cities in the world, Amman has been conquered by various empires, including the Greeks, the Romans, and the Umayyads, each of whom left their mark. Standing near the ruins of a Greek temple, a Byzantine church, and an Umayyad palace, Obama spoke about his recent visits to Afghanistan and Iraq and took questions from the press. He stressed the importance of the peace process, saying, "My goal is to make sure that we work, starting from the minute I'm sworn into office, to try to find some breakthroughs."

Following the press conference, I met with Obama at Beit Al Urdun, my residence in the suburbs of Amman. I stressed the importance of a just and lasting peace between Israel and the Palestinians, not just for the sake of peace alone, but because it would bring stability to the region and mitigate dangers from other regional hot spots. From my perspective, I told him, it was extremely important to have a coordinated U.S. foreign policy. During the Clinton administration, a series of envoys would show up in the region, from Dennis Ross to Martin Indyk to Madeleine Albright, each carrying a different message. I described how the same problem carried over into the Bush administration, when the president told me, "My man is Colin Powell. He's the only one who's going to talk foreign policy, and he is directly empowered by me." But Powell was contradicted by others in the administration who carried very different messages.

I advised Obama to select his lead person on the Middle East peace process and stick with that person. He outlined some of his thoughts on how to move forward. It was clear that he understood the issues, and I was left with the strong impression that this was a man who spoke the language of peace. We concluded our discussion and joined the other senators and their aides for a private dinner.

After dinner, I offered to drive Obama, whose next stop was Israel, to the airport. Driving senior guests around is something I do all the time — but his security detail was somewhat nonplussed. Being king, however, has its advantages. To Obama's surprise, I jumped behind the wheel of a gray Mercedes sedan and invited him to take the passenger seat. We drove to the airport, followed by a convoy of other vehicles. In the half-hour drive to the airport we talked about our families and more personal topics, and got to know each other better.

One week after the U.S. election, I traveled to New York for a meeting of the United Nations General Assembly on interfaith dialogue, sponsored by King Abdullah of Saudi Arabia. While I was there, I met with former president Bill Clinton, who urged me not to waste the next two and a half months before the inauguration and to begin to engage with the transition team immediately. This was long before Clinton's wife, Hillary, had been identified as the next secretary of state. "You have to start moving," he told me. Clinton, who came closer than any other American president to getting the two sides to hammer out a deal, is a man whose advice I take seriously, and I began to reach out informally to members of the incoming Obama administration.

On November 12, while I was in the United States, I spoke by phone with Obama. I congratulated him on his recent victory and said I was looking forward to working with him on Middle Eastern issues. I said that while I understood he had a plethora of problems facing him as he launched a new administration — ranging from the global economic crisis to America's budgetary woes and the conflicts in Iraq and Afghanistan — I hoped he would make time to quickly push forward negotiations between the Israelis and Palestinians.

Our conversation left me extremely hopeful. I felt that we would have an American president who really understood that the conflict between Israel and the Palestinians was the root cause of instability in the region, and that achieving a just, comprehensive, and lasting peace would be in America's national interest. It was a stark contrast to the previous eight years, when America's policy had all too often seemed to be to support Israel, right or wrong. But before Obama would come to office, in January 2009, the situation would deteriorate radically.

The Egyptian-brokered cease-fire between Hamas and Israel expired in December 2008 and the two sides again exchanged blows. The cease-fire had been in jeopardy since November, when Israel killed six Hamas activists and Hamas fired rockets into Israel. Gaza had been blockaded economically by Israel since 2007 — even medical supplies were severely limited — and was a ticking time bomb, waiting to explode.

Taking advantage of the political transition period in America and the Christmas and New Year holidays, when most heads of state are vacationing, Israel's prime minister, Ehud Olmert, decided to launch an all-out attack on Gaza on December 27. A weeklong aerial bombardment was followed in early January by a full-scale invasion of Gaza by the Israeli army. A UN fact-finding commission, set up in April 2009 and headed by the eminent South African justice Richard Goldstone, reported that in three weeks of fierce fighting some fourteen hundred Palestinians were killed, including nine hundred to one thousand civilians, over six hundred of whom were women and children. The Israeli army lost ten soldiers, four to friendly fire, and Hamas rockets killed three Israeli civilians. In addition, Israeli fighters bombed the main prison and the Palestinian Legislative Council building as well as a United Nations Relief and Works Agency (UNRWA) school in Gaza City, an action that was judged by the UN investigation to be illegal and in breach of the Geneva Conventions. The Goldstone Report, published in September 2009, concluded that the Israeli armed forces breached internationally recognized codes of military conduct by attacking a hospital in Gaza City with white phosphorus shells and carrying out deliberate attacks against civilians in Gaza, including firing a missile at a mosque during evening prayers, killing fifteen people.

Satellite news networks broadcast images of civilian suffering in Gaza, sparking furious outrage. Across the Arab world people united in demanding a stern response to the Israeli actions. For the first time, a group of Arab countries mounted a concerted attempt to revoke the 2002 Arab Peace Initiative, setting themselves against the moderates and pushing for a rejection of peace with Israel. The moderate Arab countries, including Jordan, Egypt, Saudi Arabia, and the United

Arab Emirates, among others, wondered whether Israel had managed to destroy the peace process for good.

Qatar called for an emergency summit of the Arab League, to be held in Doha on January 16. Fearing a hidden political agenda, Egypt, Saudi Arabia, Jordan, and other like-minded countries stayed away. Only thirteen Arab countries agreed to attend the summit. That was two countries short of the quorum required to make the meeting an official Arab League summit. In the end Qatar widened the guest list to include Iranian president Mahmoud Ahmadinejad and Hamas leader Khaled Meshaal, who traveled to Doha from his base in Damascus.

Some Arab leaders declared the Arab Peace Initiative "already dead," and called for severing all links with Israel, including the closure of Arab embassies (Egyptian and Jordanian) in Israel. But as this was not an official summit, the Arab Peace Initiative could not be formally rejected. If we thought that severing ties with Israel would help bring justice to the Palestinians or peace to the region, we would not hesitate to do so. But the opposite is true. Our treaty with Israel has meant that on many occasions the Palestinians have relied on us to represent their viewpoint and pass on messages. Now, when Gazans were in desperate need of support, the fact that Jordan had diplomatic relations with Israel allowed us to help them.

We opposed the war on Gaza but could do nothing to stop it. We demanded that Israel halt all military operations against Gaza and strongly protested to the Israelis that they should not target civilians. We also provided a channel for relief that was used to deliver most of the Arab, European, and international relief supplies. Hundreds of tons of humanitarian and medical supplies from Jordan and the rest of the world entered Gaza by way of Jordan. We also dispatched a military field hospital — still operating in Gaza — that treated over a thousand patients a day immediately after opening. As of October 2010, 340,000 Gazans have received medical care at the hospital.

On January 19, 2009, Arab heads of state gathered in Kuwait for what was intended to be an economic summit that would devise a response to the global financial crisis. But we could not ignore the continuing crisis in Gaza. King Abdullah of Saudi Arabia voiced the concerns of many when he said, "The Arab Initiative will not remain on the table indefinitely."

The emir of Kuwait, Sheikh Sabah Al-Ahmad Al-Jaber Al-Sabah, resisted the pressure from countries calling for the Arab Peace Initiative to be scrapped, and the final communiqué confined itself to calling for a cease-fire in Gaza, immediate Israeli withdrawal, and an investigation into possible war crimes committed by the Israeli army.

The next day, as Israeli troops at last withdrew from Gaza, around a million people gathered in Washington to watch Barack Obama being sworn in as the forty-fourth president of the United States. President Obama honored his campaign promise, and his first calls the following morning were to the leaders of Jordan, Egypt, Israel, and the Palestinian Authority.

Typically, recent U.S. presidents have waited until the middle of their second term to take on the Israeli-Palestinian conflict, with one eye on the present and the other on their historical legacy. But by engaging forcefully from day one, Obama seemed to be presenting the region with a rare opportunity to make progress on this most difficult and intractable of problems. We all had to wonder: Would leaders in the region be able to seize this chance?

Developments in Israeli politics were not encouraging. The optimistic spirit of Annapolis was long gone. The negotiations that had been launched at Annapolis in late 2007 ended in July 2008, when Olmert, following allegations of corruption, announced that he would not seek reelection as Kadima leader and that he would resign as prime minister after the party elected a successor. In September, his foreign minister, Tzipi Livni, won the leadership of the Kadima Party. But Livni was unable to form a coalition. Olmert stayed on as prime minister in accordance with the law, which mandates that the incumbent remain in office until a new prime minister is sworn in. On February 10, 2009, Israelis went to the polls. Although Kadima won the most seats in the Knesset, Livni was again unable to form a coalition. So Israeli president Shimon Peres asked the Likud leader, Benjamin Netanyahu, to attempt to form a coalition government.

On March 16, Netanyahu signed a coalition agreement with Israel's third largest party, Yisrael Beiteinu (Israel is Our Home), a far-right nationalist party led by Avigdor Lieberman, who was offered the position of foreign minister. In a sign of the changing sentiments of the Israeli public, the historic Labor Party, home of my father's old peace partner Yitzhak Rabin and of Ehud Barak, which had been the dominant political party from 1948 until the late 1970s, was now only the fourth largest, behind Kadima, Likud, and Yisrael Beiteinu. The return after a decade of a hard-liner who had done so much to undermine Oslo, and the inclusion of right-wing Israeli nationalists in his coalition government, did not bode well for the peace process.

While Netanyahu was finalizing his coalition, the twenty-two members of the Arab League prepared to meet for their annual summit in Doha. Mindful of the previous attempts of some Arab countries to withdraw the Arab Peace Initiative, I knew the peace-seeking members would have to act aggressively if there were to be any chance of keeping the process alive.

A few days before every Arab League summit, the foreign ministers come together to prepare for the full meeting of the heads of state. I instructed my foreign minister, Nasser Judeh, to ensure that everybody at the foreign ministers' meeting understood that the new president of the United States had to be supported in his early engagement in the peace process. We should not allow ourselves to be overcome by emotion, horrendous though Israel's war on Gaza was. Nobody would benefit from continued occupation and misery. You have to make sure, I told him, that the Arab summit comes up with a pragmatic statement that pushes for

a collective effort at reviving the peace talks.

In Doha, the mood was very negative. Some Arab foreign ministers argued that there was no point in pursuing peace in view of the Israeli government's intransigence and its continuing refusal to abide by international law. Some argued that the Arab Peace Initiative should be pulled off the table. Netanyahu had just been elected, they said, and that meant Israel would soon be even more right-wing and intransigent. Forget trying to make peace with such a government. Our foreign minister and a few others argued that even though the general mood was pessimistic, we should still try to use any window of opportunity.

At the summit my objective was to convince my fellow Arab leaders to think strategically and maintain a unified stance, to show the world once and for all who was the roadblock to peace. We all blasted Israel for its war on Gaza, but I urged my fellow heads of state to look for a ray of hope amid the general darkness. We must give Obama a chance, I argued. He had been in office for just six weeks and was already doing some good things. He had appointed George Mitchell, a former senator with a track record of success in Northern Ireland and deep familiarity with the Middle East, as his

special envoy on the peace process and had deployed him to the region immediately. He was saying that Israeli settlements were illegal and should stop. His secretary of state, Hillary Clinton, knew the region and the issues extremely well from her time as a senator and as first lady. Everyone remembered how close President Clinton had come; we should not do what many expected from the Arabs, reject new initiatives out of hand. "Let's show some prudence and restraint, reaffirm our commitment to the Arab Peace Initiative, and see where this current initiative is going," I said.

In the end, this argument carried the day, and our commitment to the Arab Peace Initiative was reaffirmed. But the strong emotional reaction across the region to Israel's conduct in the Gaza war suggested that the initiative would not survive another major assault.

I told my fellow heads of state that President Obama had called me a few days before and invited me to visit Washington. How could we use this visit to advance the cause of peace?

Prince Saud Al-Faisal, the wise and experienced foreign minister of Saudi Arabia, came over during the summit and suggested to me that we carry a message from the

summit to President Obama. We invited the foreign ministers from Lebanon, Qatar, Palestine, Saudi Arabia, Syria, and Egypt, as well as the secretary-general of the Arab League, to come to Jordan to work out a joint Arab position. Some of these foreign ministers had also been in contact with British foreign secretary David Miliband, who was actively involved in efforts to revive the peace process.

The ministers (other than the Syrian foreign minister, who was unable to attend) met in Amman on April 11. They discussed talking to the United States about a number of confidence-building measures between Israel and the Arab states that might be offered in the event that Israel should freeze its settlement construction in anticipation of resumed negotiations, allowing a return to the situation before the outbreak of the second intifada in 2000. Those measures would include revitalizing some of the ties that had been developed in 1994 after our peace treaty with Israel. At that time Israeli trade offices were opened in some Arab countries; there was increased movement of people and goods, and Israeli visitors were welcomed in Arab countries even in the absence of diplomatic relations. But most of that had ended abruptly in 2000 after the breakdown of the Camp David negotiations and the outbreak of the second intifada. The trade offices were closed and there was little or no interaction between Israel and Arab countries, other than Jordan and Egypt, but our relations with Israel had also suffered. What we were offering was not normalization, but measures to serve as a positive background to negotiations.

I agreed to convey this proposal to the new president.

In late April 2009, I arrived in Washington, the first Arab leader to visit the White House since the election. I met with Obama privately in the president's dining room, a small room next to the Oval Office. The atmosphere was refreshingly relaxed. President Obama is knowledgeable about the world beyond America's borders and balanced in his approach. A personable man, he gives the impression that you and he are old friends. He told me that he was facing many challenges in the Middle East, but before discussing them, he wanted to hear what I had to say.

I told him that I believed it was imperative to relaunch negotiations between Israel and the Palestinians as soon as possible. We would have to move forward quickly on a two-state solution, as the growing antagonism between Israel and the Palestinians was throwing the whole notion of a negotiated agreement into question. Further undermining the situation was the cancer of Israeli settlements spreading across the Occupied Territories.

I said there was an increasing pessimism among Arab leaders about the possibility of peace. Since the Gaza war, some had even urged that the Arab Peace Initiative be withdrawn. But others were still hopeful and put stock in his early engagement with the peace process. If the Israeli government were to take a bold step, I said, such as freezing settlement construction, which the Palestinians, the Arabs, and many in the international community had long demanded, then we would be prepared to return to the spirit that had existed before the second intifada and would offer some concrete confidence-building measures to help improve the environment for the resumption of peace talks.

Drawing on my past experience, I then spoke to him candidly about the new Israeli prime minister, who was scheduled to visit Washington a few weeks later. "Mr. President," I said, "Netanyahu will come to you and he will want to talk about four things: Iran, Iran, Iran, and the claim that he has no Palestinian partner." I said it would be a mistake to focus the conversation on Iran. The best way, in my view, to address all the major issues in the Middle East would be to resolve the Israeli-Palestinian conflict. As to a Palestinian partner, I said, this partner would be greatly empowered if the Israelis would for once get serious about peace. In fact, one could argue that since Sharon's election in 2001, the Palestinians had not had an Israeli partner for peace.

The president said he would not jump to conclusions before Netanyahu's visit, and that he would give him the benefit of the doubt. But he added that he planned to be tough on settlements. I reminded the president that I had experience with Netanyahu and urged him not to take everything the Israeli leader promised as certain. He had reneged on many previous commitments. The president said that he would vigorously pursue a two-state solution.

Our private meeting ended not long after that and we joined our staff members for an expanded discussion. The meeting was followed by a press conference at which Obama said:

I am a strong supporter of a two-state solution. . . . What we want to do is to step
back from the abyss; to say, as hard as it
is, as difficult as it may be, the prospect
of peace still exists — but it's going to
require some hard choices, it's going to
require resolution on the part of all the actors involved, and it's going to require that
we create some concrete steps that all
parties can take that are evidence of that
resolution. And the United States is going
to deeply engage in this process to see if
we can make progress.

I took heart and dared to hope that we
would soon be back at the negotiating table
in earnest. I said that the task at hand was to
sequence events over the next two months in
order to allow Israelis and Palestinians and
Israelis and Arabs to sit around the table and
move this process forward.

Next I headed to the State Department to
meet with Secretary Clinton. We had first
met many years before, under very different
circumstances, and it was good to see an old
friend while on official business. We talked
about how to improve conditions for the
Palestinians and how to create the necessary
environment for a successful agreement. I
said that I believed the Palestinian National

541

Authority was a credible partner in the peace efforts and that we would work together with other Arab countries to shore up support for the government of Palestinian prime minister Salam Fayyad, who had submitted his resignation to Palestinian president Mahmoud Abbas to allow for the formation of a unity government with Hamas. But talks with Hamas were not getting anywhere. A few weeks after we returned from the United States, Abbas moved to form a cabinet without Hamas, and Fayyad was sworn in as prime minister on May 19. His government, which enjoyed the support of most Arab countries, would be a ready and able partner in the peace process. Fayyad is committed to peaceful negotiations as a means to solving the conflict with Israel on the basis of the two-state solution. In his first term as prime minister, which began in June 2007, after the Hamas takeover of Gaza, he won the respect of Arab and Western governments for building Palestinian institutions and ensuring good governance.

Although the region had suffered from a brutal war in Gaza in January, in many ways the prospects for peace were better than they had been in a decade. We had a new American president who had immediately begun to engage seriously with the peace process, and who intended to approach the Muslim world on the basis of mutual respect and shared interests. We had a supportive Palestinian leadership, which was ready to make sacrifices for peace. And we had the strong support of the wider Arab world, which had signaled its desire to normalize relations with Israel and fully integrate it into the region on the basis of the Arab Peace Initiative.

The one wild card was the newly elected Israeli prime minister, Benjamin Netanyahu. In his previous tenure as prime minister, he had gained a reputation as an aggressive hard-liner, unwilling to compromise. As I headed back to Amman I wondered whether the previous decade had changed him. I would have to wait and see.

On May 14, Netanyahu flew to Amman. I was not particularly optimistic about the meeting, as our previous interactions had not been productive. We began with a tête-à-tête. Netanyahu seemed a little uncomfortable, perhaps also remembering our last encounter.

"Mr. Prime Minister," I said, hoping to break the ice, "congratulations on your election." He smiled noncommittally and I decided to dive right in. "I know that for you the life of every Israeli is sacred," I said, "but

543

I believe that the best way to protect your citizens is to come to terms with the Palestinians, to make a just and enduring peace based on the establishment of a Palestinian state." I told him my goal was to help forge a peace between Israel and the Arabs and said that Arab countries were committed to a comprehensive peace, which would allow Israel to have full, normal relations with Arab and Muslim countries, not just an exchange of embassies and icy stares. I said I strongly believed that peaceful relations between Israel and its Arab neighbors would ensure our collective security and bring economic benefits for all. I spoke of the benefits to the Israeli economy of Arab investment and the potential for Israeli investment in the Arab world.

Once Netanyahu understood that, regardless of our differences, I was trying to find common ground, he began to relax. He told me that, at fifty-nine, he was almost as old as the state of Israel. And he believed that this was the first time in his almost sixty years that he had seen Israel and the Arabs face a common threat. I had warned President Obama that Netanyahu would most likely try to focus their discussion on Iran. Now he was doing the same thing with me.

"If you want us to feel that Iran is a common threat," I said, "we will first have to solve the problem at the heart of our region's woes, and that is the Arab-Israeli conflict. It is what matters most to us, and it is what you can do the most to impact." I urged him to take serious steps toward reaching peace with the Palestinians and told him he would have to stop building new settlements in the West Bank and East Jerusalem, as they were eating away at land that should be part of the future Palestinian state and threatening the viability of a two-state solution. I also stressed the need to understand the sanctity of Jerusalem to all Muslims and to halt all unilateral actions in the holy city.

Netanyahu told me that there were some things he could not say in public, because of domestic political pressures. So talking about the need for a two-state solution and a freeze on settlements would not be easy for him. But he wanted to move forward and said he understood the importance of peace.

"If you genuinely want peace," I said, "there are some important signals you can send to the Arab world. Convince us that you are committed to making something happen in the next several months. Otherwise the support of all Arab states, including Saudi Arabia, for the Arab Peace Initiative will start to wane."

Our meeting went much better than I had expected. Netanyahu came across as a different man from the one I had known ten years before. He did not reject everything I said out of hand. He seemed eager to make progress, but I knew that the proof of his intent would be in his actions, not his words.

After forty minutes alone, we moved into an expanded session with members of our staff. We had begun to discuss the details of the peace process when Netanyahu said that he intended to focus on the economic track.

I argued that economic opportunities could not be an alternative to political independence for the Palestinians. "What about the political track?" I pressed. "Given your history, the Arabs expect you to focus on economic and security issues at the expense of peace talks."

Netanyahu took my comments in stride and said that perhaps he should start with the political track. But he offered no concrete indication of what he might be prepared to do.

"That would be the prudent thing to do," I said, hoping to hammer the message home.

Once he had left, I reflected on where we stood. Netanyahu was a right-winger through and through, but I hoped we would be able to work together to bring a lasting peace to the region. We had the Arab Peace Initiative. We had an engaged U.S. president. Was it too much to hope that we might also have a pragmatic Israeli prime minister who would want to leave behind him a legacy of peace?

# CHAPTER 27
## FORTRESS ISRAEL OR A FIFTY-SEVEN-STATE SOLUTION?

Throughout the spring and early summer of 2009, I remained optimistic that we were on the brink of a breakthrough. There were reasons to believe that the Americans would roll out their peace plan soon. On June 4, three weeks after Netanyahu's visit to Jordan, President Obama traveled to Cairo to deliver a major speech to the Arab and Muslim world. The president spoke about the urgent need to bring peace between Israel and the Palestinians, saying:

> But if we see this conflict only from one side or the other, then we will be blind to the truth: The only resolution is for the aspirations of both sides to be met through two states, where Israelis and Palestinians each live in peace and security.
>
> That is in Israel's interest, Palestine's interest, America's interest, and the world's interest. And that is why I intend to per-

sonally pursue this outcome with all the patience and dedication that the task requires.

Yet as June became July, and July became August, the progress we had hoped for a few months earlier began to look ever more distant. The Israelis refused to commit to a total settlement freeze — a necessary element in the eyes of the Arab world for creating an environment conducive to serious talks. The Israeli position defied the direct demands of President Obama, the European Union, and the rest of the international community. But this almost unanimous international stand did little to change the position of Netanyahu, who would only go as far as announcing, on November 25, 2009, after much arm-twisting by the United States and very public confrontation, a ten-month partial moratorium on the building of new settlements in the West Bank. This moratorium excluded building in East Jerusalem and did not apply to twenty-nine hundred buildings already under construction.

The peacemaking efforts appeared deadlocked, and the hope of a breakthrough was fading. The credibility of Obama and moderate Arab leaders in the Arab world was dealt a blow. We were not working in a vacuum, and spoilers in the region did not waste any time in attacking the whole peace process as a faulty approach that was yet again proving ineffective in ending the occupation.

At one point there were indications that an American peace plan would be announced in late September when world leaders, including Israeli prime minister Netanyahu and Palestinian president Abbas, would gather for the UN General Assembly meeting in New York. At Obama's urging, Abbas and Netanyahu held their first meeting since Netanyahu's election six month earlier. But the meeting produced no results. The Israeli government would not do what was necessary to restart peace negotiations. In addition to the halting of settlement building, the Palestinians wanted the Israeli government to confirm that it recognized previous agreements. They also demanded a clear Israeli commitment to the establishment of an independent Palestinian state on the territories occupied in 1967 with agreed-upon land swaps. Netanyahu was adamant that he could not change his position on settlements and he would not commit to previous agreements or to any terms of reference for the negotiations.

Ever since Israel occupied the West Bank and East Jerusalem in 1967, successive Israeli governments have approved the construction of settlements in occupied Palestinian territory. There are now about one hundred and twenty settlements and around a hundred "outposts," Israeli communities built in the West Bank by Israeli settlers without official Israeli authorization, as well as more than twenty settlements in Jerusalem — altogether housing more than half a million settlers, over two hundred thousand of whom live in Jerusalem. These settlements are illegal under international law, as they have been built on land from which the UN has repeatedly called on Israel to withdraw. A freeze on settlement building was an essential component of the road map of 2003. The Palestinians' position has been that ending both the construction and expansion of settlements is a necessary prerequisite to successful negotiations. The problem is that the settlements are undermining the viability of a sovereign Palestinian state. Israel likes to present a settlement freeze as a major concession (and one that, so far, it has been unwilling to make), but in fact it would simply be abiding by international law.

In the weeks leading up to the UN General Assembly meeting in September 2009, despite intense American pressure, Netanyahu refused to agree to a total settlement freeze. In fact, new settlement construction was authorized. The problem these settlements presented to the Palestinians and their Arab supporters was obvious: How could Mahmoud Abbas sit down and negotiate a peace agreement with a partner who was daily creating new facts on the ground that were changing the demography and geography of the very land where the Palestinian state would be established? If the Israeli government were truly committed to a two-state solution, why would it continue to build settlements on land that would belong to a future Palestinian state? Was the Israeli government building free housing for the Palestinians? Not likely. Its refusal to halt settlement activity raised legitimate doubts about its commitment to the creation of a Palestinian state.

On September 23, President Obama delivered an important speech. In his address to the UN General Assembly, he declared:

We continue to call on Palestinians to end incitement against Israel, and we continue to emphasize that America does not accept the legitimacy of continued Israeli settlements.

The time has come — the time has come to re-launch negotiations without preconditions that address the permanent status issues: security for Israelis and Palestinians, borders, refugees, and Jerusalem. And the goal is clear: Two states living side by side in peace and security — a Jewish state of Israel, with true security for all Israelis; and a viable, independent Palestinian state with contiguous territory that ends the occupation that began in 1967 and realizes the potential of the Palestinian people.

In this speech and in that of June 2009, Obama set out U.S. policy in clear terms. We in Jordan describe this policy position as the "Obama terms of reference" for negotiations to reach a just and lasting peace that would be in the interests of Israel, Palestine, America, and the world.

As the hope of spring turned into the disappointment of fall, the American administration became preoccupied by a whole raft of urgent problems: Afghanistan and Pakistan; new developments in Iran's nuclear program; health care reform, which Obama placed at the top of his domestic agenda; and the continuing global economic crisis.

These remained the overriding concerns for the United States through the first months of 2010, preventing the administration from giving the peace process its full attention. By now we were facing a major crisis. As encouraging as Obama's words had been, they had done very little to change the reality on the ground. Frustration replaced hope.

As this book goes to press, we are just one year short of the twentieth anniversary of a peace process that started in Madrid in October 1991. But the contrast between now and then could not be greater. We are in a far darker place than we were nearly twenty years ago. Then, Palestinians and Israelis met face-to-face to begin negotiating a shared future. Both sides looked to the future with anticipation. By any measure we have regressed when we no longer speak of direct negotiations but of "proximity talks," as an intermediary (the United States) shuttles between Israelis and Palestinians.

The proximity talks initiative emerged in early 2010, following a nearly yearlong effort by U.S. Middle East special envoy George Mitchell to launch direct negotiations. Thus far, his efforts have not produced the necessary progress, as Netanyahu has essentially maintained his uncompromising position on settlement building in the West Bank and East Jerusalem and continues to refuse to resume negotiations on the basis of the agreements the Palestinians reached with previous Israeli governments after the Oslo Accords.

All Arab states backed the Palestinian leadership's participation in the proximity talks as an alternative to no talks at all, with the hope that they would soon transition to direct and serious negotiations. But we knew we were grasping at straws. We supported proximity talks because we believed a vacuum in peace efforts would only benefit hard-liners, who would exploit the failure to revive the negotiations to push their extremist agendas. And Netanyahu would benefit most from a Palestinian decision not to engage in proximity talks. As he came under increased American and international pressure for continuing to build settlements and thereby blocking the resumption of negotiations, he was eager to provoke the Palestinians and Arab countries into withdrawing from the peace efforts, so that he could once again claim he had no negotiating partner.

In April 2010, I traveled to the United States and met with President Obama in Washington. Again, the Palestinian-Israeli conflict was at the center of our discussion.

We were both disappointed and concerned that more progress had not been made in the last year and hoped that the proximity talks would soon pave the way to direct negotiations. After the meeting, it was clear to me that the United States was not yet ready to roll out its plan to push the parties toward a final settlement. The administration wanted the parties to begin proximity talks and would then assess the situation at some point before throwing its own ideas into the negotiations.

I came out of the meeting assured of the president's continued commitment to resolving the Palestinian-Israeli conflict. But I knew that it would be some time before real progress could be achieved, given Netanyahu's intransigence. Accordingly, I felt that our task would be to keep the hope alive until America was ready to bring its full weight to bear on the parties to resume serious negotiations with the intention of advancing toward a settlement. The region could not afford to lose hope yet again. That would mean war.

Back in March, right when U.S. vice president Joe Biden was visiting Jerusalem, the Israelis announced plans to build sixteen hundred new settlement homes in occupied East Jerusalem. The Israeli move embarrassed and angered the vice president and effectively challenged American authority. George Mitchell canceled his next trip to the region and Hillary Clinton called Netanyahu to lodge a formal complaint. Harsh exchanges followed between Washington and Tel Aviv. The diplomatic row came on the heels of a very public disagreement between the U.S. administration and Israel the previous fall over the question of a settlement freeze, amid increased international criticism of Israel for derailing the peace process. The European Union was particularly vocal in slamming Israeli settlement policies and their impact on peacemaking efforts. On December 8, 2009, during the Swedish presidency of the EU, its Foreign Affairs Council expressed serious concern about the lack of progress and called for the urgent resumption of negotiations that would lead "within an agreed time-frame to a two-state solution with the State of Israel and an independent, democratic, contiguous and viable State of Palestine, living side by side in peace and security."

The council said that "settlements, the separation barrier where built on occupied land, demolitions of homes and evictions are illegal under international law, constitute an obstacle to peace and threaten to make a two-state solution impossible." It urged the government of Israel "to immediately end all settlement activities, in East Jerusalem and the rest of the West Bank and including natural growth, and to dismantle all outposts erected since March 2001," as required by phase one of the road map of 2003.

The council noted that it had never recognized Israel's annexation of East Jerusalem, emphasizing that "if there is to be a genuine peace, a way must be found through negotiations to resolve the status of Jerusalem as the future capital of two states." In subsequent statements, the EU strongly condemned Israel's announcement of new settlement plans.

In April 2010, former Israeli foreign minister Tzipi Livni lamented Israel's deteriorating standing in the international community. "The world today," Livni wrote in an article, "does not, at best, know what the policy of the Israeli government is, and, at worst, does not trust its intentions."

Shortly before my trip to Washington, I attended an Arab League Summit meeting in Sirte, Libya. The summit reiterated its support for the Arab Peace Initiative, but with every passing day that sees no progress, pressure builds to abandon negotiations as a means to solve the conflict. Tensions in the region are running high on more than one front. Gaza continues to be a virtual prison, with its more than one and a half million people living in desperate conditions. Jerusalem is a tinderbox and Israel is playing with fire by trying to change its identity and empty it of its Christian and Muslim population through house demolitions and evictions, and by refusing to allow Arabs to build in the city. Further afield, on the Lebanese-Israeli front, we appear to be on the verge of witnessing another confrontation as Israel continues to occupy Lebanese territory in the south and Hezbollah develops its military capabilities. In the background of all of this is the crisis with Iran and its implications for regional security.

Proximity talks were officially launched in May after a number of visits by Mitchell to the region. Abbas went into the talks with the support of the Arab League, whose ministerial committee on the Arab Peace Initiative met on May 1 and said it would reconvene in four months to assess progress. The hope was that these talks would agree on terms of reference for direct final status negotiations.

We supported these talks, as they seemed to be the only alternative to complete disengagement, which would have been a dangerous blow to our decades-long efforts to achieve peace. The hope was that the talks would bring the two sides close enough for them to resume direct negotiations. And yet by July, no agreement had been reached on the terms of reference for direct negotiations. Jordan's position was that failure was not an option, and we continued to work with all parties to ensure that progress was made to bring the Israelis and Palestinians back to the negotiating table.

Senator Mitchell worked with the Palestinians and the Israelis to an agreement on conditions for the resumption of direct negotiations. His efforts hit a deadlock. The Palestinians wanted the proximity talks to address the borders, security, refugees, Jerusalem, and other complex final status issues. Abbas presented Mitchell with fully developed position papers on all these issues. He told him that he wanted borders and security addressed first, because an agreement on the borders of the future Palestinian state would facilitate the resolution of the problem of settlements, while an agreement on security arrangements would tackle Israel's top concern.

Netanyahu, however, would not engage in any substantive discussion on the issues. He continued to speak in general terms about his commitment to peace but would not put any ideas on the table. He held that such engagement would have to be made in direct negotiations.

The Palestinians and others in the region were growing more frustrated by the day with the failure to make progress. Hopes that the U.S. administration would salvage the situation by putting forward its own proposals to get the process moving vanished as Mitchell and other U.S. officials made it clear that Washington would not risk offering proposals that either party could reject out of hand.

As the September deadline for the end of the settlement moratorium loomed, in what many in the region saw as a major turnaround in the U.S. position, Washington stopped demanding a total freeze of settlement building as a requirement for the two sides to engage in direct negotiations. The Obama administration started to push for a resumption of direct talks even absent a settlement freeze, and to pressure Abbas to agree to the new terms. The Palestinians argued that they could not directly engage the Israelis without ending settlement activities or at least announcing clear terms of reference for the new round of talks.

All of us who had supported the proximity talks were severely criticized by those in the region who believed the exercise was futile. Abbas in particular was accused of succumbing to U.S. pressure and compromising the interests of his people. He felt it would be political suicide for him to move to direct negotiations without identifying as the objective of these negotiations the establishment of a Palestinian state on the basis of the 1967 borders with minor land swaps. The picture was getting bleak again. But we knew we had to keep the hope alive to find a way out of this hole. Abandoning the process before exploring it to the fullest was not an option. This would have meant surrendering the region to a state of hopelessness that would put it on a new vicious course of conflict and war.

On July 23, I received a phone call from Obama. The president was by now determined that direct negotiations were the only way to break the impasse. He reiterated his commitment to resolving the Israeli-Palestinian conflict, stressing that he would go all the way to make sure a solution was reached. But unless the Palestinians agreed to talk to the Israelis directly, his administration would end its involvement in the process. Obama was clear: the Palestinians could either work with him to solve this issue through direct negotiations and count on his full commitment, or walk away and be on their own. The president delivered the same message to other leaders in the region.

A choice had to be made. Three days later, on July 26, I received Abbas in Amman. We agreed that the conditions were not ideal for transitioning to direct negotiations. Netanyahu's refusal to accept the earlier terms of reference and to stop building new settlements was discouraging, as was the unwillingness of the United States to commit to rolling out its own bridging proposals to rescue the negotiations should they reach a dead end. But to say no to Washington would be very costly to the Palestinian people and their quest for statehood. Abandoning the peace process was not a decision to be made lightly. The biggest winner would be Netanyahu, who would blame the Palestinians for aborting the peace efforts, and would go on creating new facts on the ground that would make the establishment of a Palestinian state impossible. At the same time, the Palestinians could not justify moving to direct negotiations that would reinvent the wheel, disregarding progress made in previous rounds of talks over the two decades since Madrid. We agreed to explore all possible options, and to consult with other Arab leaders over the next steps. We also agreed that discussions with the American administration to find a way out should continue.

The next day I received Netanyahu in Amman. It had been over a year since his last visit, and I felt that the time was right for another face-to-face discussion, given the urgency of the situation at hand. In a one-on-one conversation we had before meeting over lunch with our staff, I told the prime minister that we had a unique opportunity to give our people the peace that they yearned for. If we missed this opportunity, the Israelis, the Palestinians — all of us in the region — would have to live with the terrible consequences of more devastating wars. Netanyahu again spoke in broad terms about his government's commitment to reaching a peace deal with the Palestinians. But he said Israel must be assured of its security first. I told him that reaching a peace agreement with the Palestinians within a comprehensive framework that would ensure normal relations with all Arab and Muslim countries would be the best guarantee of Israeli security. I urged the prime minister to halt the building of settlements so that serious discussions over borders and other essential issues could begin.

Over lunch with our staff, we discussed the economic potential of the region in the event of a peace agreement. Netanyahu spoke of his plans to build railroads up to the borders of Jordan and Syria. I mentioned that Jordan too was in the process of building railroads that would link up with a new Saudi railroad to the southeast and with Syria in the north. If we had peace in the region, Israel could link to our railroad and thus be connected with the Arab countries in the Gulf and with Europe through Syria. But under current circumstances, Israel's railroad network would stop at its border. We discussed other regional infrastructure projects that Israel could plug into if we succeed in reaching comprehensive peace. I was hoping that by emphasizing the willingness of all Arab and Muslim countries to build normal ties with Israel and by highlighting the great potential of regional cooperation, I would encourage the Israeli prime minister to take the necessary steps to push the peace efforts forward. The meeting ended in a positive spirit as we discussed the potential for growth in bilateral economic cooperation between our public and private sectors. But we needed more than lofty visions of future economic cooperation to get us out of the bind we were in. And positive words had not translated into actions in the past. But the stakes were too high and I was determined to leave no stone unturned in my efforts to push for progress.

In the meantime, pressure on Abbas was mounting. Before a meeting of the Arab League Follow-Up Committee on the Arab Peace Initiative in Cairo on July 29, Abbas spoke of the difficult choices he was facing. "Never in my life have I been faced with as much pressure as that the United States and the European Union are currently putting on me to resume direct negotiations with the Israelis," he said in a press interview. The moment was critical and the Arab foreign ministers meeting in Cairo realized that. After long discussions and hard work by Jordan, Egypt, Saudi Arabia, and the Palestinians, among other moderate countries, the foreign ministers agreed to the principle of resuming direct negotiations, but said it was up to Abbas to decide when to do so. The ministers drafted a letter that would be sent to Obama outlining the necessary conditions for the talks to resume. Among these were the articulation of clear terms of reference for the negotiations and the halting of settlement activities. Abbas was empowered by the Arab League to assess the situation and decide accordingly whether to hold direct talks with the Israelis or not.

On August 12, I met with President Mubarak in Cairo on the quickly developing situation. Mitchell and other U.S. officials had floated the idea that Egypt or Jordan host the relaunching of the direct talks and that Secretary Clinton be invited. We both felt this was not sufficient. If the talks were to be resumed, we agreed, the United States must have ownership of the process. President Obama would have to demonstrate his full support of the process if it were to have any realistic chance of success. That meant that Obama would have to either host the relaunching event in Washington or attend the event if it was to be hosted by Egypt or Jordan. We also agreed that a formula would have to be found for giving the Palestinians some assurances about the terms of reference for the negotiations. After the meeting with Mubarak, I met with Abbas, who was also in Egypt to see Mubarak.

Mubarak, Abbas, and I all recognized that continued U.S. engagement in the process was essential. And we did not want the Palestinians to be blamed for the collapse of peace efforts. Creative ideas were needed to ensure that the negotiations would not be a futile exercise that would trigger another endless process and compromise Palestinian interests.

In the days that followed, and after intense discussions that involved many Arab countries, the Palestinians, the Europeans, and the Americans, it was agreed that the talks would resume in Washington on September 2, following a relaunching event hosted by Obama the previous day and attended by Mubarak, Abbas, Netanyahu, Tony Blair (representing the Quartet of the European Union, Russia, the United States, and the United Nations), and myself. Before that, the Quartet would set the stage for the negotiations by issuing a statement declaring that the objective of the negotiations was to reach a final settlement on the basis of a two-state solution.

On August 20, the Quartet issued a statement in which it reaffirmed its members' support for "direct negotiations between the Israelis and the Palestinians to resolve all final status issues." The Quartet reiterated positions it had adopted in previous statements, particularly those announced in Moscow on March 19, 2010. These stressed that negotiations should "lead to a settlement, negotiated between the parties, that ends the occupation which began in 1967 and results in the emergence of an independent, democratic, and viable Palestinian state living side by side in peace and security with Israel and its other neighbors."

The Quartet called on the Palestinians and Israelis to join in launching direct negotiations on September 2 in Washington. It expressed its "determination to support the parties throughout the negotiations, which can be completed within one year," and urged both sides to refrain from provocative actions and inflammatory rhetoric. The Palestinians considered the Quartet's statement to be terms of reference for the negotiations.

Invitations to the negotiations were issued by Secretary Clinton on the same day. In the letters she sent to the Israelis and the Palestinians, Clinton emphasized the commitment of the U.S. administration to a comprehensive Middle East peace. She said, "As we move forward, it is important that actions by all sides help to advance our effort, not hinder it. There have been difficulties in the past; there will be difficulties ahead. Without a doubt, we will hit more obstacles. The enemies of peace will keep trying to defeat us and to derail these talks. But I ask the parties to persevere, to keep moving forward even through difficult times, and to continue working to achieve a just and lasting peace in the region."

Clinton called me that afternoon to brief me on the preparations and to deliver my invitation. I spent the following days discussing steps that could be taken to ensure progress with fellow Arab leaders. I met with King Abdullah of Saudi Arabia; King Hamad Al Khalifa of Bahrain; and the emir of Kuwait, Sheikh Sabah Al-Ahmad Al-Sabah. I also consulted on the phone with King Mohammed VI of Morocco and Syrian president Bashar al-Assad. None of us had any illusions as to how difficult the situation was. But most were of the view that despite the apparent concessions the Palestinians had to make by engaging in the negotiations without a full settlement freeze or terms of reference or even an agenda for the negotiations, the talks represent an opportunity that must be supported.

I left for Washington on August 29. Before leaving, I felt it was important to address the Israeli public directly, to try to explain how important it was for them to support courageous decisions. In an interview with Israeli television that aired on August 28, I said that more than ever, we needed politicians with backbones who were prepared to make the difficult decisions necessary for peace. And because politicians tend to get nervous when they face issues of any real magnitude or controversy, they would need to know they had the support of the people to muster up the courage to move forward.

Unfortunately, people on both sides had lost faith in the process. Failure to deliver over numerous rounds of previous talks had led to an alarming erosion of public support for negotiations. Since the Oslo Accords, Israel had gradually shifted to the right — abandoning the Labor Party in favor of more nationalist and religious alternatives. Many of those who had supported the peace process after Rabin's assassination had given up hope or left the country. The Arab world had also been shaken by decades of false promises and reversals. The "security barrier," the land seizures and arbitrary arrests, the Gaza war and the invasion of Lebanon had all taken their toll — and so too had the climate of suspicion and antagonism surrounding the Iraq War. Skepticism was particularly high this time around due to Netanyahu's reputation as an uncompromising hard-liner and to the perception that the Palestinians had been forced to make major concessions by giving up on the requirement that settlement activities halt before talks could begin.

I knew that by supporting direct talks against the backdrop of such public opposition, Mubarak, Abbas, and I would lose political capital among our people, who did not believe much would come out of the negotiations. But we felt the price of abandoning this last chance was too great. We could not afford another period of U.S. disengagement. Here we had a U.S. president who was putting his personal weight behind the process. We could not throw this opportunity away; it would only benefit the spoilers. When I had seen Obama in Washington in April 2009, I had told him that this time the Arabs would not leave him to do the heavy lifting on his own. We were at a decisive crossroads. And we had to make sure we moved in the right direction.

All eyes were on us when Obama, Mubarak, Abbas, Netanyahu, and I walked through the door to a room full of cameras at the White House on the evening of September 1. We were there to send a message of hope and to show that serious action was being taken to resolve a conflict that had for decades evaded the efforts of many good men. That was not an easy message to send amid the general mood of disappointment and disbelief prevailing in the region. People wanted action, not words, and action was what we hoped to achieve in the intense rounds of discussions that would immediately follow.

President Obama spoke of his unwavering commitment to resolving the conflict. Mubarak was clear in stressing Arab support for a solution, and I pointed to the difficulties ahead but warned of the disastrous consequences of failure. Netanyahu went to extreme lengths to present himself as a man of peace and addressed Abbas directly, saying he came to Washington to work for a historic peace. Abbas was grand and said he wanted dignity, freedom, and peace for his people and for the Israelis alike.

The public speeches were followed by a dinner hosted by President Obama. Abbas and Netanyahu sat next to each other. Obama emphasized the need for the two leaders to help each other succeed, and said that we would all be there with them as they moved on the difficult path of peace. Abbas and Netanyahu engaged in serious discussions throughout the dinner. Could these two men succeed in brokering a peace deal that would finally free our region from the threat of war? We would have to wait and see. A litmus test was only twenty-three days away. On September 26, the partial moratorium on the building of settlements that Netanyahu had announced in November would expire. The future of the negotiations would hang on his decision of whether or not to renew that moratorium.

The next morning, Abbas and Netanyahu met at the State Department for the first round of negotiations. After an expanded meeting that included members of the Palestinian, Israeli, and American delegations, Netanyahu, Abbas, Clinton, and Mitchell held a smaller meeting before Abbas and Netanyahu met on their own. The parties agreed to refrain from any public statements in order to avoid any provocative announcements that could jeopardize the process. Only Senator Mitchell would make a statement to the press.

Mitchell characterized the talks as "long and productive." He reiterated his belief that the negotiations could be completed in one year and said that Abbas and Netanyahu were committed to approaching the negotiations in good faith. He reiterated their commitment to the "goal of two states for two peoples and to a solution to the conflict that resolves all issues, ends all claims, and establishes a viable state of Palestine alongside a secure state of Israel."

The parties agreed to start working on a framework for a permanent status agreement. Abbas and Netanyahu agreed to meet every two weeks, and the next meeting was set for September 14 and 15. The next round of talks took place in Sharm El Sheikh on September 14 in the presence of Clinton, and continued the next day in Jerusalem under the shadow of the fast-approaching deadline for the end of the moratorium. Mitchell was again the only one to report to the press. This time, he said that the two leaders had reiterated the commitments made in Washington and started to tackle tough issues. He said that the United States would remain engaged as a serious partner. He tried to sound optimistic, but everybody in the region was concerned that the talks were nearing collapse, as all indications from Israel were that settlement building would resume on September 26.

Once the two leaders began to tackle details, the difficulties became more apparent. Abbas told Netanyahu he wanted to move forward on final status issues and presented the Israeli prime minister with the Palestinian positions. He again suggested that they begin with borders and security. But the talks ended on a negative note as Netanyahu insisted that any security arrangement must ensure a continued Israeli presence on future Palestinian eastern and western borders to guard against potential threats. Abbas said he would agree to security mechanisms, including the presence of international forces, but could not accept the presence of any Israeli soldiers on Palestinian land.

The situation deteriorated further over the following days as Israeli politicians made inflammatory public statements saying that settlement building would resume immediately after the end of the moratorium. The Palestinians were emphatic that they would walk out of the negotiations if the Israelis did not extend the moratorium. A crisis seemed inevitable.

President Obama, like all of us, was concerned that all the difficult work that had gone into getting the two sides to the table would be useless unless we could find a way out of the moratorium dilemma. He took advantage of the UN General Assembly meeting in New York to send a powerful message about the need to proceed with the negotiations. "We believe the moratorium should be extended," he said. "We also believe that talks should press on until completed." He told all the gathered heads of state and diplomats, "This time we should search for what's best within ourselves. If we do, when we come back next year, we can have an agreement that will lead to a new member of the United Nations — an independent, sovereign state of Palestine, living in peace with Israel."

Unfortunately, the Israeli government did not heed the call of the U.S. president, of the international community, and of all of us in the region. No sooner had the moratorium ended than announcements were made that more than 840 new units would be built in the West Bank and East Jerusalem. The Palestinians immediately suspended the negotiations but delayed a formal decision to abandon them to give efforts to resolve the deadlock a chance.

I met Abbas on October 3, six days before a scheduled Arab summit in Libya on October 9. He was frustrated with Israel's failure to renew the moratorium for even a limited period of two to three months during which time he hoped to tackle borders. We explored creative scenarios that could offer diplomacy a new chance. The challenge was to keep the door open for a breakthrough. But the ball was in Israel's court. Before meeting Abbas that day, I received Senator Mitchell, who had just concluded rounds of talks with Israeli leaders and was set to see Abbas in Amman following our meeting. We were all committed to finding a way to break the impasse. I told him that it would be impossible for Abbas to continue with the talks if the issue of settlements was not resolved.

Mitchell said he would continue his efforts.

On October 8, Abbas told the Arab League committee that he would withdraw from the negotiations if the Israeli government did not renew the moratorium on settlements. If the freeze was not extended, Abbas said the Palestinians would consider other options, starting with requesting a unilateral U.S. recognition of a Palestinian state. Should the United States refuse to do so, the Palestinians would ask the Arab League members to collectively demand a UN Security Council resolution recognizing a Palestinian state and would seek a UN General Assembly resolution to put the Palestinian Occupied Territories under a UN trusteeship if the United States vetoed such a resolution. "We have exhausted all options," Abbas said. The Arab League committee backed Abbas's decision, but decided to give the United States a month to try and salvage the negotiations before moving on to the options presented by Abbas.

As this book goes to press, direct negotiations are on the verge of collapse. We are two weeks away from the expiration of the one-month period given by the Arab League to the United States to get the negotiations back on track. Netanyahu shows no sign of compromise. His argument is that his coalition partners would not support an extension of the moratorium and his government would collapse if he pushed for such a decision. He would need to offer them sufficient incentive to convince them to extend the moratorium, incentives that the United States would have to provide in the form of a new package of financial and military assistance. In frenzied back-channel negotiations, the United States has offered major inducements to Israel to extend, even for as little as three months, the settlement freeze. But Israel, astonishingly, has so far thumbed its nose at these offers.

The United States continues to conduct extensive diplomatic efforts to break the deadlock, but the chances of success are getting slimmer by the day. Many in the Arab world are concerned that the staff changes that are expected to follow the U.S. midterm elections will give a more prominent role in the peace process to Dennis Ross, currently a special assistant to Obama. Because his hard-line positions did not help in moving the peace efforts forward in the past, the fear is that a growing influence by Ross will only be a complicating factor.

It is astonishing that a peace agreement that would open the door for Israel to have normal relations with all of its neighbors was not incentive enough for the Israeli government to give the peace talks a chance by halting settlements for even a limited period. That is a very negative signal to send to the Arab world and to all members of the international community who seek peace in the Middle East as a pillar of global stability. It is a message that will only empower those who have all along bet on our failure. It is also a major blow to all forces of moderation in the region, particularly Abbas. If the Israeli government collapses, Israelis will elect a new government. But if Abbas loses his credibility with his people or is so demoralized that he decides to step down, the whole world would lose a credible partner for peace that cannot easily be replaced.

Abbas told me personally and has made it clear in public that he will make all necessary sacrifices for peace. But he cannot do it on his own. Claims by some in Israel that he could not deliver because of the challenge to his authority by Hamas are mere excuses not to go forward. What Abbas needs is a credible deal to present to his people. Were he to secure such an agreement, he would put it to the people to vote on in a referendum. Nobody would then be able to stand between the Palestinian people and their right to freedom and statehood. But in the absence of an agreement, we will all have to reckon with the real possibility of the total collapse of public support for the peace process and the complete bankruptcy of moderate policies, setting the stage for extremists to take over.

I had hoped, when I set out to write this book, that we would by now be celebrating the resolution of the Palestinian-Israeli conflict and marking a new era of comprehensive peace in the Middle East. Instead, everyone in the region increasingly fears that we will soon be plagued by yet another devastating war. Israeli policies are mainly to blame for this gloomy reality.

So to the people of Israel I say: do not let your politicians endanger your nation's security through blind and thoughtless choices that continue to isolate your country. Almost one-third of the countries in the world do not have normal relations with Israel. Even North Korea has a better standing in the international community. A two-state solution with the Palestinians essentially means a fifty-seven-state solution, ensuring that Israel has normal relations with fifty-seven Arab and Muslim states that support the Arab Peace Initiative. If your leaders continue to choose conflict and war, each of you can make a decision to choose peace. For, in the end, only a fair peace with your neighbors can guarantee Israel the security it aspires to.

We don't need to look far into the future to see the problems on Israel's horizon. Simple demographics will alter the composition of Israeli society over the next decade. Currently, Arab Israelis make up around 20 percent of Israeli society. If there is no peace, and Israel continues to control the West Bank, then Arabs will become the majority. How will the Israeli government tackle this situation? If we fail to come to terms and to hammer out a two-state solution, which offers the promise of peace and security for all, the only other option is a one-state solution. That means that the Israeli government will have to give the Palestinians their full political rights as citizens, thereby eroding the Jewish character of the state. The other option would be for Israel to continue to disenfranchise a large proportion of its population, keeping the Palestinians under military occupation and denying them equal rights as citizens, thereby creating a new apartheid state and keeping the whole region hostage to the threat of war.

There are no alternatives. Some voices in Israel have spoken of what they call the "Jordan option," whereby Jordan would become the homeland for the Palestinians. That simply will not happen. We will not allow it; the Palestinians do not want it; and Israel cannot force it, for any attempt to do so will mean war and will expand the area of conflict. Nor will Jordan play any security role in the West Bank. We will not replace Israeli tanks with Jordanians tanks. The only role we will play is to continue to work for regional peace by helping the Palestinians in their effort to establish a viable independent state that will live in peace side by side with a secure Israel.

Israel has a clear choice. Does it want to remain fortress Israel, peering over the ramparts at increasingly hostile and aggressive neighbors? Or is it prepared to accept the hand of peace offered by all fifty-seven Muslim states and finally integrate itself into its region, accepted and accepting?

My father spent more than forty years searching for a lasting peace between Israel and the Palestinians, and for a comprehensive peace in the region. But even though he struggled until his dying day, he did not see it come to pass. My great-grandfather, Abdullah I, was assassinated in Jerusalem, paying the ultimate price for his pursuit of peace in a climate of war. We all hope that this conflict does not claim more brave leaders and continue through future generations.

In 2009, I named my oldest son, Hussein, crown prince in accordance with the Constitution, which states that "the Royal Title shall pass from the holder of the Throne to his eldest son" but gives the king the right to select one of his brothers as heir apparent. This was a difficult decision. I would have preferred that he avoid the extra scrutiny that goes with the position, and be blessed with teen years as unpressured as mine were. But in the end I felt that it was best for the country, and for my son, to be clear about where I saw destiny taking the Hashemite Kingdom of Jordan. Hussein is now sixteen. My most fervent hope is that when, in the fullness of time, he assumes his responsibilities, he will not be struggling with the same conflict that took his great-great-grandfather's life.

Over a decade ago, in the last months of his life, my father raised himself from his sickbed to address Yasser Arafat and Benjamin Netanyahu at the signing of the Wye Accords. He understood how fragile the dream of peace could be and was under no illusions as to the difficulties that lay ahead. He said, "I think such a step as is concluded today will inevitably trigger those who want to destroy life, destroy hope, create fear in the hearts and minds of people, and trigger in them their worst instincts. They will be skeptical on the surface, but if they can, they will cause damage, wherever they are and wherever they belong."

My father spoke at a time when trust between Israelis and Palestinians was high and many hoped the leaders on both sides would build on this foundation to achieve a lasting peace. The last decade of neglect has seen trust and hope fall to new lows and has strengthened those bent on destruction.

Every family, in East Jerusalem and in Tel Aviv, in Ramallah and in Jaffa, in the end, wants the same things: a peaceful and dignified life; the ability to fulfill their potential and to secure a better future for their children. Our better nature compels us to always look toward the light. I cannot believe that the people of Israel and Palestine want to continue to kill and be killed. We must all pray that their political leaders will give them the opportunity to live in peace and dignity.

Unless we see some positive breakthrough in the next year, I fear that we will miss our last chance for peace in a generation, and condemn our region to suffer another cycle of violence, war, and death. I fear that we are slipping into the darkness. But that does not have to be the future for our region. Our people want peace. It is our responsibility as leaders to make this much-eroded dream come true.

# ACKNOWLEDGMENTS

Not that long ago, I was speaking to some friends about how remarkable it was to me that more than ten years had passed since I had become king. We talked about the extraordinary series of events that Jordan, the Middle East, and the world had been through in that decade and my hopes that the next ten years would see greater safety, prosperity, and opportunity for all our citizens. Most of all, we talked about my conviction that the world is at a crossroads. In early 2009, it seemed to me that the stars could be uniquely aligned to give us a chance to solve the Palestinian-Israeli conflict and to achieve the regional peace that had eluded past generations. I said that I would continue to do everything I could to make that happen.

During that discussion, one of my friends suggested that this would be a good time for me to write a book about what I had seen and done, and what I dreamed about for the future.

I had never given much thought to writing a book. My army training leads me to prefer courses of action with timelier outcomes. And besides, I thought, I'm a young man who, God willing, has only just begun his time as King of Jordan. But someone pointed out that my father had published a book, *Uneasy Lies the Head,* in 1962, the year I was born, describing his first ten years as king. I have always found following my father's example to be a wise course, so I began to give it serious thought.

The first step was to find a publisher who might be interested in bringing this story to a wider audience, and Andrew Wylie and Scott Moyers of Wylie & Company, one of America's most respected literary agencies, helped me to navigate the complex waters of international publishing. With their help, I was introduced to Clare Ferraro and Joy de Menil of Viking Penguin. Clare immediately believed that I had a story to tell that would be of interest to the reading public and we began to work together on the process of producing a book. Joy was assigned as my editor, and throughout I have benefitted greatly from her razor-sharp intellect, broad knowledge of politics and history, and keen sense of how to present complex facts in a simple manner. She helped me pull together the threads of a varied life into a coherent narrative. Her assistant, Chris Russell, was also a tremendous help.

Relying on one's memory alone would be a very bad way to produce a memoir. I have sought the help of countless people to refresh my recollections and sharpen my judgments. I have also drawn on many documents and records from our archives to provide context, color, and clarity where memories might fade. I have endeavored to make this book as accurate as possible. But I know that whenever you have more than one person in a room, particularly when trying to reconstruct complex and important discussions on topics like Middle East peace, you can count on multiple recollections of what transpired. All I can say is that this book is my best effort to share with you my memories, impressions, and views.

Countless people played important roles in helping bring this project to fruition. Space allows me to thank by name just a few of them — but I am deeply grateful to many others whose contributions have been significant and who will go unnamed.

First, I must single out several members of my staff at the Royal Court whose contributions were extraordinary. Ayman Safadi, my adviser, has been the overall project manager, whose tireless work, energy, attention to detail, and persistence in bringing the book to a higher level made this project possible. Without his involvement, the book would never have gone to print. Mohammad Abu Taleb, keeper of the Royal Privy Purse, has been tremendously energetic, optimistic, and enthusiastic as he shepherded this complex project smoothly to a conclusion. I could not have asked for a better person to help make sure that everyone involved met their deadlines and remained focused. Nadine Khamis, projects manager at the Royal Privy Purse, has been invaluable in sorting through the complex legal nuances of publishing a book in many different countries and languages. My private secretary, Shereen Shuwayhat, did a fantastic job transcribing many, many hours of conversations, which were the basis for the written material in the book. She also helped me track down resource documents and kept track of the many drafts of the various chapters as I worked on them to make sure that I was accurately conveying my thoughts.

The chief of royal protocol, Amer Al-Fayez, and his staff, particularly Seeta Talhouni

Mirza, were essential in coordinating the scores of interviews with current and former Jordanian officials to ensure that the book thoroughly reflected the views of those who were most knowledgeable about the events I describe. Widad Maria Salah and Shaza Moghraby at the Media and Communication Directorate at the Royal Court did a tremendous job in researching and reviewing materials for the book. My thanks also go to Dr. Jafar Hassan, former director of the International Affairs Directorate at the Royal Court, and as of December 14, 2009, minister of planning and international cooperation, who helped in retrieving scores of critical documents from the royal archives. Also deserving appreciation is Haron Hassan, who has helped create a Web site for the book.

Many friends, family members, and current and former Jordanian officials shared their recollections to help flesh out my memories of events past. A partial list of them includes: HM Queen Rania, HRH Princess Muna, HRH Prince Feisal, HRH Prince Ali, HRH Prince Ghazi, HH Prince Zeid, Zaid Rifai, Field Marshal Abdul Hafez Kaabneh, Dr. Samir Mutawi, General Ahmed Sarhan, Dr. Marwan Muasher, Nasser Judeh, Samir Rifai, Karim Kawar,

Dr. Bassem Awadallah, Brigadier Ali Jaradat, Lt. Col. Nathem Rawashdeh, Dr. Mutayyam al O'ran, Dr. Eric Widmer, and Robert Richer.

Special thanks go to Drosten Fisher for his invaluable help with the writing of what has become *Our Last Best Chance*. Drosten attended Oxford and Georgetown Universities. An Arabic speaker and a thoughtful student of the Middle East, Drosten kindly took a leave of absence from his work at a consulting firm to help me with the project. He has proven to be a terrific choice in helping me to assemble, shape, and present my thoughts on paper.

As in all things, I am enormously grateful to my extended family. Readers of this book will know that my six sisters, four brothers, and numerous aunts, uncles, and cousins have played a critical role in making me who I am and in helping me achieve whatever good I have accomplished in my life. My father, His Late Majesty King Hussein, and my mother, Her Royal Highness Princess Muna, gave me an opportunity to live an extraordinary life, to see what few have seen, and to do my best to serve the people of Jordan.

God has given me many blessings. But

the greatest of all is to b
and father to our childr
Salma, and Hashem. The
my life.

# ABOUT THE AUTHOR

**King Abdullah II** spent his formative years in the United States, where he went to Eaglebrook and Deerfield, and in England, where he trained to be an officer at Sandhurst. A cavalry officer in the Jordanian army, he eventually became commander of the Jordanian Special Forces, a position that allowed him to forge invaluable relationships with intelligence and military officers around the world. The head of the Hashemite family, he is the forty-third-generation direct descendant of the Prophet Mohammad. His family ruled the holy city of Mecca for more than eight hundred years and his great-grandfather led the Arab revolt for independence from Ottoman rule.

The employees of Thorndike Press hope you have enjoyed this Large Print book. All our Thorndike, Wheeler, and Kennebec Large Print titles are designed for easy reading, and all our books are made to last. Other Thorndike Press Large Print books are available at your library, through selected bookstores, or directly from us.

For information about titles, please call:
  (800) 223-1244

or visit our Web site at:
  http://gale.cengage.com/thorndike

To share your comments, please write:
  Publisher
  Thorndike Press
  295 Kennedy Memorial Drive
  Waterville, ME  04901